HAAK
195565166

THE IMPLEMENTATION OF PROJECT MANAGEMENT:

THE PROFESSIONAL'S HANDBOOK

THE IMPLEMENTATION OF PROJECT MANAGEMENT:
THE PROFESSIONAL'S HANDBOOK

Edited by
Linn C. Stuckenbruck, Ph.D.

Institute of Safety and Systems
Management
University of Southern California
Los Angeles, California

Project Management Institute
P.O. Box 43, Drexel Hill, PA 19026

ADDISON-WESLEY PUBLISHING COMPANY
Reading, Massachusetts • Menlo Park, California
London • Amsterdam • Don Mills, Ontario • Sydney

Library of Congress Cataloging in Publication Data

Main entry under title:

The Implementation of project management.

At head of title: Project Management Institute,
Southern California Chapter.
Bibliography: p.
1. Industrial project management—Addresses, essays,
lectures. I. Stuckenbruck, Linn C. II. Project
Management Institute.   Southern California Chapter.
HD69.P75I457   658.4'04   80-14898
ISBN 0-201-07260-2

Sixth Printing, December 1986

ISBN 0-201-07260-2
  FGHIJK-AL-89876

*To my wife and severest critic—Marlys,
and a typist who cares—Roger Buckhaus.*

CONTENTS

CONTENTS
x

FOREWORD

There is an often used sequence in *Through the Looking Glass* where Alice and the Red Queen are running as fast as they can, but the trees and other things appear to move along with them. Alice says, "In our country, you'd generally get to somewhere else—if you ran very fast for a long time, as we've been doing." "A slow sort of country," said the Queen. "Now, here, you see, it takes all the running you can do to keep in the same place." Project Management is not "a slow sort of country"; management innovations, in theory and practice, happen relatively fast. In an endeavor to keep pace with these rapid changes, the Project Management Institute (PMI) was formed in 1969 as a group of concerned managers and erstwhile managers intent on improving the quality of management at all levels.

The Project Management Institute's objectives are to: (1) foster professionalism in project management; (2) provide a forum for the free exchange of project management problems, solutions, and applications; (3) encourage industrial and academic research; (4) improve communications through dialogs and discussions about terminology and techniques; (5) provide an interface between users and suppliers of hardware and software systems; and (6) provide guidelines for instruction and education, and to encourage career developments in the field of project management. This book, representing two years of conscientious effort by the Southern California Chapter of PMI, provides a concise coverage of these objectives. It will help the expert or the novice to advance the understanding of the nature of project management.

The purpose of this book is to serve as a guide for project managers, at all levels, who are considering the implementation of project management in their company or organization. It is also a how-to-do-it manual for practicing managers newly catapulted into project management, as well as a textbook for graduate level courses in management. The emphasis is not on any given field or industry but represents the cumulative experience of the authors in the general field of project management. It provides the basic ground rules for developing the right type of project management organization with particular emphasis on "selling" all levels of management on the advantages of, and the necessity for, project management. Many projects that have been initiated with the best of intentions have faltered and failed because the project manager, or upper management, did not provide a workable organization with adequate lines of communication. The adage that a chain is only as strong as its weakest link is of great relevance in project management. This book is meant to identify and strengthen the weak links before they cause the chain to fail and the project to falter.

I would like to express my appreciation to the authors who contributed to the book. They are all practitioners in the field of project management and have been through the trials and tribulations of implementing project management and have faced the short- and long-range problems of a project manager. They are therefore considered to be very well qualified to help newly appointed project managers (and their "top management") to solve the problems of getting started on the right foot. Of special note are the efforts of Linn C. Stuckenbruck for his persistence and conscientious efforts to coordinate the work of the Southern California Chapter of PMI in making the book possible. By his dedication, the articles have been readied for publication in a format that I am sure you will find interesting, informative, and thought-provoking.

Thanks are also extended for the steadying and steadfast guidance provided by Mr. Jim Snyder, the overworked, unpaid Executive Director of PMI. This book is a result of his desires for many years to publish, in a systemized format, writings by PMI members on the subject of project management.

John R. (Dick) McCandless
Chairman 1980
Board of Directors, PMI

CHAPTER ONE
INTRODUCTION

Linn C. Stuckenbruck, Ph.D.

Institute of Safety and Systems Management
University of Southern California
Los Angeles, California

Executives considering the implementation of project management in their organization must understand what they are getting into. They must understand what project management is, and under what conditions it can be the answer to some of their problems. They must understand that it will not always work, and that to assure its success it must be planned and implemented with great care. This book will discuss the methods and procedures used by successful project managers, and will point out the pitfalls to be avoided in implementing a project.

WHAT IS A PROJECT?

The authors define a project as a *one-shot, time-limited, goal-directed, major undertaking*, requiring the commitment of varied skills and resources. A project has also been described as "a combination of human and nonhuman resources pulled together in a temporary organization to achieve a specified purpose."[1] A project has a single set of objectives, and when these objectives are reached, the project is completed. Therefore, a project has a finite and well-defined life span. In addition, management must have a very clear idea

1

as to what these objectives are so that there can be no question as to when the project is completed.

For the purposes of this book, the words *project* and *program* are considered to be synonymous. However, the two words have had different acceptance depending on the industry involved. The Department of Defense and their aerospace and electronics customers prefer to use *program management*. Construction, public works, and product industries prefer the term *project management*. There is a growing acceptance of the differentiation of a "project" from a "program" in that a program is usually much larger in scope, is activity oriented, and is not necessarily time limited. A program, however, may encompass a number of projects.

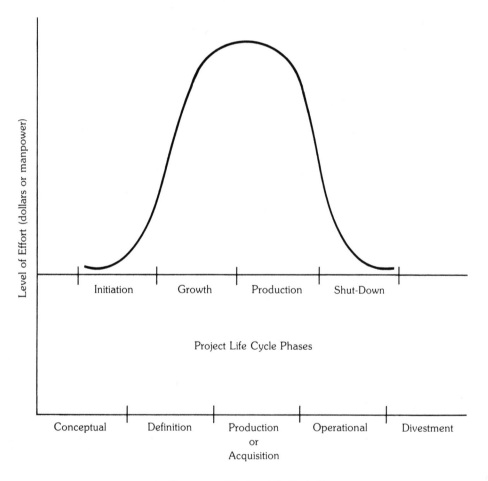

Figure 1-1. Project Phases

THE PROJECT
LIFE CYCLE

A project consists of sequential phases as shown in Figure 1-1. These phases are extremely useful in planning a project since they provide a framework for budgeting, manpower and resource allocation, and for scheduling project milestones and project reviews. The method of division of a project into phases may differ somewhat from industry to industry, and from product to product, but the phases shown in Figure 1-1 are basic. If government contracts are involved, the project life cycle will fit into the government system life cycle as also shown in Figure 1-1. In addition, it must be realized that these phases are not strictly sequential; there may be considerable overlap, particularly in large and complex projects.

What must be done during these phases? There are certain actions that must be taken by top management, and as the project matures, by the project manager. These actions are shown in Table 1-1.

TABLE 1-1. PROJECT PHASE ACTIONS

Concept or Initiation	Growth or Organization	Production or Operational	Shut-Down
Management decides that a project is needed. Management establishes goals and estimates of resources needed. Management "sells" the organization on the need for project management. Management makes key appointments.	Organizational approach defined. Project plan and schedule for operational phase defined. Project objectives, tasks (WBS), and resources defined. Project team built up.	The major work of the project accomplished (i.e., design, development, construction, production, testing, site activation, etc.).	Project terminated. Manpower, resources, and commitments transferred to other organizations.

This book is primarily concerned with the actions that take place during implementation of a project, which is a combination of the concept or initiation phase and the growth or organization phase.

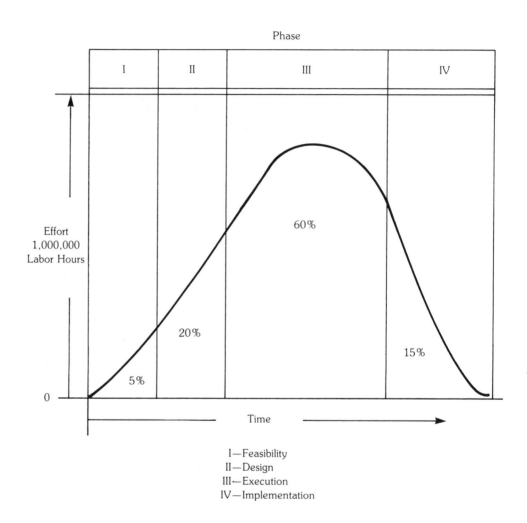

I—Feasibility
II—Design
III—Execution
IV—Implementation

Figure 1-2. Project Life Cycle

It is often useful to divide the project into phases as shown in Figure 1-2. This scheme of phases fits projects such as construction, and by plotting the phases versus total effort, a very clear picture can be obtained as to where the money goes.

PROJECT MANAGEMENT

Project management evolved as an answer to some of the management problems resulting from today's complex systems, and the increasingly complex efforts required to solve those systems' problems. Project management is periodically rediscovered whenever a member of top management, contemplating a big job in deep trouble, says, "What I need is someone who can take charge of this whole infernal mess and keep me informed as to what's going on." Project management is thus the investiture in a single person of the responsibility for success or failure of a project.

THE PROJECT MANAGER

Project success depends on selecting the right person as a project manager. Management means getting things done through the *active support* of other people. It would be difficult to find a better statement which more accurately describes the project manager's job. Unlike the functional manager who has power through position in the hierarchy and direct authority over people, the project manager usually has only position power which usually comes from endorsement of the role by top management. However, formal announcements and directives bestowing this authority on the project manager seldom guarantee results. Direct personal signals from the top executives of the company are necessary to convey the message to others in the functional organization. Although this authority is necessary to do the job and make things happen, the better project managers use another source of power—their own leadership ability and charisma—to command attention and gain respect.

The project manager of a major project is chosen by top management, and is thus their direct and very real representative. Therefore, the project manager must relate unequivocally with corporate goals. It has been pointed out that every project has a "customer."[2] This statement is obvious if we are dealing with a contractual project, but not so obvious when dealing with a new commercial product. It is easy to forget that the public is the ultimate customer for most projects. Therefore, the project manager must also strongly relate with the customer's goals.

Having ultimate responsibility for success or failure, the project manager must provide project direction; planning; control of all costs, schedules, and resources; and customer satisfaction.

The job of the project manager may best be described as the same as that of any manager with the addition of a unique function, that of integrator. The process of integration involves direction and coordination of the efforts of the project team so that all parts of the project effort fit together and all the subsystems can be finally integrated into a total working system. Problem solving and decision making are critical to the integration process since most project problems occur at subsystem or organizational interfaces. The project manager is the only person in the key position to solve such interface problems. The project manager's integration function is discussed in Chapter 9.

THE PROJECT TEAM

It is only the first step to appoint a project manager. The really important step is to develop an effective team, consisting of all the people involved in the project. This may be the most important action that the project manager makes because the success of the entire project will depend on the hard work and dedication of the project team. The members of the project team come from different parts of the organization, and may work part time or full time on the project. It is the job of the project manager to weld this heterogeneous group into a cohesive team that can work closely together to meet project goals.

PROJECT MANAGEMENT IS NOT FOR EVERYONE

Is project management the answer to my problems? This question must be given very serious consideration by the organization contemplating the implementation of project management. To find the answer, top management should ask three additional questions:

1. Does my organization really need project management?

2. If so, how much project management?

3. What type of project management is necessary?

Project management does not work in every organization, nor does every organization need project management. Project management should only be utilized if it is really needed, and can provide solutions to pressing management problems. A simple operation limited to one or two departments in an organization is not a project as defined by the authors of this book. A project is defined as a complex system involving the coordination of a number of separate department entities throughout the organization, and which must be completed within prescribed schedule and cost constraints. If an organization's job or problem does not meet these criteria, it probably does not need project management, and for these types of tasks, project management will probably hinder rather than help.

HOW MUCH PROJECT MANAGEMENT?

The project manager must be given adequate authority by top management to do his or her job. The amount of authority needed must be carefully considered by top management, and will depend on customer requirements, project urgency, management information needs, and importance of the project to the organization. For various reasons top management may want to limit the authority of project managers. Top management may not be willing to give up some of their decision-making prerogatives, or they may not want to take power away from their line/functional management. Therefore, project managers cover a spectrum from very strong to very weak, depending on the needs of the project and the deliberate decisions of top management. This situation is not necessarily bad since every project is different in needs and organizational environment.

A small or unimportant project, for instance, probably does not need a strong project manager; a weak position such as a project coordinator may be adequate. As a project becomes bigger and more important, more authority should be given to the project manager. However, top management should always ensure that the project manager has adequate authority to carry out the job and its assigned responsibilities.

WHAT TYPE OF PROJECT MANAGEMENT?

The organization considering the implementation of project management is not limited to a single alternative. Project management can take various forms to fit specific organizational and project needs. These organizational alternatives differ primarily in the amount of authority (power) and autonomy given to the project manager and the project office. The major choice is between a "pure" project organization and some form of the matrix. In a pure project, everyone works for the project office and the project manager runs the whole show. This organizational form has been very successful in managing big projects, particularly government contracts where the contracting agency has a similar organization. In a matrix, a project organization is superimposed on top of the normal line/functional organization, and it is very efficient for small or medium-sized projects.

THE MATRIX

As indicated by the discussions in Chapters 5 and 6, this book places considerable emphasis on the matrix form of project management since it appears to be gaining ever-widening acceptance in today's profit-motivated, complex organizations. The matrix is usually the only way in which project management can be effectively utilized for small- and medium-sized research and development efforts.

The implementation of a matrix requires that an organization make major changes in the way it functions. Management priorities, procedures, and controls must undergo drastic modification to accommodate project needs, since a new dimension has been added to management decision making. The potential for conflict has been increased because of the new management interfaces that have been established. Top management must learn to deal with the conflicting goals, priorities, and resource demands of functional and project management.

It has been proposed that the matrix has evolved in response to the inherent conflict that haunts every large modern organization—the needs of specialization versus the needs of coordination.[3] Top management cannot make all decisions, and they cannot be sure that they are obtaining an optimizing decision since they may not have sufficient information. The experts or specialists, whatever their role in the functional organization, also cannot make optimizing decisions since project and overall company needs are beyond their area of expertise. The matrix provides a mechanism for minimizing this conflict by making the project manager "act as a decision broker—working problems through the experts who in their respective fields know more than he does."[4]

MULTIPROJECT MANAGEMENT

An organization which has many relatively small repetitive or essentially similar projects should consider utilizing multiproject management.[5] Many projects in construction, public works, product development, and manufacturing are this type, and do not need a full-time project manager. Multiproject management functions by having a single project manager or project office be responsible for a number of projects, usually in a matrix organization. The rationale is that an organization's projects, particularly similar projects, are interrelated and are competing for resources and management time. The project office provides for management attention at an appropriate level in the organization to ensure that all projects are completed on time and with maximum benefit for the entire organization.

WHAT CAN GO WRONG?

Why doesn't project management always work? It is such a simple concept that it would seem to be a panacea for most organizations' problems. That it does not always work can be shown by the number of organizations that have initiated project management and then have given up, often in disgust, and returned to a line/functional organization.

What went wrong? Causes of project management failure are mixed; however, hindsight indicates that failure can usually be ascribed to one or both of the following causes:

1. Internal Conflict	Strong and continuous conflict existed between the project management and line/functional organizations, characterized by foot-dragging on the part of the line organizations, resulting in poor schedule and budgetary control.
2. Inadequate Authority	The project manager was given inadequate authority to accomplish goals and responsibilities. Top management failed to provide the necessary backing to the project office for the commitment of money, resources, personnel, and facilities to the project.

Both of these causes of failure may be regarded as symptoms of the problems resulting from a single basic mistake—the project management approach was inadequately sold to *all* key members of the organization. This problem will be discussed further in Chapter 4.

In the first case, conflict resulted from a failure to sell the line/functional-oriented managers on the importance of project management to the total organization. They must realize that the project organization is just as important to them as to the overall organization, and that it does not constitute a threat to their authority and future advancement. In fact, the utilization of the project approach may be vital to the continued existence of the organization. Every member of the line organization has to understand how the project management office functions, and what real authority it has. The overlapping of line and project authority must be understood, and working relationships worked out. It is theoretically possible to so specifically delineate authority and responsibility that there will be no overlapping and no conflict. In the real world, however, this ideal can only be approached. The division of authority and responsibility can be broken down as follows:

Project Management Is Responsible For	Line Management Is Responsible For
What?	Who?
When?	Where?
At What Cost?	How?

Major conflicts can, therefore, be resolved based on these guidelines. However, there will always be problems of interpretation of responsibilities, and there will always be some true divisions of authority, necessitating negotiations between line and project management. For instance, can the line manager make an arbitrary decision on "how" a job is to be accomplished without negotiating with the project manager in terms of cost and impact on other portions of the system?

It must be understood that project management involves direction of the project and not just coordination. The project manager has firm responsibilities and must be provided with the authority necessary to get the job done, on time, within budget, and to the satisfaction of the client or customer.

In the second case, inadequate delegation of authority resulted from a failure to convince top management of the advantages and true functions of project management. Top management is naturally reluctant to delegate what they consider to be their prerogatives, or to take authority away from line managers who have functioned faithfully and successfully for many years. Top management must thoroughly understand as well as unwaiveringly support project management. It may be clear to top management that project management is needed. However, it may not be so clear what the mechanism of implementation should be or the necessity of clearly spelling out the degree of delegation of responsibility and authority. Many so-called projects are not really project managed since the project manager has no real authority, and only functions as a coordinator and information source. It is impossible to go halfway in implementing project management. Without adequate authority, the project manager has two strikes against him or her. Then top management wonders why project management failed. The project manager must report at a high enough level in the organizational hierarchy to have equal or greater authority than other managers participating in the project. The project manager must be more than an ineffectual coordinator who ends up as a scapegoat to take the blame when things go wrong.

It is of importance that the necessity for and the advantages of the project management approach be sold equally well up and down the hierarchy of management. Failure to accomplish either step may doom the project to failure.

WHAT CAN GO RIGHT? Project management at its best, and where it is really needed, will result in outstanding performance and profit. If there is one outstanding characteristic of successful project management, it is its ability to get the job done on time, at lower cost, and with improved efficiency. In addition, it can mean new life and vitality for the organization that correctly utilizes it. The rewards also are great in terms of personal satisfaction and organizational accomplishment.

GETTING STARTED ON THE RIGHT FOOT

As indicated in the various chapters of this book, there are many things that can go wrong. However, almost all problems start or occur during the process of planning and implementation of project management in the organization. If project management gets off on the right foot, and is effectively implemented, it almost always works. Therefore, this book addresses this most important and often neglected aspect of project management—its successful planning and implementation. What precautions can be taken to assure the successful implementation of project management once a decision has been made to go ahead?

A number of very important actions must be taken "up front," some of them long before the project is formally implemented. These actions, some the responsibility of top management and others of the project manager, are discussed in Chapter 4.

The most important of these actions is ensuring that the organization is ready for project management. Then the management position must be made very clear to the entire organization by the issuance of a Project Charter which delineates the authority and responsibilities of the project manager and all other managers involved in the project. Then top management faces the important problem of choosing the "right" project manager. From this point on, the newly appointed project manager must take over and carry the ball. However, top management has the additional responsibility of following up on their good intentions by providing the project manager with positive and continuous support—right to the end of the project.

SCOPE OF THE BOOK

Getting project management off to the right start is absolutely vital to its ultimate success. It is not enough to appoint project managers, hand them the ball, and tell them to run with it. They will probably fall flat on their face, unless a great deal of preparation and careful planning is accomplished first. It is the perplexing problems of planning and implementation of project management that this book examines in detail. The authors have all been through this process of project planning and implementation in different types of organizations. Hopefully they have learned enough from their mistakes to be able to lay out a road map (through the project management jungle) to guide organizations contemplating the use of project management. This book is directed to the needs of executives and managers who must understand the advantages and problems of project management if they are to successfully implement it in their organization. In addition, this book is organized to serve as a guide for prospective or newly-appointed project managers to help them get their project started on the right foot. Therefore, it is essentially a "how to" book. The scope of this book will thus be confined to the critical initial steps of planning, organizing, and implementing project management.

This book will not be concerned with contracts, marketing, or other steps in obtaining the project. It is only concerned with the actions that must be taken after an organization has made the decision that project management is the way to go. This book will attempt to highlight the pitfalls and suggest approaches that have resulted in the successful implementation of project management.

If there is a single most important admonition that this book can make, it is *keep it simple*. The greatest hazard to any system is to initiate controls so complex that they limit or decrease efficiency and effectiveness of the project.

ENDNOTES

1. David I. Cleland and William R. King, *Systems Analysis and Project Management*, 2nd ed. (New York: McGraw-Hill Book Co., 1975), p. 184.

2. Charles C. Martin, *Project Management—How to Make It Work* (New York: Amacon, 1976), p. 8.

3. Leonard R. Sayles, "Matrix Management: The Structure With a Future," *Organizational Dynamics* (Autumn 1976): 2-17.

4. Ibid.

5. Russel D. Archibald, *Managing High-Technology Programs and Projects* (New York: John Wiley and Sons, 1976), pp. 59-78.

CHAPTER TWO THE NEED FOR PROJECT MANAGEMENT

James L. Easton Division Engineer
Los Angeles County Flood Control District
Los Angeles, California

Robert L. Day Project Manager
Southern California Edison Company
Rosemead, California

INTRODUCTION Solutions for the staggering problems facing the world today have called for the development of ever larger and more complex systems. It is debatable whether project management (or systems management) was developed as a result of management's need for a technique to handle such complex problems. However, like the chicken and the egg, it is a useless argument. What is not debatable is the fact that today's big, complex problems require integrated, multidisciplinary efforts. Project management provides just such an approach to problems.

RECOGNIZING THE NEED In establishing the need for project management, there are some basic premises that must be recognized. First, every organization, whether public or private, produces a product, or provides a service, or does both. All of these organizations *want* to perform so that their goods or services are provided at the right time, at minimum cost (maximum profit), and to the satisfaction of the customer, client, or consumer. Evidence of lack of success in meeting these goals is found in business failures, firing or replacement of top executives, reduced profits, and rapidly expanding government bureaucracies. Sometimes the reasons for these failures are external, but more often than not, the fault is within the organization itself.

A major factor influencing the need for project management is the size of the organization. A very small organizational entity such as a consulting firm, engineering office, or even a small contractor who has a budget, a schedule, and limited requirements to control quality and production, probably could get along very well without using formal project management techniques. By virtue of its smallness, the few people involved can communicate rapidly and efficiently. Often, the same person is responsible for several interdisciplinary actions. The planner becomes the implementer (designer), scheduler, monitor, procurer, and director of construction on a simple noncomplex project. A whole hierarchy of organizations having projects of varying complexity can be listed, and at some point in this listing the need for project management becomes more and more evident. In an electric utility (a large organization) in which one department has a project involving one or maybe two disciplines, there really is no need for formal project management as previously defined. There is a clear point of responsibility (to whom the assignment was given). This individual (engineer) can be held responsible for control over the immediate subordinates (draftsmen, designer, typist, junior engineer, etc.). Actually, this person is the project manager, project engineer, and lead-discipline engineer for the work. In contrast, the same utility that is responsible for the design of a large complex nuclear-generating project involving a score of departments and many disciplines, will require project management in its most formal sense. Management found that they needed a formalized method to manage complex one-of-a-kind jobs. Size was not the key factor in the need for project management, rather it was organizational and project complexity.

COMPLEX PROJECTS

What happens when an organization is faced with accomplishing a very complex, multidisciplinary project? For instance, the Atlas missile program provides an early example of the use of project management in the aerospace industry. Up to this time the aerospace companies had attacked their problems within their hierarchical management organizations. They would set up task forces, giving functional managers responsibility for certain portions of the project, but with top management retaining overall responsibility. It worked, but with considerable difficulty, and with more or less constant organizational conflict.

Pure projects (fully projectized), such as the Manhattan project (or even the construction of the pyramids), where everyone on the project worked directly for the project manager, existed long before the Atlas program. However, the Atlas program has been said to be the beginning of modern project management,[1] in that it was the first successful use of matrix management in an immensely complex "crash" program. The Atlas program was started in 1954 under Air Force Brig. Gen. Bernard A. Schreiver to develop the free world's first ICBM. "Because the Atlas program had started late and faced early and critical deadlines, the Air Force had to scrap accepted management principles and develop its own."[2] Many management innovations were initiated, including: (1) direct program control by the Air Force and by a Special Projects Office, (2) the creation of the Ramo-Wooldridge Corporation to give overall technical advice to the program, (3) a speed-up of the development cycle by the use of "concurrency" by which major decisions were frozen early in the program and work on many different components went ahead simultaneously, and (4) the establishment (with Air Force insistence) of project offices by each contractor on the program.

As a result of the success of this and other government-sponsored programs, project management is now regarded as an essential part of all major systems acquisitions. Defense systems contractors rapidly recognized that project management had many advantages, and they established "mirror-image" organizations to their government customer. The defense contractors went one step further and developed what is now known as the matrix organization (discussed in Chapters 5 and 6). The matrix has expanded the applicability of project management to the point where it can be successfully utilized by a wide variety of organizations.

WHO NEEDS PROJECT MANAGEMENT?

Project management has a very wide range of applicability; its present use only scratches the surface. It is equally useful in small or large organizations, and for small or large rich projects. Small projects can also benefit from the concentrated attention of a project manager with the attendant advantages of better budgetary and schedule control and better allocation of resources.

The principles of project management are applicable to every organization dealing with complexity. In the past, project management has been widely used in the defense department, the aerospace industry, and in major construction projects. Now project management is gaining acceptance in product development, public works, nonprofit organizations, financial institutions, and in all sectors of government. It is particularly useful whenever considerable coordination is required between government agencies, between a government agency and a customer, or between a contractor and a client.

ORGANIZATIONAL CONSIDERATIONS

In today's world of rapidly expanding technology and expanding influence and control by federal, state, and local government, organizations find it increasingly difficult to meet the complexities of a rapidly changing business environment. Most industrial, public service, and government organizations have met the problems of complexity by utilizing the hierarchical management structure inherited from the military. Top management has been very comfortable with the hierarchy because of its simple one-boss reporting system. The hierarchy also lends itself to convenient subdivision of an organization into groups or departments, each of which represents a specialty, discipline, or function. What could be more natural than to subdivide an organization into the same specialized disciplines that serve as departments in the university system? Staffing is simplified and specialists relate best to other specialists in their same discipline.

These so-called line, functional, or disciplinary divisions often enhance efficiency and maximize productivity, but they also have some of the following inherent problems:

1. The ability of specialized organizational groups (line or functional divisions) to work together and to coordinate effectively with government regulatory agencies and/or clients is critical to the success of the organization. Line managers often suffer from "tunnel vision" in that they either don't know or don't subscribe to overall organizational goals. Often what's good for the division as perceived by the division manager may take precedence over what's best for the project or the entire organization.

2. Competition or feuding between line divisions may result in efficiency or failure to communicate vital information.

3. The responsibility for important external coordination may become muddled because of overlapping or inadequately defined responsibilities.

4. The division of responsibility for a job that overlaps several line or functional divisions (a project) usually slows and complicates the process of making decisions that affect the entire project. This may increase the possibility of inadequate or tardy response to chang-

ing conditions which could make the difference between project success or failure.

5. As organizations grow in size and organizational complexity, it becomes increasingly difficult for top management to concern themselves with the day-to-day problems of individual projects.

For any of these reasons, a chief executive may become faced with project failure and, in attempting to determine the cause for the failure, may find the division managers pointing the finger of blame at each other. Precious little objective information may be found as to what really went wrong.

IS PROJECT MANAGEMENT REALLY NEEDED?

It can be a very traumatic experience for top management to realize that they really don't know what is going on. A chief executive in this position, faced with the problem of poor project performance, usually comes to the conclusion that a single point of information and control is needed if complex projects are going to be successfully conducted. Among the alternatives which can be considered is formalized project management. However, as previously indicated, project management is not for everyone, and should be used only if the situation demands it.

In determining the need for project management, one should examine the project *and* the organization carefully and ask the following types of questions:

1. Is the job very large?

2. Is the job technically very complex?

3. Is the job a true system in that it has many separate parts or subsystems which must be integrated to complete the operational whole?

4. Is the job a part of a larger system and must it be closely integrated, particularly if the larger system has a project-oriented organization?

5. Does top management strongly feel the necessity of having a single point of information and responsibility for a total job?

6. Are strong budgetary and fiscal controls required?

7. Are tight schedule and budgetary constraints foreseen?

8. Are quick responses to changing conditions necessary?

9. Does the job cross many disciplinary as well as organizational boundaries?

10. Will the proposed job drastically disrupt the present organizational structure?

11. Are more than two divisions involved, and is more than one division going to be dealing directly with the client or customer?

12. Are there other complex projects being conducted concurrently with this one?

13. Is there likely to be conflict between line managers concerning this project?

14. Is the organization committed to a firm completion date?

15. Is it likely that changing conditions may seriously affect the project before its completion?

16. Are there major buys and procurements that must be made outside the company?

17. Are there major portions of the system which must be subcontracted outside the organization?

18. Is it necessary to have the project reviewed or approved by government regulatory agencies? Will these review processes and approvals be likely to generate problems and controversy?

If the answer to many of these questions is "yes," or even if there are only several "yes" answers concerning a phase of the project that is particularly critical, then project management should be seriously considered.

ALTERNATIVES TO PROJECT MANAGEMENT

The decision to introduce project management is a difficult one because it will require top management to give up some of its prerogatives, and line management to be partially or wholly subordinated to project management. It is an even more traumatic situation if the decision is to introduce a matrix organization, which is sure to be resisted by many old line, conservative managers. As previously indicated, project management is not for everyone, and it should only be used if it is really needed. There are four alternative methods of reorganizing which provide some of the benefits of project management. One of these alternatives should certainly be considered if top management does not want to relinquish authority, or if they decide that their projects are not sufficiently complex for project management.

The alternatives to project management are:

1. Establishment of a "lead" division or discipline with responsibility to coordinate and sometimes direct the activities of the other affected divisions. This may suffice for smaller projects or in small organizations, but for large complex projects, conflict between project goal and the vested interests of the "lead" technical division may result in more problems than it solves.

2. Direct control over the project by top management. This is fine if top management has enough time to get involved in day-to-day project problems. If there is not adequate time, then the project and/or the entire organization may suffer if this alternative is chosen.

3. *Clear* definition of responsibility and authority of each organizational entity involved in the project. Even the clearest instructions may be misinterpreted or misunderstood, especially if the project is a complex one. This alternative is satisfactory if *everyone* is willing to cooperate fully, but most of the time this method sounds much better in theory than in actual application.

4. Establishment of a project coordinator who can accomplish one of the principal duties of a project manager, i.e., keep top management informed. However, the project manager cannot be held responsible for a project since she or he does not have decision-making power or authority for project direction.

WHAT DOES PROJECT MANAGEMENT DO FOR YOU?

Once top management has decided that they should consider the use of project management, they must review what it can do for them. Are the benefits worth the trauma of implementing something new and very upsetting to their organization? What do they gain by implementing project management? What are the benefits?

Probably the most singular benefit provided by project management and its philosophy is its concerted and organized planning and control function. This is provided through a consistent and constant point of leadership by the project manager.

Project management will centralize responsibility for the following key items in one individual:

READ
AGAIN

1. Budgeting cost control

2. Schedules

3. Resource allocation

4. Technical quality

5. Client, customer, or public relations.

BUDGETING COST CONTROL

If a project has complete definition, it has budgetary responsibility and/or at least cost-control responsibility. With many groups or organizational entities within a corporate structure, all having some degree of cost impact on the project, cost control must be implemented. The control responsibility can be delegated to subgroups, *but converges at the project manager's office*. Traditionally, the greatest impact to a project's cost comes from engineering and from construction units.

Budgeting is a part of the planning function, and also serves as a control mechanism giving the basis from which actual performance can be compared, measured, explained, and corrected. Control accounts are identified and established, each having component accounts needed for optimum control. The budget should be viewed and used as a program for planned expenditures. When the budget is combined with a schedule it serves as a program of physical completion and provides a most important tool of project management.

SCHEDULES

No cost control program is effective if not coupled with the definitive schedule showing distinct, measurable, identifiable milestones. In addition, the schedule should show the interrelationship of one group's planned achievements with the other groups', thus identifying key interfaces. The complexity of the project will set the detail of this schedule. A schedule, however, must be a living document, easily understood, *previously committed to by its participants*, and readily adjusted to reflect current project conditions.

Developing construction schedules is relatively easy; however, developing engineering or design schedules is more difficult and least understood.

Other important aspects deal with interfaces and constraints. If all a project manager does is to think out each of the key steps of design and construction, then establish the rational and logical activity sequence, the significant progress milestones toward completing the planning of the project will have been achieved. This, at least, establishes a reference point from which to make changes, and a basis to keep the interfaces clearly defined.

RESOURCE ALLOCATION

In addition to money and time the most important project resources are materials (and equipment) and manpower. Each project requires that some orderly process be followed in the procurement of materials, equipment, and services if it is to succeed. Without that orderly organization it is highly probable that planned costs and/or schedules will not be met due to the delay of delivery of key items.

After it has been determined what needs to be procured for a project, sequence and lead time must be determined to meet required delivery dates for the construction schedule. A Material Procurement Forecast is an extremely important document to manage this resource. It can identify key steps in the procurement process from development of specifications, through the bid cycle, vender prints, ending with delivery dates for any level of detail in material and equipment desired. Of course, the Material Procurement Forecast must be close-coupled with the project schedule.

The other aspect of this resource category involves manpower. The engineering/design manpower and construction or production labor make up the bulk of this resource. For the most part, this is a scarce and costly resource that is in high demand. Manpower requirements must be planned for in advance, often having to make compromises and tradeoffs according to priorities established.

In a large electric utility having many projects of varying importance and a relatively fixed number of personnel, project priorities were set up, ranking each of the projects according to importance and cost risks. The infighting and competition for manpower becomes much more objective and orderly when project management is used.

TECHNICAL QUALITY

Once a quality control system has been designed and documented, a design review process is in order. This should bring together experts and second-level supervision to review as a committee a predesignated segment of work.

With respect to manufacture and construction, a good "hold and witness" control plan must be developed with each specification. During construction, specific documented tests and witnessed operations are imperative. Any plan should include both source inspection and on-site inspection. Documented evidence of tests is also mandatory. In the nuclear power field, the subject of inspection has a very high priority and is almost of equal importance to getting the job done.

Start-up and acceptance testing should be outlined well in advance. Methodology and special measuring devices must be adequate. Prequalification of bidders can alleviate many of the future problems before they materialize. Procedures for inspection of delivered materials and equipment and documented damage reports are a must.

CLIENT, CUSTOMER, OR PUBLIC RELATIONS

One of the most important aspects of the project manager's job is the responsibility, as a representative of top management, to maintain good client, customer, or public relations. Top management occasionally interfaces with the client or customer, but the project manager is the day-by-day contact, particularly at the working level. The project manager must recognize and carefully plan for this phase of activity. If the client or customer finds that the project manager must continually refer to some member of the project team whenever a question is asked, the client or customer can rightly assume that the project manager is acting more as coordinator than as a manager. The project manager will eventually become bypassed when the client or customer needs information. It is quite likely that top management will then find the project manager's usefulness has ended.

Public relations are not always of concern to the project manager, however if the project is sensitive to the public interest because of environmental, marketing, or safety factors, then the project manager is deeply involved. The fact that there is a public aspect to almost every project cannot be ignored.

CONCLUSIONS

Formalized project management is not the solution to every organization's problems. Small, simple projects do not need formalized project management, but it is needed for large, complex, and multidisciplinary problems. There are many criteria that can be used as tip-offs indicating whether project management is really needed. The most important criteria are project complexity and top management's need for a single point of information, responsibility, and control for each project. There are four viable alternatives to project management, including the establishment of a lead division, direct control by top management, very clear definitions of responsibility and authority, and a project coordinator. However, each alternative has problems of implementation, and sound better in theory than in actual application. The need for project management is most apparent in the project manager's planning and control function which centralizes responsibility for the following key items in one individual: (1) budgeting cost control; (2) schedules; (3) resource allocation; (4) technical quality; and (5) client, customer, or public relations.

ENDNOTES

1. John Stanley Baumgartner, *Systems Management* (Washington, D.C.: The Bureau of National Affairs, Inc., 1979), p. 4.

2. Wernher Von Braun, and Frederick I. Ordway, III, *History of Rocketry and Space Travel* (New York: Thomas Y. Crowell Company, 1969), pp. 132-136.

CHAPTER THREE PLANNING FOR PROJECT MANAGEMENT

James L. Easton Division Engineer
Los Angeles County Flood Control District
Los Angeles, California

Robert L. Day Project Manager
Southern California Edison Company
Rosemead, California

INTRODUCTION "OK boss, we've decided to use project management, what now?" The boss should answer, "Before we take any drastic actions, we've got to do a lot of careful planning."

Once the need for project management has been established, the organization must be careful not to jump too precipitously into project management. It is risky for a chief executive to merely issue a memo creating a project and a project manager, and then expect everything to go well. This would probably result in complete disruption of the entire organization. Top management must realize that their management and their specialists very probably prefer the status quo. As indicated previously, line or functional management is very comfortable with the hierarchical organization, and will be strongly resistant to change. It also must be recognized that the implemen-

24

tation of project management is a rather drastic change. Therefore, it must be carefully planned.

THE GAME PLAN

Once an organization is committed to project management, someone in management must ensure that project management "gets off on the right foot." The first thing that must be done is to carefully plan the implementation process. It makes little difference whether this planning is done by top management, staff personnel, middle management, or a consultant; a game plan for implementing project management is necessary. The game plan does not delineate how the project is to be carried out, only how project management is to be implemented and how will the problems of initiating this new concept be solved.

The game plan or project implementation plan must answer such important questions as:

1. How will a firm top management commitment be obtained?

2. How will middle- and lower-level management and potential project personnel be "sold" on project management?

3. What will the first project be?

4. How will the first project manager be chosen?

5. How much real authority will the project manager have?

6. How will the project manager interface with top management and with the customer or client, if there is one?

7. How will the project be organized?

8. What control tools and what reporting system will be used?

TOP MANAGEMENT COMMITMENT

The implementation of project management may or may not start at the top management level in an organization, but in any case, it cannot succeed without an absolute commitment from top management. They must be ready to delegate sufficient "clout" or authority to project managers. This delegation of authority can be done informally or by means of a formal Project Charter, but there can be no doubt in anyone's mind that this is the way the "boss" wants to go. Too many organizations have given up in despair after having tried project management only to have it fail because the project managers were not given adequate authority. Project management must start with top management.

It is a fortunate organization where top management recognizes the need for project management, and can give it their unqualified support without being subjected to a prolonged selling effort. Fortunately top management is usually more oriented toward acceptance of change than middle management, and often will be the first to recognize that a better way of handling one-of-a-kind jobs is needed. (See Case History #1 in Chapter 13.)

However, in many organizations the idea to implement project management originates with middle- or lower-level management, and they then face the problem of convincing top management that project management is the way to go. This is the first problem to be faced in the game plan, and may involve convincing one man (i.e. the chief executive) or a whole roomful of senior vice presidents. It might involve a considerable period of education and learning, utilizing seminars and training sessions. For this purpose, one manager developed a slide program with an accompanying primer telling the story of project management. After securing top management support, the same material, with different words, was successfully used to "sell" middle- and lower-level management. (See Case History #1 in Chapter 13.)

OBTAINING GENERAL PROJECT SUPPORT

The next important part of the game plan after obtaining top management support is communicating it to the entire company or organization as a whole. The entire organization must not only be told about project management, but must be "sold" on the need for it. First, all members of management must be convinced that project management is there to help them, and that it is not a threat to their authority or to their "empires." Prospective project specialists and other personnel must be convinced that they can live with a new boss (or two bosses if a matrix organization is chosen). A very important aspect of the game plan should be a workable approach for obtaining support from both management and project personnel. This action may be the most important aspect of implementing project management, and it is the most often neglected.

THE FIRST PROJECT

The decision as to which project will be first should not be taken lightly. There are two major alternatives that should be considered in the process of deciding how to implement project management: (1) convert all projects in the organization at the same time, or (2) convert only a single project and use it as a trial of the concept. The three case histories presented in Chapter 13 are examples of each approach. The choice of which approach to use depends upon the type of organization involved, the success with which project management has been sold within the organization, and the extent of the top management commitment.

Converting all the projects in an organization to project management at one time is risky. There is just too much chance that the organization will come up short in one of the major resources needed, i.e., enough good project managers. The sudden full-scale implementation of project management also stretches other resources such as line manpower, facilities, equipment, and supporting activities. It can also be somewhat more expensive, at least initially. In addition, the organization must be sure that it is totally ready for project management.

If top management shows signs of timidity or if the organization has inadequate resources, then a single project converted to project management may be the best solution.

Whatever approach is used for the selection of the first project or projects, the effort must result in success if the organization is to continue to use project management. Nothing succeeds like success or nothing will kill project management faster than an initial failure.

THE FIRST PROJECT MANAGER

The choice of the first project manager may be very critical to the future of project management in an organization. If project management has not been previously used, there will probably be no experienced project managers available. The alternatives would be to hire someone with experience, or take the path of least resistance, and appoint an experienced line manager to do the job. There is risk in either case. Bringing in a project manager from outside the organization may have adverse effects on morale, and it may take the new project manager some time to come up-to-speed with the idiosyncracies and problems of the organization. On the other hand, an experienced line manager who knows the organization very well will not necessarily become a good project manager, at least not immediately. The demands and the stress content of the two jobs are so very different. A line manager who is very comfortable managing an organization consisting of specialists may be very ineffective in a high-pressure, multidisciplinary project atmosphere. If a line manager is chosen to be the new project manager, the person should come from as high a level in the organization as possible in order to minimize the risks. A high-level manager will be much more likely to have the necessary multidisciplinary orientation, whereas lower-level managers are usually specialists. 195565166

PROJECT MANAGEMENT AUTHORITY

Organizations considering project management must recognize the effect (which may be traumatic) on the organization's power structure. Top management must be willing to delegate sufficient authority to the project managers so that they will be able to effectively represent management in the accomplishment of project goals. Simply stated, these goals are:

1. Produce the results that were intended.

2. Meet schedules.

3. Stay within the budget.

4. Keep the client or customer satisfied.

To be most effective, the project manager needs enough latitude and independence to accomplish these goals without excessive administrative involvement; however, management must get enough feedback to satisfy itself that the project's goals are being met. This is essential to the maintenance of effective but not excessive control over project management. There is a thin gray line on one side of which is overinvolvement by management, while on the other side is dangerous abdication of management responsibility. Status reports are the key to proper management involvement. These need to be frequent during the early stages of implementation, but they may evolve into an exception reporting system once project management is well established.

THE PROJECT INTERFACES

If a project is viewed as a group of building blocks representing the elements essential to the project, then the principal domain of the project manager is the interfaces between the blocks. The blocks represent the various line or functional organizational units and the various work packages involved in the project. The project manager must be concerned not only that the blocks contain the specified elements, but that the blocks fit together correctly at the proper time and within the budget. The principal job of the project manager can thus be viewed as that of interface management. It is essential that this process of interface management be an important part of the implementation plan. The critical interfaces most likely to cause problems should be identified, and plans should then be developed for minimizing their impact on the project.

In addition to interfaces within the project, there are three important interfaces external to the project which are extremely important since they interface directly with the project manager. These interfaces are between the project manager and top management, subcontractors, and the client or customer.

All project interfaces are important since most problems occur at interfaces, usually a result of two organizational units, each with differing goals and objectives, going in different directions. The project implementation plan should provide clear guidance to all organizational units to minimize potential conflict and smooth conflicting management styles and aspirations.

The subject of interface management or project integration as it pertains to the principal job of the project manager will be further discussed in Chapter 9.

ORGANIZATIONAL ALTERNATIVES

Obtaining a decision as to which organizational form will be utilized is one of the most important aspects of planning for project management. This decision cannot be put off because the entire project operation will be dependent on the organizational form. This subject is so important that the organizational alternatives are examined in detail in Chapters 5 and 6. A pure project organization or "projectized" approach involves the creation of a little company within the larger organization. This approach is highly desirable for very large projects, particularly if the government or other customer has a similar organization and is willing to pay for its high cost. It also must be recognized that the implementation of a pure project constitutes a major organizational disruption which top management may not want to accept. The economies and other advantages of the matrix organization make it a very desirable form for small or multiple projects. It creates the least disruption of the total company organization in that it does not upset the existing functional organization. It merely adds another reporting dimension.

The decisions that must be made by top management involve:

1. To what extent do they wish to disrupt the existing organization? In other words, how much of a change do they really want to make?

2. How important is the project or program to the health and future of the company? That is, how much power in terms of authority and responsibility do they wish to give the project manager?

These are not trivial decisions, and they must be made well in advance of the initiation of the project and certainly prior to issuing the Project Charter. If top management wants a weak matrix, they must recognize that the project manager becomes primarily only a coordinator, and that they must live with the limitations of that organizational form. Project authority and responsibilities cannot be delineated until the type of organizational form has been well thought out and a decision made.

INEVITABLE
CONFLICT

This commitment from top management is a vital prerequisite because project management will be controversial and will be opposed. Conflict will occur even if middle and top management in the line divisions have been thoroughly indoctrinated in the need for it and perhaps have even participated in the decision to implement it. The project manager must plan for opposition and accommodate it because conflict is inevitable and cannot be completely eliminated. A little healthy competition may be good for the organization.

One of the first conflicts encountered when setting up project management must deal with how the line organization perceives its new roles within the project management structure. Often the line organization tends to react as if it were losing some of its power relationship with top management and its control of its own organization.

The conflict that will arise during the planning and implementation of project management can be useful if line managers are encouraged to air their objections and reservations (some of which may be valid and result in modifying project management systems and procedures). If these objections are considered fairly and objectively by top management without weakening its commitment to project management, it may do much to reduce the difficulties that will be encountered during implementation of project management.

Another important aspect of the introduction of project management is the effect on "power politics" as viewed by the line manager. The line manager has a new "boss" (the project manager) who may or may not have line authority over him or her, but who definitely influences what, when, and how things are done on a particular project. Unless the line manager thoroughly understands and supports the need for project management, this new relationship will probably be troublesome. The line manager may think that making personal views known to top management or even to his or her own boss are being inhibited by the project manager. In fact, such an observation may be correct because the project manager represents top management for the project.

The line manager may also view the project manager as an obstacle to gain favorable exposure to top management and therefore a threat to future promotional opportunities. Perhaps the line manager considers the project manager unqualified to make decisions on specialized technical matters. Any or all of these things may impede willing cooperation by line managers. The sensitivity and importance of these new relationships cannot be overemphasized and need to be planned carefully and discussed thoroughly with managers at all levels before implementing project management.

For those companies who cannot achieve this balance of operational conflict, organizational development sessions are designed to sort out those problems. This usually requires the services of a disinterested party to referee sessions between the two sides. A consultant or consulting firm can be very useful at this point to give an orientation program to all personnel involved in the project.

PLANNING FOR CONTROL   The heart of the project management concept is good control, therefore it must be carefully planned. Very elaborate and complex control tools are not needed; the control tools should be adequate only to assure compliance with the overall project plan. Therefore, the project implementation plan should provide the basic elements of the control process. It is important that the organization be informed as to the extent that a Work Breakdown Structure (WBS) will be used, and how small will the units or work packages be. This subject will be discussed in detail in Chapter 7. Will the project control system utilize the existing organizational accounting and reporting system, or will the project have additional input and output requirements to ensure control? A separate project accounting and control system should be avoided if at all possible.

GETTING STARTED ON THE RIGHT FOOT   There are numerous ways of implementing project management. These vary from a completely in-house approach to heavy involvement by a consultant. The method chosen depends on the characteristics of the organization and the degree of sophistication that is desired in the proposed project management system.

Each organization must decide for itself which approach is best suited to set project management in motion. One utility decided it would conduct a series of orientation sessions in two stages. The first set of sessions involved "two-way communications" between middle management and those involved in project work, including future potential project managers. The second series of sessions were set up with other involved departments to present project management philosophy and answer questions.

Once top management has decided that they want project management, they must decide in as much detail as possible what the organizational structure and other aspects of the proposed system will be. A careful evaluation should then be made of the in-house expertise and its ability to produce all or part of the system. If it is decided to employ a consultant, the work to be done by the consultant should be carefully and completely defined. Selection of the consultant is also important and should be done with considerable care, especially regarding the consultant's experience and expertise.

If a consultant is employed, the consultant's work should be closely and carefully monitored. It should be kept constantly in mind that the consultant will never know a client organization as well as the management of that organization does. The constant scrutiny is necessary so to avoid having the consultant recommend systems and procedures that are not workable because of organizational idiosyncrasies.

On the other hand, the consultant may be able to point out organizational and/or personnel deficiencies that may not be apparent or may be overlooked by the management of the client organization.

A consultant may be very helpful in the following areas:

1. Selecting a scheduling system that is as simple as possible but with sufficient detail to provide clear definitions of the sequence of the work and the important interfaces.

2. Formulating a cost control system.

3. Selecting a reporting system that will include concise reports that will be of use to the project managers and the line management in monitoring the progress of the system.

4. The use of the computer in any or all of the above.

One of the key considerations in formulating and implementing a project management system will be the involvement of the affected line managers.

At the onset of project management it is essential that the line managers understand project management. The organizational training sessions described previously gave basic concepts of cost, scheduling, and quality commitments not otherwise understood. Once the line managers understand and support the objectives that can only be obtained by project management, then successes will increase as project management matures. The line manager's role in project management must be completely understood; the role has to be a supportive one working in concert with the project managers.

CONCLUSION

Establishing the need for project management is just the first step; the next and most important action is planning for project management. In order to carry out this action, a game plan or implementation plan is necessary. The first essential feature of the game plan is obtaining a firm commitment from top management in order to provide the project manager with sufficient authority to be effective. It is equally important that middle line management thoroughly understands project management, and that they get deeply involved in the implementation process. Conflict between the line/discipline managers and the project manager is inevitable and unavoidable and may even be helpful if line managers are encouraged to air their objections and reservations.

Other important aspects of the game plan involve such questions as: What will the first project be? Who will be the first project manager? Exactly how much authority will the project manager have? How will project interfaces be handled? How will the project be organized? How will the project be controlled?

Getting started on the right foot is the desired result of planning for project management. This step will vary greatly depending on organizational needs. It often begins with a series of meetings with top management to discuss philosophy, followed by a series of seminars to involve increasingly lower levels of management in the specific policies and procedures of project management. These sessions can often be conducted by a consultant, particularly as the sessions progress into the more technical aspects of the system. Whatever method is utilized, the end result must be that all parts of the organization understand and accept project management.

CHAPTER FOUR IMPLEMENTATION OF THE PROJECT: GETTING OFF ON THE RIGHT FOOT

Linn C.
Stuckenbruck
Ph.D.

Institute of Safety and Systems Management
University of Southern California
Los Angeles, California

INTRODUCTION

How can project management be implemented with a minimum amount of trauma and organizational conflict?

Put yourself in the position of a manager of an organization that has decided that project management is the answer to some of its problems. The suggestion to use project management may come from any level of management; it might be limited to a single department or it might involve participation by the whole company or organization. For instance, a research department could implement project management in its own organization without involving the rest of the company. The decision to implement project management and the process of selling it to the organization are totally in the hands of the research director. The research director has the choice of pure project or matrix organizational forms and can experiment with variations to determine what works best in her or his organizational climate.

However, if the project or projects are large and involve the entire company's organization, the problem becomes more difficult since many organizational boundaries must be crossed and "empires" invaded. It doesn't really matter at which management level the suggestion to adopt project management originated, if it involves the entire organization the suggestion must go first to top management for approval. Project management is often "discovered" by members of middle management who then enthusiastically recommend it to top management. They fail to understand why the concept is not greeted with equal enthusiasm by top management and other members of middle management. Selling the concept to top management and obtaining their active, unqualified, and enthusiastic support is absolutely necessary for successful implementation of project management. This problem of obtaining top management support was discussed in Chapter 3, and will be examined in detail in Chapter 11. If project management is to be successfully implemented, a number of critical actions must be taken by top management, the involved line or functional managers, and by the newly appointed project manager.

TOP MANAGEMENT ACTIONS

The most important of the many actions that must be taken in implementing project management are those which must be taken by top management. The most significant of these actions are:

1. Completely selling the project management concept to the entire organization.

2. Choice of the type or form of project organization to be utilized.

3. Issuance of a project charter to completely delineate project vs. functional authority and responsibilities.

4. Choice of project manager.

5. Choice of the right functional managers to participate in the project and/or matrix organization.

6. Supplying adequate resources to the project organization such as finances, equipment, personnel, computer support, etc.

7. Continuing support to the project manager.

This list of actions is more or less in the order that the actions must be taken, and most of them must be taken prior to the actual implementation of the project.

SELLING PROJECT MANAGEMENT

The entire organization must be prepared for project manage-ment—particularly functional or line management. It is not enough that top management and the project office are strong project management supporters. The concept must also be sold throughout the organization as a "way of life." Strong top management support can nullify the problem of a few foot-dragging managers, but for project management to be really successful it must have continuing support from all levels of management. It is too late to implement project management after the contract has been received, the selling should have begun long before. In fact, a project staff and a project manager should have been appointed long before the arrival of the contract or the job.

How does top management sell the project management concept to the organization? It is apparent that first the support of middle management is essential. A management directive, although necessary, is not enough. An educational process is needed. A management training program can be initiated, using in-house training personnel or perhaps bringing in a consultant to conduct the training sessions. However, this process is usually time consuming, and it is too easy for attendees to beg off or miss sessions due to pressing company duties. A more effective approach is to send the managers in rotation to a concentrated two- or three-day professional seminar on project management, completely away from their job location. Such seminars are numerous in the larger cities. Perhaps an even more effective approach is the management workshop, preferably held as far away from the job location as possible. The workshops can be two- or three-day concentrated sessions held in a conference room of a local restaurant or hotel.

Experience has shown, however, that the most effective approach is the weekend retreat workshop. These can be held at a nearby resort or out-of-town hotel. More and more hotels are providing capabilities for this type of event. The managers and their families check into the hotel, and the family goes its own way while the managers are free to spend their entire day, including evenings, learning about project management. These sessions, often irreverently referred to as "charm school" or "brainwashing," allow a concentrated dose of project management to be administered without interference from work. Top management should be present, not as instructors, but as participants in the discussions, and to demonstrate to their management that the implementation of project management is a joint undertaking of all management and that it has their unqualified support. The principal advantage of weekend sessions is that all involved management can participate at one time rather than in rotation. Top management can lead the discussions or they can call upon a knowledgeable management consultant to be the conference leader. In either case, participation and presentations by outside experts should be an important part of the program. The most important aspect of the program, however, should be the discussions in which management as a group decides how best to implement project management in their own particular organizational climate. Top management must realize that complete acceptance of the project management concept will come only after considerable soul searching and study by the management team. One weekend session may prove to be insufficient, and two sessions separated by time for thought and for homework may be more effective.

CHOICE OF TYPE OF PROJECT ORGANIZATION

The choice of the particular type or form of project management that top management wishes to implement depends entirely on decisions that only top management can make. These decisions should have been made during the initial project planning process, and were discussed in Chapter 3.

ISSUANCE OF A PROJECT CHARTER (SEE APPENDIX A)

Top management must provide a clear charter to the project manager. The charter may be simply a memo from the president or chief executive officer, or it may be an elaborate working document. In any case, a project organization charter should state "the purpose and meaning of organizational activities and ultimately direct the loyalties within and the stability of the structure."[1] At the very least, the charter must spell out the responsibilities and authority of both project and functional managers. In addition, it can indicate, as much as possible, the project manager's relationships with the various functional managers involved in the project. That is, the charter should designate the desired organizational form. The initiation period of a project is no time for organizational experimentation. Not that the Project Charter should be "etched in stone," rather it should be sufficiently flexible to allow for periodic revision or organizational tinkering as indicated by management experience as the project progresses.

It is readily apparent that the project manager should be given adequate authority to do the job he or she is expected to do. The amount of authority is the question that must be faced by top management. How much of their own authority do they want to delegate, and to what extent do they wish to limit the authority and responsibilities of functional management? Top management is understandably reluctant to relinquish any of their authority or take it away from experienced and loyal functional managers. Top management must recognize that when they create a project manager who is expected to be held accountable for the success or failure of the project, they must give that project manager adequate authority. The causes for many a "sick" project can be traced to top management who held back and did not release sufficient authority to do the job. The project manager, being forced to check out most decisions with top management, becomes powerless to prevent disaster, and will probably end up as a convenient scapegoat when the project fails.

CHOOSING THE PROJECT MANAGER

After providing a project charter, the next important action is that of choosing a project manager. Top management must ensure that the right project manager is chosen, and that the selection is early in the formation of the project. Preferably the project manager should be the first person chosen so that she or he may then organize the project team.

Unfortunately it usually does not happen this way. A project is initiated, either as a result of a customer request (the receipt of a government contract or a successful bid on a client's project) or a product need (a potential commercial product indicated by marketing research). Hopefully, at this time a project or product manager would be chosen and the project would get off to a fast and positive start. As previously indicated, this does not always happen. Therefore, the project blunders on until a project manager is selected, and only then does the project really get underway.

It would be much better if the project manager was assigned at the conception of the idea for the project. As soon as a customer or client need is determined, a project manager should be assigned. In this manner a single point of top management and customer or client contact is established as early as possible, and the project will be ready to function at full speed when the project is initiated.

CHOOSING THE RIGHT FUNCTIONAL MANAGERS

It is often just as important to choose the right functional managers to work with the project as it is to choose the right project manager. A functional manager who is not a "believer" in project management, or perceives it as a threat, will be a roadblock to project progress, particularly when functioning in a matrix organization. Therefore, the nonbelievers should not be utilized in a matrix organization. Top management must recognize the nonbelievers in their management team and use them only in the type of functional organizational situation in which they can operate comfortably and effectively.

SUPPLYING
ADEQUATE
RESOURCES

A vital function of top management is to supply adequate resources to their project managers. These resources may take many forms, but most important are financial support, project staff, service group support, and realistic priorities.

A certain amount of financial support is usually needed by projects to supplement direct project costs. This support often takes the form of burden or overhead charges for costs that could not be charged dircectly to the project because of contract or client constraints. Such costs could occur for the following types of needs:

1. Trips for attending conferences with clients, subcontractors, etc.

2. Trips and other costs to attend conferences and seminars to keep up with the state-of-the-art in the project area.

3. Hiring of consultants to solve special project problems.

Closely related to financial support is the provision for adequate staff support for the project office. Many of the project manager's problems involve lack of sufficient time to do the job right. Having adequate staff will alleviate this problem. Quite often job classifications such as administrative assistants, analysts, and planners cannot be charged directly to the project. Similarly, secretaries, clerks, and typists normally charge to overhead.

Another type of support effort not always charged to contract is that of service organizations within the company. The problem is not just that a service effort may not be fully chargeable to a project, but that the service effort be of high quality and adequate to meet project needs. The following types of service-oriented functions must be provided to assure project success:

1. Editorial and printing support to prepare progress and other reports

2. Photographic support for test data and for report illustrations

3. Accounting support to provide timely reporting of project status

4. Computer service support to provide special programming expertise

5. Experimental machine shop and model shop support

6. Research and analytical laboratory support

7. Material and processes control laboratory support

8. Testing laboratory support

9. Purchasing support.

In addition, such organizations as quality control, logistics, value engineering, reliability, configuration management, and safety may or may not be part of the main stream of the project effort, but certainly have to be available and adequate for project needs.

Adequate service is dependent not only on the existence of adequate supporting organizations, but on the priority given the project in these organizations. Top management has the responsibility of ensuring that the relative priorities between projects and between project and functional organizations are realistic. Priorities are not only important for service support, but also for the use of materials and equipment, both company and government owned. Priorities must be adequate to ensure that materials and equipment can be purchased on schedule according to the Project Material Procurement Forecast and the Project Plan. Priorities should also ensure that the best qualified available personnel will be assigned to the project. Project priorities must guide the tradeoffs in materials, equipment, and personnel that must be made to determine which project gets what resources.

CONTINUING TOP MANAGEMENT SUPPORT

Top management cannot simply implement project management by giving it their blessing and then forget about it. Continuing support is necessary and applies to all of the resources previously mentioned. Project needs and priorities should be continuously or frequently reviewed by top management to assure that the project remains healthy.

ACTIONS BY FUNCTIONAL MANAGEMENT

Functional management in a matrix organization must also take an important action. The attainment of project goals and objectives can be endangered by inaction or "foot-dragging" on the part of functional management and personnel serving on the project team. Therefore, functional management must not only accept the concept of project management, but they must obtain complete support from their organizational personnel.

ACTIONS BY THE PROJECT MANAGER Now that the top management has successfully implemented project management and has given it full support, the action passes to the newly appointed project manager. There are a number of specific actions that must be initiated by the project manager to start the project on the road to success. The most critical of these actions are:

1. Issuance of the Project Implementation Plan

2. Creation of the Project Work Breakdown Structure (WBS)

3. Development of the project organization

4. Issuance of the Project Procedures Guide

5. Implementation of reporting and review procedures

6. Issuance of the Project Material Procurement Forecast

7. Issuance of Work Authorizations.

These actions are more or less sequential, although they are strongly interrelated and must be worked on at the same time. The most important consideration is that documentation implementing these actions be issued as early in the project life cycle as possible. Hopefully, much of this effort will be accomplished prior to the initiation of the project, such as during proposal preparation. Even so, a great deal of effort is required during the "front end" of a project to accomplish these actions.

ISSUANCE OF THE PROJECT IMPLEMENTATION PLAN The project manager, recognizing the responsibility of taking the first step toward getting the project going, puts together an initial project document usually called the Project Implementation Plan. This is the first step in developing an overall project plan, which will come a little later in the project (see Chapter 7). The implementation plan is necessary in either a pure project or a matrix organization, but is absolutely unavoidable in a matrix where there are many functional managers who must be informed about the following types of project information:

1. What must be accomplished?

2. What are the specific goals and objectives?

3. What are the important constraints in terms of the schedule and budgets?

4. What specific organizational units will be involved in the project?

5. What are the important milestones in the project?

6. What are the important interface events in the project where hardware, facility, or other completions must be integrated?

7. What detailed planning must the project organizational units accomplish in support of the project and how early in the project?

8. How does the actual contract differ from the proposed work statement?

In the Project Implementation Plan the first cut must be made at breaking the project down into manageable pieces or work packages, usually only major subsystems at this point. The project should also be broken down into a rough time schedule for the completion of each subsystem or task, which will usually be presented as a simple bar chart. As can be seen, the major purpose of the Project Implementation Plan is to alert management as to the actual scope of the project and the role of their organizational unit in conducting the effort. Much of this effort will have been accomplished during the proposal stage. However the details must be covered in this official document which, in reality, serves to turn the project on and informs the project team what they must accomplish.

CREATION OF
THE PROJECT
WORK
BREAKDOWN
STRUCTURE

The project manager's next important task is to produce a detailed Work Breakdown Structure (WBS). The purpose of the WBS is to break the total project down into sufficiently small subdivisions to permit accurate cost estimates, and to permit adequate visability and control. A second purpose of the WBS is to ensure that the smallest subdivisions represent tasks that can be readily accomplished within the estimated cost and schedule. Thus, the WBS is not only an important control tool, but it is extremely useful as a planning and estimating method. That is the reason for placing it in the position of the second project implementation action.

The development of a WBS is a contractual requirement for the acquisition of most defense material items, particularly research and development.

In developing the WBS, the project office must work very closely with the functional and/or project subdivision managers who must actually perform the cost estimates and can best plan the work breakdown. An important goal is to keep the smallest work packages within single organizational units, if possible, in order to simplify cost and schedule estimating and control.

The technique of accomplishing the WBS consists of subdividing the project into major subdivisions (subsystems or subprojects), then to subdivide further into tasks, then into subtasks, and so on until the smallest practical unit (work package) is reached. The WBS is extremely important as it can tie all of the implementing and control actions of the project manager together. It can be the common framework for the Project Implementation Plan, for the project organization, and for the issuance of schedules, budgets, and work authorizations. This results in an integrated WBS, schedule, and budget. (Appendix B is an example of a construction WBS.)

DEVELOPMENT OF THE PROJECT ORGANIZATION

Only good people can ensure project success. While this statement is true for any type of organization, the consequences resulting from inadequate personnel can be much more disastrous in a project since a relatively small slippage can mean project failure. In a pure project, the project manager has a free hand in developing his or her organization, and in selecting and/or hiring the project personnel. However, in a matrix the project manager can only select the project office personnel, and must negotiate with functional managers for the people who will do most of the work on the project.

How does the project manager know who are good people? In most cases, the functional manager's advice must be taken. But the project manager should always be on the lookout for people with the particular technical ability or managerial talent that is needed. In particular, project management and top management should always be watching for those people in the functional organizations who possess the unique qualities which can lead to their being successful project and assistant project managers. This talent is always in short supply, as discussed later in this chapter. In any case, the reservoir of people is in the functional organizations, and the project manager must negotiate with the functional managers for the services of the people she or he wants to work on the project.

A formal document should be issued by the project manager in which the project organization is outlined in detail and the status of everyone working on the project is clarified.

ISSUANCE OF THE PROJECT PROCEDURES GUIDE

The fourth important implementing document that should be produced by the project office is the Project Procedures Guide. This document is designed to detail how the daily business of the project should be carried out, and it should contain the following types of procedures:

1. The duties and responsibilities of staff reporting to the project office

2. The duties and responsibilities of functional personnel working on the project

3. Time-keeping methods

4. Methods of obtaining priorities

5. Methods for resolving priority and conflict problems

6. Type and frequency of computer feedback of project expenditure and schedule status

7. The formal or contractual reporting and review procedures

8. The informal reporting and review procedures.

For the most part, these procedures need no further comment. The exception is the reporting and review procedures, which will be discussed in the next section.

IMPLEMENTATION OF REPORTING AND REVIEW PROCEDURES

The project manager needs effective reporting and review procedures to effectively keep on top of activities and their status in the project. These procedures should be implemented early in the project and not allowed to be set aside whenever a crisis occurs. Reporting procedures must mesh with contractual requirements for customer reports and reviews, and will consist of formal reports, project review conferences, and informal contacts.

Formal Reports and Reviews

Formal reporting procedures are usually customer or client requirements and are out of the hands of the project office. However, the project manager usually needs to implement his or her own formal reporting procedures. All report inputs must go to the project office prior to being made a part of formal reports. The project manager must schedule regular project reviews as often as necessary. These meetings should be scheduled well ahead of time, and the desired attendees should be informed of their responsibilities for presentations. Regular reporting of project status and of significant or interesting events in their area of responsibility should be reported. Special formal reviews should be scheduled if the project finds itself in a crisis.

Informal Reports and Reviews

Informal reports are equally important, but differ primarily in that they are not regularly scheduled and have no standard format. The project manager should be in close enough contact with the principal members of the project team so that daily or more frequent informal reports are received. The project team should make sure that the project manager is never placed in the position of being surprised. That is, the project manager should be the first to know of any problems, and always be on top of every aspect of the project. The project manager who, unaware of a potential problem, is called in for an informal briefing to top management will be extremely unhappy.

Informal reviews will only be called if a special problem arises, and the project manager feels the necessity of obtaining immediate consultation with all concerned parties.

The War Room

Most projects, regardless of size, require the use of a single, central conference room to hold design reviews, progress report meetings, and meetings with the customer or client. The project manager's office is usually too small for such meetings unless the project is very small. A general-use conference room, while adequate for holding meetings, is of no use as a tool for promoting good communications, project togetherness, and esprit de corps. It is a valuable asset to have a room that is solely used for the project. The project manager and personnel cannot only hold project meetings, but can also maintain briefing charts, data, models, and various project progress displays in this room. The room would be available to all members of the project team, and all levels of technical and administrative personnel would be encouraged to utilize it. Such rooms are variously referred to as the project room, the war room, or the project control room. It should be a comfortable room, of adequate size to hold the largest group desired, quiet, and with comfortable chairs. In addition to provisions for projecting and displaying data, it should have an abundance of blackboard space to encourage group discussions.

During the implementation stage of a project the war room can be of great help in creating a project team spirit. It serves as a symbol of the project to both top management and the customer. All members of the project team should become used to meeting regularly in the same place where they can communicate and solve problems together in familiar surroundings.

ISSUANCE OF THE PROJECT MATERIAL PROCUREMENT FORECAST

In order to ensure an orderly and well-run project, a Project Material Procurement Forecast should be issued early in the project life cycle. The successful integration of most interfaces are dependent upon carefully scheduled procurements. This forecast is not only a necessary planning tool for alerting functional managers to the procurement schedule, but it also serves to highlight critical and long-lead time items. Such items as raw stock for fabrication may be overlooked without this forecast.

ISSUANCE OF WORK AUTHORIZATIONS

The last of the implementing actions of the project manager is the issuance of work authorizations, although as a result of project urgency, this action often precedes some of the other actions previously discussed. The work authorization allocates project funds to the functional and/or project organizational unit for the accomplishment of their portion of the effort. The work authorizations allocate funds to the individual work packages indicated in the WBS.

SELECTION AND TRAINING OF PROJECT MANAGERS

THE JOB OF THE PROJECT MANAGER

The project manager's job consists primarily of following good management practice. First and foremost, the project manager, like any manager, must be skilled at getting the job done through people. However, there are several key differences between the job of the project manager and that of general or functional/line management. As discussed in Chapter 9, the project manager must be very concerned with and skilled at carrying out the function of systems integration. As the single point of systems responsibility and authority, the project manager is the only person in the right spot to assure that integration takes place. Another characteristic of the job of project manager is to act as the center of a vital communications network linking together all parts of the project, including top management and the customer.

In addition, the project manager usually has very large, wide-ranging responsibilities much more extensive than equivalent level functional managers. The responsibilities sometimes appear to be overwhelming, yet there is not a commensurate high level of authority and salary. If the project is successful, the project manager seldom receives accolades or cash awards; she or he merely goes on to the next project. It only takes one unsuccessful project to cut a career short as a project manager, and the project manager runs the risk of being the scapegoat if the project fails. Project management is a high-pressure job, full of risk and uncertainty, and it is very often a thankless job.

WHY BE A PROJECT MANAGER?

It would seem that a prospective project manager should consider very carefully whether to accept the position. However, there are very real rewards in project management. Project management is where the action is, and where there are unlimited opportunities to excel. There is great satisfaction in having successfully completed a total project, a satisfaction seldom realized by functional management. In addition, project management's wide-ranging nature gives great freedom of action and wide opportunities for creative accomplishment. This has been very well supported by Charles Martin: "Projects daringly conceived and imaginatively executed offer great opportunities for talented people. Indeed, the freeing of creative people from inhibiting rules and bureaucratically restrictive environments can be the best reason for establishing a project. When a project achieves the delicate balance between bringing out the best of inventive thinking and providing adequate controls to ensure that efforts are directed toward project goals, then it is headed for a striking record of success."[2] Thus, the rewards in project management are found in the personal satisfaction obtained from superior performance in a difficult job.

SELECTION OF THE PROJECT MANAGER

Why should it be difficult to select a good project manager? Can't any competent, experienced manager do the job? If so, why do project managers usually seem to be in short supply? Recognizing promising candidates should be an easy matter if there are means of identifying the characteristics necessary for successful performance in project management.

It is risky to attempt to list all of the personal characteristics necessary for success in project management. Since everyone has different management styles it is impossible to stereotype the proficient project manager. How then can prospective project managers be selected? There have been several attempts to suggest the type of person who would make the best project manager.[3,4,5] These studies concluded that the project manager needs to have all the attributes of any middle-level good manager, but with particular strength in human relations skills. Therefore, the project manager should be strong in communicating, motivating, and team-building skills. The project manager must also be multidisciplinary oriented and innovative, possess integrative skills (see Chapter 9), and have a high tolerance for rapid change and frustration.

The principal reservoir of project talent is in the line/functional organization, although project managers can be brought in from outside the organization. There are two approaches: (1) choose proven, successful line managers as project managers, and (2) develop a cadre of potential project managers by bringing promising candidates into the project office to gain experience as assistant project managers, planners, or other functions.

The first approach is the simplest in that mature, experienced managers of proven ability can be utilized. After the completion of the project, the manager can return to a line position if so desired. The alternative of having a line manager wear a second hat as a project manager is often utilized. Choosing the right manager can be a problem since success in a line/functional position does not necessarily guarantee success as a good project manager.

The second approach is more expensive, but it is more assured of success. A cadre of potential project managers is continuously maintained by viewing the project staff as trainees for the big job. Everyone brought into the project office is screened for his or her potential and continuously reviewed for suitability for project management. The problem involves first locating promising candidates, and then extricating them from their positions in the line/functional organization.

The potential project manager is faced with a career decision. One can remain in the line/functional organization and be assured of a relatively certain career path up the functional line of management, or one can enter the project office. For project management to be an attractive career path, it must have compensations and rewards. The rewards to be gained from personal satisfaction can be great and can be very important to the right person. For the generalist who is interested in the "big picture," project management is a very rewarding job, and it can be a career path leading to top management.

The challenge to top management is to identify individuals relatively early in their careers who have the basic attributes to become project managers.

Project management is not for everyone. The men or women who like their jobs to be disciplined, orderly, unchanging, and conducted according to relatively fixed sets of rules, will not be comfortable in project management. This probably explains why functional managers often have difficulty making a transition to project management. Their management style was more suited to the ordered life typical of a specialist/functional organization. It is usually a traumatic experience to drastically change one's management style. In addition, the temporary nature of projects does not appeal to many people.

Change is the name of the game in project management. Project success is often dependent on rapid change. Prompt action by the project manager is necessary whenever a project runs into trouble. Delay usually only makes the problems worse. The project manager must be willing to change the rules, or break them if necessary, to get the job done.

The background of a project manager will usually include a degree in science, engineering, business, or whatever preparation necessary to understand the basic technology of "business."[6] It is most important that the project manager be able to communicate with the technical specialists working on the project. Therefore, the project manager's educational background will be most likely to match the major technical needs of the project. Since most large projects have a very significant technical content, the project managers quite often are engineers. Engineers also often have the necessary total-system, multidisciplinary orientation.

TRAINING OF PROSPECTIVE PROJECT MANAGERS

The identification of promising candidates for the position of project manager is just the first step. The next question is can project management skills be increased or developed? Such skills can be developed by either a training program, by experience, or both. Training programs are particularly useful to help the members of the project team who are working up the ladder. Such programs might consist of combinations of university courses, professional seminars or short courses, presentations by consultants, and in-house presentations by key project and top managers.

However, the real essence of the job of project manager can only be learned by experience. Therefore, the use of the project office as a training ground is very important. Prospective project managers can be given successively more responsible positions until they are fully prepared for the big job.

CONCLUSION

Project management can be implemented with a minimum of trauma and organizational conflict. If project management is to get started on the right foot, it depends upon top management, functional management, and project management making a number of critical actions very early in the life of the project. The most important action to be taken by top management is that of completely selling the project management concept to the entire organization. A number of other actions must be taken by top management which all involve firm and continuing support of the project manager and the project concept. The action then passes to functional and the newly appointed project manager. Functional management must ensure that their organizations provide full support to the project manager. The project manager has seven very important actions, all of which involve ensuring that everyone on the project team knows what has to be done and when it has to be done.

ENDNOTES

1. Stewart P. Blake, *Managing for Responsive Research and Development* (San Francicso: W. H. Freeman and Company, 1978), p. 176.

2. Charles C. Martin, *Project Management: How to Make It Work* (New York: Amacon, 1976), p. 39.

3. Frank A. Stickney, and William R. Johnson, "Identification and Development of Individuals for Project Management Positions," *Proceedings of the Project Management Institute,* Chicago, 1977, pp. 416-424.

4. Linn C. Stuckenbruck, "The Effective Project Manager," *Project Management Quarterly* (March 1976): 26-27.

5. Linn C. Stuckenbruck, "The Ten Attributes of the Proficient Project Manager," *Proceedings of the Project Management Institute,* Montreal, Canada, 1976, pp. 40-47.

6. David I. Cleland, and William R. King, *Systems Analysis and Project Management,* 2nd ed. (New York: McGraw-Hill Book Company, 1975), p. 6.

CHAPTER FIVE ORGANIZING FOR PROJECT MANAGEMENT

James N. Salapatas Manager, Project Control Services
Florida Power and Light
Miami, Florida

INTRODUCTION In the past, companies involved in the management of projects placed little importance on the organizational implications of this new form of management. A company merely decided to take on a project, appointed a project manager, assigned personnel, and staked a claim on project management. Although the concepts are simple, project management can be very complex in its application, particularly in its initial appearance in the organization. Ineptly conceived or poorly executed, project management is doomed to failure.

The most traumatic aspect of the process of implementing project management is the extensive reorganization or realigning of the existing organization that is necessary. However, it pays not to get too carried away in completely reorganizing; the more drastic the changes, the more the likelihood of failure. In addition, it must be remembered that the project management organization is an integral part of the existing management structure, and must be compatible with it. The form of project management must be chosen to fit the requirements of each particular organization and management structure. An organization does not completely start over with entirely new rules and new management. Most of the old rules and the old top management structure will still be there, and project management must be adapted to fit these organizational constraints (see Chapter 13, Case History #1).

Implementing project management need not change the original parent organization, but it may greatly alter it. A project organization will emerge emphasizing accomplishment of project objectives rather than optimizing the performance of functional departments. This is good because the project organization promotes the company viewpoint. Project management not only creates a new decision-making process, but complicates interpersonal relationships and new organizational interfaces. All these changes are complex and, to a degree, disruptive, but they are tolerated because of their contribution to overall effectiveness and efficiency.

This chapter presents some important organizational issues that need consideration before embarking on project management. The most critical facet of project management is the character of the project. There is a variety of project management "forms" which lead to the effective management of projects. The cause and effect of project objectives, information, and decision making are translated into organizational relationship roles called liaison personnel, expediters, coordinators, project administrators, project managers, project teams, and matrix management.

While these labels may be new to some organizations, the roles have usually been present in successful companies. In today's more complex and fast-moving business world, these relationship roles play a more significant part in achieving overall organizational goals by their sheer integrating force. Things get *done* because somebody is watching over the myriad of activities that traditionally overlap unyielding department boundaries. Things get *done better* because of the synergistic effect of team work.

This chapter concludes by directing these organizational issues into one focal point—the project manager—and ultimately proposes that results still depend on *effective* leadership of a *single* manager and her or his innate ability to influence the outcome of a project through the *active support* of other people.

THE PROJECT DEFINITION MODEL

With the existing state-of-the-art in project management and organizational theory, it should be possible to develop a model that most companies can follow to manage their projects. However, this is not the same as implementing project management in a company, but the model can be useful in deciding what elements of project management are needed. The implementation of project management should be considered *only* if the characteristics of a potential project require a change in the organization and the information systems of the company. Otherwise, the project can be assigned to a "can do" type department head and handled with the existing organization.

The project definition model, Figure 5-1, can be used as a basis for determining whether there is a compelling reason to use project management at all. At this point, a conscious decision must be made to supplement the organization and the information *before* implementation. This decision must come from top management with emphasis and clarity that project management is the direction in which the company is heading. Once the decision is made, a certain amount of fanfare is acceptable to set the stage, but top management must follow-up with active and visible support. Part of top management's decision process should include an assessment of the company's organizational climate with a corresponding directive as to the type of project organization to carry out the effort.

Therefore, matching the project characteristics to the organization is an essential step in determining the extent and type of project management necessary. Project characteristics are:

1. Objective—expected results

2. Schedule—time span and when needed

3. Complexity—technological requirements

4. Size and nature of the task

5. Resources required—people and money

6. Organizational structure

7. Information and control systems.

Figure 5-1 represents a model for defining these project characteristics. All projects essentially follow this process. This Project Definition Model provides a clearer definition of the project, its impact on the organization, and the plan for its accomplishment.

USING THE PROJECT DEFINITION MODEL (PDM)

Since all projects have similar characteristics it is axiomatic that they follow a similar development and maturing process. This process is illustrated by the Project Definition Model (PDM). The PDM may be used as a framework for analysis and will result in a clear description of the project work, a plan for its accomplishment, and the impact of the project on the sponsoring company.

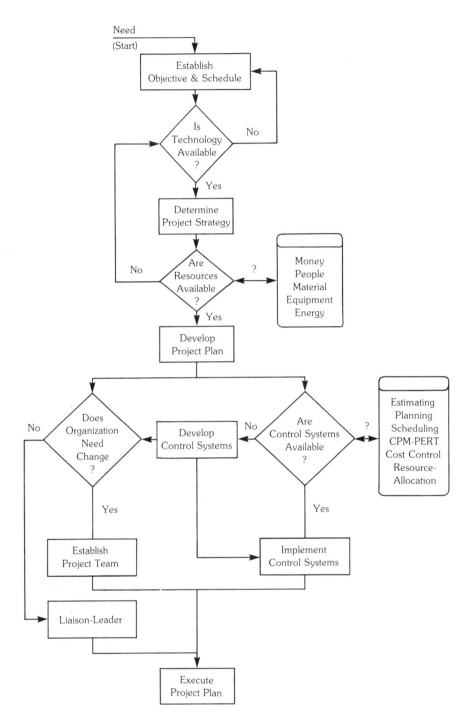

Figure 5-1. Project Definition Model

Every project is a manifestation of some management need or a desire to accomplish some specific task. It could be simply the design and programming of a computer system to control inventory, as complex as harnessing the sun to produce electric energy for commercial use, or even as remote as a research and development project to find a new drug for curing the common cold.

All projects start with some objectives and a schedule. The schedule at this early stage may be just a timeframe or a target date when results are desired. In any event, the first step in the PDM is to establish an objective and a schedule.

The next PDM step is a conceptual question that demands a definitive answer. Is the technology available to accomplish the objective and the schedule? Without the available technology it becomes necessary to go back and reconsider the purpose and necessity of the objective. Can an alternative be found which will achieve similar results? How important is the schedule? A brief survey of the computer state-of-the-art usually indicates that adequate technology is available for an inventory control system. However, in the case of harnessing the sun for producing electric energy, new technology must be developed. As a result, while it is still possible to desire the same objective, the schedule will have to be extended to accommodate the development of new technology. A good crystal ball or a soothsayer would be helpful at this point. If all else fails, a useful rule of thumb indicates that results from research and development efforts take approximately fifteen to twenty years to become commercially available. Except in rare R&D situations, a general approach would be to assume that the adequate technology is available and proceed to the next step, which is determining project strategy.

Determining project strategy means creating a step-by-step plan which will be used to meet the objective and schedule. Such a plan should include the sequence of these steps, how long each will take, and when the work will be done. The plan might also identify what kinds of skills and talents are needed to perform the project work. Upon completion of the project strategy, the next question concerns the availability of resources such as money, people, material, equipment and energy. If the company does not have enough systems analysts and programmers to design their computer system, perhaps there is enough money to purchase a ready-made system, or to contract for its programming and implementation. In the case of solar energy, while solar technology exists in controlled laboratory settings or in limited quantities, extensive production for commercial use will require considerably more applied scientific knowledge and funds. Many sponsors must be found to commit these vast resources before proceeding with the project work. Thus, it can be seen that executing project strategy relies heavily on having the available resources. The project strategy must match the available resources, but it also depends on the available technology. If resources are not sufficient, then it becomes necessary to return to the available technology question and start over. Before the project plan is ever developed, it is highly probable that in most of the complex programs the first steps of the PDM are iterative in nature. There must be a match between all constraints such as objective, schedule, technology, strategy, and resources, until a plan is finalized. Thus, the project plan depends on having a reasonable fixed objective and schedule with available technology and available resources.

According to accepted management practices, organizational *structure* follows operating *strategy*. In the PDM the project plan essentially represents the strategy of a project. How then should the organization be structured to accommodate the project plan? The foremost question becomes: Can the project be handled through the normal information and decision-making processes of the existing organization? If the present organization can support the project without change, a liaison leader can be assigned to execute the project plan. However, if the organization needs to be changed in order to handle the project work, a project team should be established. Running concurrently with this organizational question, there is also the question of systems. Are the control systems available for monitoring, reporting, analyzing, and controlling the progress of the project? Are there systems in place that can perform the functions of estimating, planning, scheduling, cost control, and resource allocation? Are these systems operational so that they can be used by the organization to control the project? If the answer is no, then control systems need to be developed to support either the existing or the new organization. The project team should be involved in the overall development and implementation of the control systems. It is unwise to execute the project plan until the project team has been established and the control systems are implemented.

The very existence of project management is contingent on two critical issues: (1) whether the organization needs changing, and (2) whether new control systems need to be developed, separate and apart from the existing systems of the sponsoring company. The degree of project success is directly proportional to the *effectiveness* of the information and decision-making processes. Efficient and effective management of projects demands strict attention and adherence to the PDM. However, in most cases, while all the steps are performed, they need not necessarily be completed in the order started.

The PDM can be used to determine project management needs because it brings to the surface the "hard" questions that need management attention. Ultimately, the right answers are furnished to get the job done.

THE PROJECT Consider an R&D project in the materials handling field.[1] The customer, a large trucking company was looking for a method to transport small freight shipments cross-country with a minimum of handling. One solution was some form of containerization. But the size, shape, weight, and handling mechanisms required engineering design, tooling, operations, testing, etc. The technology was researched and found lacking except for some exotic containers used by the military in airlift operations. A project strategy was determined to design and build several prototypes for testing on high-volume freight routes. The project plan and schedule were developed to fabricate and test a dozen containers.

The project, assigned to a lead engineer, lasted six months and cost under $100,000. No organizational changes or new control systems were necessary for its execution. The result was a satisfactory design for freight containers which became the forerunner of today's modular truck container equipment. The container project may be considered an example of a small, uncomplicated project, requiring only a very limited project organization.

On the other hand, a project to build a nuclear-generating station costing approximately $1 billion with a ten-year schedule produces a different set of conditions. Although the same Project Definition Model is applicable, the complexity of the project, its magnitude, and the amount of resources required demands a different organization to direct the project effort separately and apart from the normal functional departments of the company.

Special information and control systems are needed to support the project team and to keep top management abreast of progress. While the following is not a comprehensive systems description, it illustrates the magnitude of the systems effort. Elaborate network cost and schedule systems with resource allocation capability are developed to handle upward of 20,000 engineering and construction activities at different levels of detail. Special computer programs are used to perform electric cable design and isometric interference studies (necessary to prevent pipes, cable, and equipment from literally running into each other during construction). Gigantic one-time inventory control systems are created to track and account for the approximately 100,000 material line items. Finally, detailed project information must be summarized into simple but meaningful progress reports for management. A full-time project manager, with decision-making authority, is necessary to lead the project team of selected experts from the functional departments. The nuclear project may be considered an example of a very large and complex project requiring very strong project management.

While these two examples differ widely in size and scope, the Project Definition Model still applies and illustrates the organizational flexibility available. The trucking firm's R&D containerization project is typical of the limited use of project management. Factory expansion projects or developing new products are borderline situations. It may be prudent to consider project management if the project is a one-time effort and the stretching of supervisory controls and interdepartment communications links appears risky. This is especially important since final results and existing information systems seldom meet the needs for urgent project decisions.

At the other end of the scale are very large and complex projects which have a compelling need for project management. However, as projects increase in size and duration, they eventually fall prey to the same bureaucratic system that their parent companies turned away from when they adopted project management.[2] This occurs because the project is as large and complex as the parent organization without becoming a separate division or subsidiary company. In the planning are several large construction efforts where a single project, involving billions of dollars and spanning a dozen years, has a project organization which is almost a duplicate of its hierarchical parent company.

Admittedly, there are some ideas that never develop into projects. Use of the Project Definition Model will help to identify most of these situations. However, ideal use of the model assumes a fixed objective and schedule. This is not always practical. Sometimes original objectives never reach the strategy stage because technology is unavailable. In one case, a large company cancelled its Management Information Systems Project because the computer software technology was not available to meet its processing requirements. It had to settle for modified computer programs with manual support systems.

THE CHANGING PROJECT ORGANIZATION The unique and complex character of projects creates considerable uncertainty in decision making and forces business organizations and their information systems into a different mold. This uncertainty is amplified by the sense of urgency inherent in project work. Considerable pressure is placed on the decision maker by time and schedule constraints.

As uncertainty increases, business organizations respond in two ways.[3] They either reduce the amount of information needed for project decisions, hoping for the best, or they increase their capacity to handle information through some other more costly means. Reducing the amount of information is unacceptable because it results in poor decisions, lowers performance, and increases the risk of project failure.

Project management fills the need to bring information closer to the decision maker. One step toward meeting this requirement is through development of formal information systems and procedures called Project Control Systems. Traditionally, Project Control Systems have consisted of individual and independent information processing subsystems solving specific operational problems. The individual solutions have not been necessarily compatible with each other. The systems approach suggests that every system or subsystem of project control directly affects the performance of other systems. The effective project control systems integrate the planning, scheduling, cost control, estimating, administration, status reporting, and contract effort of the project manager. The system should consist of an integrated and balanced set of methods and procedures incorporating the following elements: (1) manual and computerized systems, (2) control of forms and reports, (3) information flow, (4) records management, (5) specifications, (6) procedures, (7) standards, (8) manuals, (9) mechanization requirements, and (10) personnel organization.[4]

The need to bring information closer to the decision maker is much more than formal information systems and using computers. It depends on vertical and horizontal communications between people in different functional groups and different levels in the organization. Traditional patterns which follow organizational lines have been deficient for making decisions in a project environment. The final step then is the creation of new communication links, lateral relationships, between the people in the project who can carry the information to decision makers in a more timely and effective manner anywhere in the organization.

Most often, management of a project takes on different forms in different organizations depending upon who the decision maker is and where the decision is made. A small project may be handled by direct contact between managers who share information for its accomplishment. A problem in the shop can be handled simply between the engineer and the foreman. From a project viewpoint, the information is at the level where the decision can be made.

When the volume of contacts between any two departments grows, it becomes more economical to set up specialized roles to handle this communication. Liaison personnel are typical examples of these specialized roles designed to facilitate communications between the departments and bypass the upward lines of communication normally involved in decision making. To illustrate this specialized role, in the steel industry when a salesperson books an order for coils, sheet, or plate steel, it is turned over to a customer service representative who maintains contact with the customer and the factory production department until final shipment is made. The customer service representative acts as the liaison between the salesperson and the factory because traditionally in steel sales there is a high volume of changes in shipment quantities, production schedules, and specifications after an order has been booked.

When projects or problems arise which involve more than several departments and their resources, the decision-making capacity of direct contacts is exceeded. Task forces are formed to handle such interdependent tasks on the horizontal basis. Task forces are made up of representatives from each of the involved departments. Some are full-time members and others are part-time members. The task force is a temporary group and exists only as long as the project may take or as the problem remains.

During the development of a computer estimating system in a large utility company, it became evident that prior to computer system design, the estimating subassembly standards required information from engineering, construction, purchasing and stores, and accounting. A task force was established to identify and categorize the labor and material for each subassembly prior to assigning account numbers, purchasing identification, and other coding needed for setting the standard. The effort took longer than originally expected, but the results were very favorable to the company. The material identification numbers were streamlined, ineffective labor practices were uncovered and corrected, surplus material was found and disposed of, and new subassemblies were designed to fill in some operating deficiencies. With completion of the project or solution of the problem, each participant returned to his or her department and normal tasks. To the extent that they are successful, task forces remove problems from higher levels of the hierarchy. They make the decisions at the lower levels in the organization. Group problem-solving techniques are used as the information is available where the decisions are made.

As certain decisions consistently arise in the business organization, task forces tend to become permanent. These are labeled *standing committees* or *teams*. The group decision process becomes permanent. The task force (from the previous example) which developed the estimating subassembly standards had disbanded, but was recalled periodically to review new subassemblies which were being designed to keep up with the latest technology. They also convened to review current standards which were changing because of new material specifications or construction practices. This increase in effort resulted in establishing a standing committee to review subassemblies. The committee leader was usually the manager of the department responsible for causing the change. However, there are many organizational concerns involved with this type of team decision making, such as: (1) At what level do team members operate? (2) Who participates? (3) Who will be the leader?

Occasionally, the leadership passes from one manager to another. Consensus decisions still prevail, but occasionally when this was not possible and the protem leader could not make the decision, the information went up to the executive level for a final decision. Both consensus and executive-level decisions were costly and time consuming. Consensus decision making may be acceptable for a subassembly standards committee, however, for projects such as a million-dollar factory expansion or development of a new product line, consensus decisions are not desirable because the conditions are entirely different. These projects are usually complex efforts requiring significant contributions from different functional departments who in turn must set their own priorities and allocate their resources. Since each project has a specific objective and schedule and competes with other projects, time, resources, and productivity become critical.

Timely decision making requires full-time leadership. In most organizations, their full-time leadership is solved by creating a new integrating role called Project Coordinator, Project Engineer, Project Leader, etc. The issue with this role is to create enough power in the role to influence the decision process. Project coordinators have power because they report to the executive level even when no one reports to them. They collect information to equalize power differences with functional department heads. With preferential access to knowledge and information, the quality of joint decision is improved. Power equilization occurs only if the integrating role is staffed with someone who can exercise expert power in the form of persuasion and influence rather than exert the power of rank and authority.

As the task becomes more complex and uncertain, it becomes more difficult to exercise "expert power." The integrator must obtain more power of the formal authority type in order to be more effective in coordinating the joint decisions which had occurred at the lower levels of the organization. This becomes position power and changes the nature of the role. Labels such as Project Manager and Program Manager are found in this situation.

Unlike the integrating role, the project manager possesses formal position power, but is different from the line manager because the participants still do not report directly to him or her. The power is added by the following successive changes: the project manager has approval over budgets formed by other departments, controls the planning and budgeting process, initiates the budgeting cycle, and buys the resources from the functional groups. These steps permit the project manager to exercise considerable influence even though no one really works for her or him. The role is concerned with integration, and it exercises power through the formal power of position.

However, if this power is not sufficient to integrate the subtasks, and the creation of self-contained groups is not feasible, there is a final step. This is called the matrix organization which creates the dual authority relationship between the project manager and the functional manager. In a matrix organization, personnel assigned to the project have formal reporting relationships to the project manager. In effect, they have two bosses. They receive function direction and support from their home (functional) department, and project direction from the project manager. In theory, the project manager tells them what project work to do, and when; while the functional manager tells them how and sets the standards for technical performance. The expected result is a balance of power between the project manager and the functional line organization. The matrix covers a wide spectrum of integrating roles resulting from the wide range in the balance of power possible between project and line organizations.

THE ALTERNATIVES

Project management requires a special organization, but there is no single unique project organization; rather there is a spectrum of organizational alternatives. Even the terms *pure project* or *matrix* do not refer to single, clearly defined organizational forms; each may have many variations. It has been proposed that organizations fit on a continuum with the functional organization and the pure project organization at the two excesses.[5] As shown in Figure 5-2, the matrix fits in between these two extremes. However, the point of this figure is that there are not just these three alternatives but a whole spectrum of alternatives depending upon the amount of power given the so-called project manager. The continuum of matrix organizations varying from weak to strong is discussed in the next chapter. The balance of power tips toward the project manager in the strong matrix and toward functional management in the weak matrix.

SELECTING THE RIGHT ORGANIZATIONAL FORM

How is the right organizational form of project management chosen, once the decision to implement project management has been made? The organizational form chosen must be appropriate for the company, the project or service, and its management. The type of organization needed will emerge rather clearly as answers to the following questions are obtained:

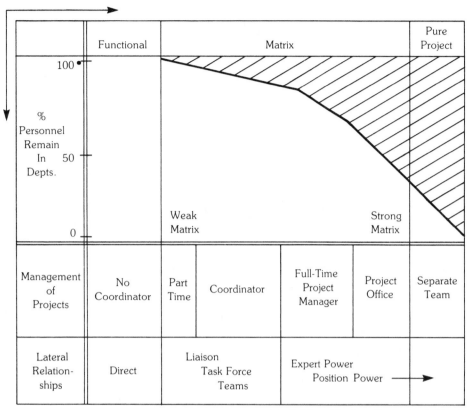

Adapted from Youker. See end note No. 5.

Figure 5-2. Project Management Organizational Continuum

1. Is the organization ready for project management?

2. How big are the projects?

3. How complex are the projects?

4. How many projects are there?

5. What does the customer or client want?

6. What does top management want?

The answer to the question of whether the organization is ready for project management lies partly in the past history of the company or organization. Has project management been previously used in the organization, and was it successful or unsuccessful? If a previous attempt was unsuccessful, is the organization better prepared at this point in time, or will the same mistakes be made? Is the organization ready for a major reorganization? These questions concern whether management at all levels recognizes that changes are needed, and whether they are ready to accept organizational changes. It then becomes a decision as to how drastic a change will the organization tolerate without an extensive orientation program. In other words, if a rather lengthy and expensive orientation and educational program is not desired, the project organizational form should be kept as simple as possible. It might be better to start with a project coordinator or a weak matrix and wait and see how everything works out.

Does the organization have just one big project? A pure project organizational form is usually the answer for that one gigantic project, whether its an aerospace or construction project. If there are a number of rather medium-sized projects, a strong matrix is usually a better answer. Whenever there are multiple projects, a matrix should be considered, particularly if the projects are technically very complex and cross many disciplinary boundaries. A number of small projects usually suggests the use of multiproject management where a single project manager has a number of small projects, none of which justify a full-time project manager. Multiproject management works best when the projects are not complex but are similar or interrelated. A multiproject manager can be very valuable in setting priorities and allocating resources.

Very complex projects, crossing many disciplinary lines, are usually best managed by a matrix organization. The advantages of the matrix are also apparent when there are a large number of projects, the principal advantage being better utilization of resources, principally people, equipment, and facilities.

The type of project organization is often mandated by the client or customer, who should be accommodated if at all possible. The government and large construction companies prefer a pure project organization, particularly if it matches their own organization. They like the "mirror image" because all members of the organization know whom to contact as their equivalent in the other organization.

The most important consideration is what does top management want? After all, the boss will get her or his way, and, as indicated in Chapter 4, the selection of the project management organizational form should be a prerogative and responsibility of top management. In any case, since top management approval is necessary, whoever does the planning should determine what reservations and constraints top management would impose on the project organization.

THE PROJECT MANAGER

The selection of the right person for project manager is very important because that person constantly works with change, copes with multiple-discipline groups, and deals with problems across functional lines. With conflict, the pressure of time and cost limitations, and a job that has more responsibility than authority, the project manager's success depends on personnel from different functional areas who must work as a team to accomplish the project objective. This requires a keenly developed sense of timing, a talent to deal with human behavior in a multidisciplinary environment, and an effective leadership style.

Project managers typically employ two leadership styles in managing projects.[6] One is characterized by going through formal organizational influence sources such as authority, reward, and punishment. The other approach focuses on the needs of team members in deriving influences for their project support.

Since project management is a function of the project, the organization, and the project manager, it should follow that these three would determine effective leadership style for managing projects—not so. The evidence shows that organizational climate is the strongest influencing factor in determining effective leadership style.[7] What this means is that it makes little difference how complex the project, or whether the project manager reports directly to the president or another manager. If the organizational climate is good, chances are the project manager will get the job done concentrating on team member needs and support. This is slightly more than a coordinating role.

However, if the organizational climate is poor, project manager success depends on using formal authority through the hierarchical organization. In this case, the higher the position power, the more effective the results. It is important to note that extremes in organizational climate (i.e., very good or very bad) are rarely the case. Thus, the project manager normally operates in a mix, and needs to be flexible in leadership approach.

Maintaining open lines of communication and reinforcing liaison relationships between project people in the matrix and their home departments is one of the most difficult tasks for the project manager. It is incredible how much time is spent defining and discussing reporting relationships between various people assigned to a project, be it at the construction site, the home office, or between the functional departments. Who reports to whom and why? Who *should* report to whom and why? Why is somebody doing that? It is not their job! Hey, why isn't somebody doing that? It is their job! This kind of conversation is typical for an organization where there is much activity and there are many bosses flexing their hierarchical muscles. This is the type of discussion normally found in a new matrix management environment. Relationships are fluid and ambiguous; the organization appears in constant change.

In order to be effective, the project manager must have a high tolerance for ambiguity and a propensity for orderliness. While the project manager needs to exercise decision-making authority, it should not be at the expense of losing matrix management flexibililty or reducing the active organizational support of the functional departments.

When major decisions come up, it is the project manager's primary job to determine the importance of the decision, what impact it will have on a project, who should be involved, and how much effort should be expended before the time is literally up and the decision must be made. There is much give and take in a matrix organization, with team members assuming an organizational role based on the situation as opposed to what their job description dictates. Decision-making authority in such an organizational situation gravitates to the person who has the best credentials to make the judgment.[8]

There is no single method for making this determination—no strict rules or written procedures. Deciding *how* to have project decisions made rather than personally making them is the project manager's real job. This entails using a systematic approach to strengthen the decision-making process. One such method offers a series of questions which, when answered, provides the manager with insight as to whom and how many should be involved in the decision-making process.[9]

1. Does it make a difference which course of action is adopted? How will it affect the project and impact the overall company?

2. Is there adequate information to make a proper analysis? What data is missing to put the pieces together and where can the information be obtained?

3. Who is going to be affected by the decision and is their commitment critical to its implementation?

4. If commitment is critical, will the response be in full compliance with whatever decision is made, or will there be conflict such that the decision may be delayed, or even reversed?

The evidence indicates acceptable answers lean toward getting more information and involving more people to improve the quality of the decision. However, the project manager must weigh the involvement of people and sketchy information against time. Decisions by the project manager are necessary only when there is not enough time to get all the information required.

The project manager is the timekeeper for project decision making. When the project stakes are high, the project manager's risks are greater. Split-second timing may sound exaggerated, but since projects have specific duration and cost objectives, decisions missed are literally gone and could be very costly.

The project manager is also in a good position to influence the organizational climate by personal actions. Establishing a reputation of credibility and trust through interpersonal relations will have a far-reaching effect on team motivation and morale. Single-mindedness in pursuit of project objectives, personnel planning to integrate the work flow and prevent conflict, and an honest concern for matching team member goals with project objectives will also help in establishing a more favorable organizational climate. The opportunity to perform these actions, however, rests with top management. Their support is a must for the project manager to make things happen.

CONCLUSION

Organizing for project management starts with analysis of project characteristics to determine the extent and type of organization needed for getting the job done. A variety of project management "forms," from simple liaison personnel who carry messages unobstructed across forbidden department boundaries to a pure project organization where the project manager controls her or his own "empire," are available and effective as a means for the management of projects. Also available is matrix management which refers to a continuum of organizational forms where the project personnel must relate to two bosses.

Prior to initiating the program, however, an important step is the assessment of organizational climate which is helpful in uncovering potential problems and developing the strategy for implementation. Top management involvement carries a dual responsibility: (1) commitment and visible endorsement of the program, and (2) selection of the most qualified individual for project manager. While the project manager's leadership effectiveness might be diluted by prevailing organizational climate, the "right" style can strongly influence climate and project decision making toward high team performance and successful results.

ENDNOTES

1. Author's personal experience, Roadway Express, Inc., Akron, Ohio, 1960.

2. Author's attendance state-of-the-art panel discussion, PMI Symposium/Seminar, Chicago, Illinois, October 1977.

3. Jay Galbraith, *Organization Design* (Reading, Mass.: Addison-Wesley, 1973).

4. A. M. Burger, and D. W. Haldin, "Data Base Methods for Complex Project Control," *Journal of the Construction Division*, ASCE, vol. 103, no. CO3 Proc. Paper 13210 (September 1977): 453-463.

5. Robert Youker, "Organizational Alternatives for Project Management," *Project Management Quarterly* 3 (March 1977): 18-24.

6. H. J. Thamhain, and D. L. Wilemon, "Leadership Effectiveness in Program Management," *Project Management Quarterly* 8 (June 1977): 25-31.

7. Ibid., p. 29.

8. David I. Cleland, "Defining a Project Management System," *Project Management Quarterly* 8 (December 1977): 37-40.

9. V. H. Vroom, and P. Yetton, *Leadership and Decision Making* (Pittsburgh: University of Pittsburgh Press, 1973).

CHAPTER SIX THE MATRIX ORGANIZATION

Linn C.
Stuckenbruck,
Ph.D.

Institute of Safety and Systems Management
University of Southern California
Los Angeles, California

WHAT IS A MATRIX ORGANIZATION?

A matrix organization is defined as one in which there is dual or multiple managerial accountability and responsibility. However, the term *matrix* means quite different things to different people and in different industries.[1,2] In a matrix there are usually two chains of command, one along functional lines and the other along project, product, or client lines. Other chains of command, such as geographic location, are also possible.

The matrix organizational form may vary from one in which the project manager holds a very strong managerial position to one in which only a coordinating role is played. To illustrate the organizational principles, first a matrix will be considered in which there is a balance of power between the project and functional managers. It must be recognized that such a balanced situation, considered by some authorities to be ideal, probably seldom occurs in practice.

THE TWO-BOSS MATRIX

In a balanced matrix organization various people in the organization have two bosses (Figure 6-1). This represents an abandonment of the age-old management concept: "Thou shalt have but one boss above thee." None of the re-

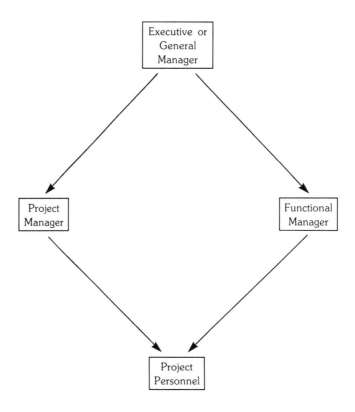

Figure 6-1. The Basic Unit of the Matrix Organization

porting relationships shown in Figure 6-1 are dotted-line relationships. Solid- and dotted-line relationships have various interpretations depending upon local management custom. However, solid lines normally connect managers with their direct subordinates, the one above being the boss. Dotted lines are usually used to indicate staff relationships or reporting relationships of lesser importance. The project manager in the matrix organization is not a staff member, and does not normally have less authority than the functional managers reporting on the same level. Nor can the relationships shown in Figure 6-1 be simply described by such terms as "the project personnel report to the functional manager only for technical direction," or "the project personnel report to the project office for budgetary and schedule control." Such descriptions are inadequate for describing how the matrix organization really works because, in reality, not just on paper, the project personnel do have two bosses.

Implicit in the definition of the matrix organization is the recognition that the project is temporary whereas the functional departments are more permanent. Although all organizations are temporary in that they are constantly changing, the matrix is designed to be temporary and a particular organizational structure lasts only for the finite life of the project.

WHY THE MATRIX? The matrix developed as a natural evolution of organizational structures in answer to a very definite real-world need. The need was for an organizational form capable of managing very large and very complex programs, projects, and problems, and for managing limited resources. The conventional hierarchical management organization could not cope with the added complexity and the enormous amount of information that had to be processed, and conventional management theory was of little help in solving these new and unique problems.

Most management theorists predicted that the lack of any clear-cut single line of responsibility and authority would result in managerial ineffectiveness. There is no evidence to indicate that multiple authority and role conflict lead to ineffectiveness.[3]

The primary reason for adopting the matrix in a large organization can be pinpointed in the fact that functions and skills are fragmented throughout the organizational structure. Individual functional departments have great difficulty in solving very large problems because of a failure to view the total system and a tendency to suboptimize or solve the problem within their particular discipline. According to an old aerospace cliché, "an engineer attacks every problem as if it had an engineering solution." How many of today's big civil and social problems have purely technical solutions?

Since it was found to be impractical to fragment the problem and have the various functional organizations work only on their portion of it, *microcompanies*[4] were formed. This represented the development of the pure project organization. It was rapidly realized that this alternative was not only very unwieldy but also had many disadvantages with respect to efficient functional operations. The matrix was the next logical development.

GROWTH OF THE MATRIX As problems and projects became more complex, the inadequacy of the hierarchical organizational structure became apparent. At the same time, the necessity for designing the organization around the task to be performed was realized. Fortunately, varied but more complex organizational alternatives have become available. The present management philosophy is that there is no "one best way" for all projects to organize; rather, there are many alternatives from which to select a specific project. Among these alternatives are various forms of the matrix.

A formalized matrix form of organization was first developed and documented in the United States aerospace industry, where it evolved during the growth of the large, complex projects of the 1950s and 1960s. If a project was very large, it usually became a pure project organization in which all of the functions and resources necessary to accomplish the objectives of the project were put into a single hierarchical organization. This alternative worked very well if the project or program was very large, if the government customer was similarly organized, and if the customer not only insisted on such an organization but was also willing to pay for its added expense.

However, the aerospace industry found that it had many more projects that were not particularly large, but were exceedingly complex, and therefore not conveniently handled within a single discipline. Today, it is rare to find a real-world problem that is unidisciplinary. In addition, top management still felt a strong need to have a single source of information and a single point of responsibility for each project or program. Some form of project management was obviously needed, and, as top management was unwilling to bear the expense of making each project a little empire of its own, the matrix was a natural evolution in management thinking. The term *matrix* began to be applied to organizations at this time, and, as indicated by Davis and Lawrence, "It probably seemed like a fitting term for mathematical trained engineers in that industry to apply to the gridlike structure that was evolving. . . ."[5]

THE MATRIX ORGANIZATION

It has been recognized that the matrix organizational structure has applications far beyond that of project (program or product) management.[6] However, in this discussion the matrix will only be considered from the viewpoint of its most highly developed application—that of project management.

The term *matrix project organization* refers to a multidisciplinary team whose members are drawn from various line or functional units of the hierarchical organization. The organization so developed is temporary in nature, since it is built around the project or specific task to be done rather than on organizational functions. The matrix is thus built up as a team of personnel drawn from both the project and the functional or disciplinary organizations. In other words, a project organization is superimposed on the conventional function hierarchical organization.

The matrix in its simplest form is shown diagrammatically in Figure 6-2, indicating how the matrix received its name. This matrix represents a general organizational structure. To be more specific, engineering, research, product, and construction matrix organizations are shown in Figures 6-3, 6-4, 6-5, and 6-6 respectively.

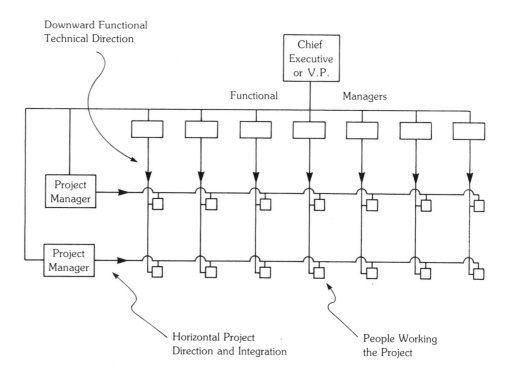

Figure 6-2. Simple Matrix Organization

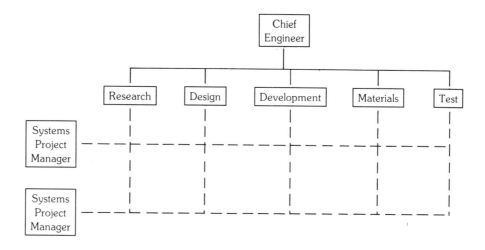

Figure 6-3. An Engineering Matrix Organization

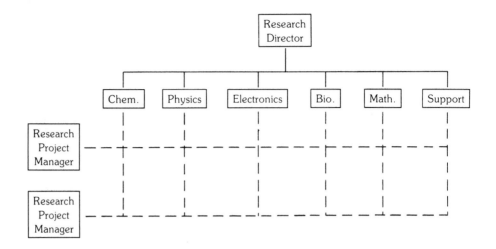

Figure 6-4. A Research Matrix Organization

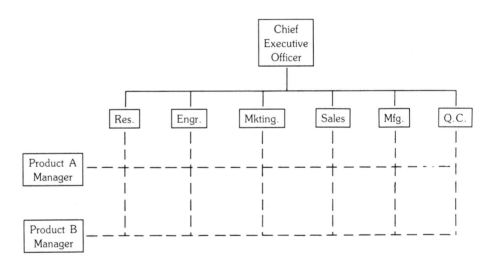

Figure 6-5. A Product Industry Matrix Organization

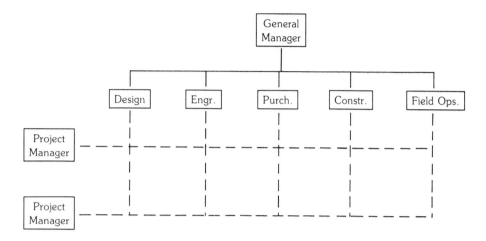

Figure 6-6. A Construction Industry Matrix Organization

The matrix is thus a multidimensional structure that tries to maximize the strengths and minimize the weaknesses of both the project and the functional structures.[7]

DOES THE MATRIX WORK?

No specific organizational form can be guaranteed to work at all times, or to improve productive output. However, it can be said that some organizational forms have a better chance of working than others, particularly if they are designed to meet the needs of project work. As previously indicated, the matrix meets a number of well-defined needs. The principal need is for an organizational structure that can handle the great complexity of a multidisciplinary effort.

If the multidisciplinary need is really there, and if project management is necessary, then the matrix is a viable organizational solution. However, the matrix is a complex organizational form and will not automatically work. The number of things that can go wrong is endless, but the most usual reasons for failure of the matrix are either foot-dragging or downright sabotage on the part of functional management and even by lower-level supervision. As indicated in the previous discussion of project management, it is necessary to thoroughly sell the concept to top management and to all involved functional management to assure that the matrix will work. If everyone involved in the matrix is "a believer," and every effort is expended to make it work, the matrix will work and will result in outstanding project accomplishment. It only takes one uncooperative disciplinary manager to make the whole project fail.

However, active, enthusiastic, and aggressive support by top management will counteract even the most recalcitrant functional manager.

ADVANTAGES OF THE MATRIX

The matrix organization has many advantages which far outweigh its principal disadvantage of complexity. Among the more universally accepted advantages that go beyond the advantages of project management in general are the following:[8,9]

1. Project Objectives Clear

Project objectives will not only be highly visible through the project office, but will also be balanced with the objectives of the functional organization.

2. Project Integration

There is a clear and workable mechanism for achieving project integration of subsystems and work packages across functional departmental lines. Coordination across functional lines can easily be achieved.

3. Efficient Use of Resources

The maximum efficient utilization can be made of scarce company resources. It is the most efficient use of manpower, since personnel can be used only part time if desired, and can be shared between projects. It is the most efficient use of facilities, machinery, equipment, and other resources, since these resources can be shared between or among projects. Allocation of scarce resources can be negotiated between project and functional management, or corporate priorities may be established. The matrix is therefore less expensive than an equivalent pure project organization.

4. Information Flow

Information dissemination should be very effective since there is provision for both horizontal and vertical flow. Horizontal flow provides for project and systems information to flow from functional unit to functional unit. Vertical flow provides for detailed disciplinary information to flow from project to project, and to various levels of management. Information of use to other projects is not locked up within a single project.

5. Retention of Disciplinary Teams   Teams of functional experts and specialists are kept together even though projects come and go. Therefore technology and know-how is not lost when a project is completed. Specialists like to work with other specialists in the same discipline, and they will be better able to continually exchange ideas and information. As a result, when teams of functional specialists work together, a synergistic effect occurs, resulting in increased innovation and productive output, even though individually they may be working on different projects.

6. High Morale   Morale problems occur less frequently, since the worker in the matrix responds first to the morale-building experience of working on a successful project resulting in visible achievements. This will be true whether the achievement is a ballistic missile, an aircraft, a power plant, or the introduction of a new soap into the marketplace. Second, worker morale is normally higher when they can work with their fellow specialists. Third, by retaining their functional "home," specialists may have a clearer career progression up the functional ladder. On the other hand, if they find that their talents and interests are multidisciplinary, they can set their career objectives toward the project office.

7. Development of Project Managers   The matrix is an excellent training ground for prospective project managers since promising candidates can easily be spotted in the multidisciplinary project environment. A common occurrence would be the transfer of a person who had demonstrated the ability to work across functional departmental lines to the project office as an assistant project manager. Career progression would then be to project manager, which is an excellent path leading to top management.

8. Project Shut-down

In a matrix organization, project termination is not the traumatic and painful event that it can be in a pure project organization. It is not uncommon for a large aerospace or construction project to have several thousand people working in a pure project organization. What do you do with several thousand people when the project is completed? Large layoffs are almost unavoidable, since only a relatively few people can be relocated unless major buildups in another project are occurring. Matrix projects are normally smaller, with fewer people involved overall. In addition, the people are spread across a whole functional organization so that each department has only a few people to relocate.

PROBLEMS OF THE MATRIX

The matrix organization does have some disadvantages and problems, but they need not be considered insurmountable. Knowing what problems may occur is half the battle in overcoming them. The following disadvantages are inherent in the matrix organization:

1. Two Bosses

The major disadvantage is that the personnel on the project are working for two bosses. In any type of conflict situation a person could easily become caught in the middle. Further problems of conflict can be caused by project personnel playing one boss against the other.

2. Complexity

The matrix organization is inherently more complex than either a functional or a pure project organization, since it is the superimposition of one on the other. This complexity shows itself in the following problems:

a. Difficulties in Monitoring and Controlling Complexity results from the number of managers and personnel involved and from the number of people that must be kept informed. Fortunately, modern computer techniques have helped to keep this problem under control, but basically it's still a "people" problem.

b. Complex Information Flow

This is a problem only because there are so many people and organizational units involved. Both the project and functional managers must be certain that they have touched bases with each other for any major decisions in their areas of responsibility.

c. Fast Reaction Difficulties

The project manager is sometimes faced with a problem of achieving fast reaction times, primarily since there are so many people to be consulted. The project manager in the matrix usually does not have strong vested authority, therefore considerable negotiation is necessary. Project management was primarily conceived to prevent this problem, but it can be a problem if the management system keeps the project manager from making any decisions without consultation with functional and top management. If the matrix is working, the problem won't occur.

d. Conflicting Guidance

The more complex organization with two lines of authority always increases the possibility of conflicting instructions and guidance.

3. Priorities

A matrix organization with a number of projects faces real problems with project priorities and resources allocation. Each project manager will obviously consider his or her project to have the highest priority. Similarly, functional managers will consider that the allocation of resources and priorities within their departments is their own business. As a result, the decisions involving project priorities and often the allocation of resources must be made at a high level. This often puts an undue and unwelcome load on the top executive officer in the matrix. This problem has led to the use of a manager of projects or a super project manager in some organizations. Principal functions would be to consult with higher levels of management to assure equitable allocation of resources and to periodically reassess project priorities. This effort can be extremely valuable in reducing conflict and anxiety within the matrix.

4. Management Goals

There is a constant, although often unperceived, struggle in balancing the goals and objectives of project and functional management. A strong project manager may place undue emphasis on time and cost constraints, while a functional manager may concentrate on technical excellence at the expense of schedules. Top management must assure that a careful balance of the goals of both project and functional management is maintained.

5. Potential for Conflict

Whenever there are two project managers competing for resources, there is potential for conflict. This conflict may evidence itself primarily as a struggle for power. However, it may also evidence itself by back-biting, foot-dragging, and project sabotage. Conflict and competition may be constructive as an aid to achieving high performance; however, it cannot be allowed to degenerate into personal antagonism and discord. In project work conflict is inevitable; keeping it constructive is the problem in matrix management.

6. Effects of Conflict on Management

Since conflict and stress are inherent in the matrix organization, considerable attention must be given to the individuals who will function as both project and functional managers. Individuals vary greatly in their ability to function effectively under stress. Conflict, particularly the role conflict typical of the two-boss situation, can produce stress, anxiety, and reduced job satisfaction. Considerable attention must be directed toward assuring that prospective managers have a high tolerance for conflict situations.

Davis and Lawrence[10] have discussed matrix problems, which they term *matrix pathologies*. They list and discuss the following problems: power struggles, anarchy, groupitis, collapse during economic crunch, excessive overhead, decision strangulation, sinking, layering, and navel gazing. They indicate that many of these difficulties occur in more conventional organizations, but that the matrix seems somewhat more vulnerable to these particular ailments.

They indicate that power struggles are inevitable in a matrix because it is different from the traditionally structured hierarchy. In the matrix, power struggles are a logical derivative of the ambiguity and shared power that have purposely been built into the design. Corporations will find it exceedingly difficult to prevent power struggles from developing, but they must prevent them from reaching destructive lengths.

Anarchy is defined as a company quite literally coming apart at the seams during a period of stress. As the authors admit, this is an unlikely occurrence, and the more explicit the organizational agreements are, the less likely it is to occur.

Groupitis refers to confusing matrix behavior with group decision making. The matrix does not require that all business decisions be hammered out in group meetings. Group decision making should be done as often as necessary, and as little as possible.

Collapse during economic crunch refers to the frequently noted fact that matrix organizations seem to blossom during periods of rapid growth and prosperity, and to be buffeted and/or cast away during periods of economic decline. It seems natural that during periods of crisis, top management should think that the organization needs a firmer hand and reinstitute the authoritarian structure. "There is no more time for organizational toys and tinkering. The matrix is done in." Thus the matrix is the readily available scapegoat for other organizational problems such as poor planning and inadequate control.

One of the concerns of organizations first encountering the matrix is that it is too costly, since it appears, on the surface, to double up on management by adding another chain of command. It is true that overhead costs do rise initially, but as the matrix matures, these overhead costs decrease and productivity gains appear.

It is suggested that moving into a matrix can lead to strangulation of the decision process. "Will all bold initiatives be watered down by too many cooks?" Three possible situations can arise: (1) the necessity for constant clearing of all issues with the functional managers, (2) escalation of conflict caused by constant referral of problems up the dual chain of command, and (3) the belief of some managers that every decision must be a crisp, unilateral decision. These managers will be very uncomfortable and ineffective in a matrix organization.

Sinking refers to the observation that there seems to be some difficulty in keeping the matrix viable at the corporate or institutional level, and a corresponding tendency for it to sink down to lower levels in the organization where it survives and thrives. This phenomenon may be indicative of top management not understanding the matrix, or the matrix may just be finding its proper place.

Layering is defined as a phenomenon in which matrices within matrices are found. By itself, layering may not be a problem, but it sometimes creates more problems than it solves because the unnecessary complexity may be more of a burden that it is worth.

Navel gazing refers to the tendency to become absorbed in the organization's internal relations at the expense of the world outside the organization, particularly clients. This concentration on the internal workings of the organization is most likely to occur in the early phases of a matrix when new behaviors have to be learned.

MAKING THE MATRIX WORK

After examining the disadvantages and problems of working in a matrix organization, one may view the problems as insurmountable. How then does a company get this complex organizational form to function? Its successful operation, like that of any management organization, depends almost entirely on actions and activities of the various people involved. First, top management must give real and immediate support to the matrix, including a clear project charter. This charter should state the purpose of the project and spell out the responsibilities and authority of the project manager. In addition, it should indicate to the fullest extent possible the project manager's relationships with the functional managers involved in the project.

Functional managers must modify much of their managerial thinking and their usual operational procedures and activities in order to make the matrix work. This may mean a considerable change in the way they determine their priorities. It may be a considerable shock to functional management to find that its priorities must change, and that the project comes first. Project managers must realize that they get their job accomplished primarily through the process of negotiation, and that they should become negotiation experts. If all major decisions are made with the concurrence of the involved functional managers, project managers will find themselves in a very strong position in insisting that the decision be carried out and that the desired goals be accomplished. In addition, the project personnel must be able to adapt to the two-boss situation, which can be a traumatic experience when first encountered.

WHO IS THE REAL BOSS? Whenever the two-boss situation is encountered, the logical question is who is the real boss? Theoretically it should be possible to divide the authority and responsibility more or less equally between the project and functional managers. However, there is no agreement among the experts as to whether a balance of power is necessary or even desirable.

Even if there is a balance of power, the question of who is the real boss may depend on other factors. For instance, the line or discipline manager is usually perceived as the real boss by the employees in a matrix organization. This is a natural situation since the discipline manager represents "home base"—the disciplinary home to which the employee returns after the project is completed. In addition, the disciplinary manager normally carries the most weight when it comes to performance evaluations and promotions. However, there are usually some employees who relate so strongly to the overall project that they perceive the project manager to be the real boss. Perhaps, then, there is no one real boss; rather, there is a continually shifting balance of power.[11]

BALANCE OF POWER At the heart of the operation of the matrix is the balance of power. Theoretically, it should be possible to divide the authority and responsibility more or less equally between the project and functional managers; in practice, however, this is difficult and seldom occurs. Attempts have been made to clearly delineate the authority and responsibilities of both project and functional management so as to assure a balance of power. Such a delineation has been presented by one management author,[12] who has divided the responsibilities as shown in Table 6-1.

TABLE 6-1 Project Manager's Responsibilities

1. What is to be done?

2. When will the task be done?

3. Why will the task be done?

4. How much money is available to do the task?

5. How well has the total project been done?

Functional Manager's Responsibilities

1. How will the task be done?

2. Where will the task be done?

3. Who will do the task?

4. How well has the functional input been integrated into the project?

Another way of stating the roles is to say that the project manager is responsible for the overall integration of the total project system and the functional manager is responsible for technical direction in his or her discipline.

The so-called responsibility chart has been proposed as a useful device in defining jurisdictional areas of management.[13,14] A simplified example of a responsibility chart is shown in Figure 6-7. Such a chart is probably more meaningful than organization charts or job descriptions, particularly if the chart is filled in during a meeting at which all concerned managers find agreement on the job responsibilities. This process results in confronting potential conflicts early, before specific problems arise.

Certainly such a delineation indicates where the major responsibilities lie, but it cannot guarantee a balance of power. In fact, there are many reasons why it is almost impossible to have a truly equal balance of power between functional and project management. Not the least of these reasons is the fact that we are dealing with people, and that all people, including man-

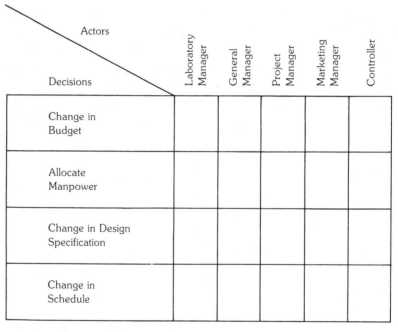

R = Responsible
A = Approve
C = Consult
I = Inform

Figure 6-7. Example of a Responsibility Chart

Source: Jay R. Galbraith, *Organizational Design* (Reading, Mass.: Addison-Wesley Publishing Co., 1977), p. 171.

agers, are different. Managers have differing personalities and differing management styles. Some management styles depend on the persuasive abilities of the manager, while others depend on or tend to fall back on strong support from top management. In addition, power is a constantly changing condition that cannot be static even if one so desired.[15]

The breakdown of responsibilities, although useful in planning and decision making, is highly simplistic. What conscientious, knowledgeable project manager would not get personally involved in "how will the task be done?" The project schedule and "when will the task be done?" responsibilities do not allow the luxury of sitting back and waiting for functional management to make every technical decision. The project manager must ensure that technical decisions are made on schedule, and then must review the key technical decisions and challenge them if necessary. As project integrator, he or she has the overriding responsibility for evaluating every key project decision to determine how it interfaces with the other project tasks, and with the schedule and budget. The project manager therefore must get involved and influence every project action, and, as a last resort, always has appeal rights or veto power—for the good of the project. The project manager even gets involved in "who will do the task?" After all, the highest achievers and most innovative personnel in the discipline organizations will be highly sought after, and the project managers will seek to obtain only the very best people for their projects.

On the other hand, what good functional managers will not get deeply involved in the details of "what, when, and for how much money?" They have a strong personal interest in these details since their organizations have to perform the tasks spelled out in the project schedules and budgets. They must assure that the task is realistically priced and technically feasible. The responsibilities listed in Table 6-1 can therefore only be used as indicators of where the major responsibilities lie.

Since the project, program, or product is usually a very important part of a company's activities, the project manager is a very important person—the one who puts the company in a position where it can make more profits, or lose money.

Therefore, in terms of the balance of power, it would seem that project managers always have the scale of power tipped in their direction, particularly with the firm support of top management. Not necessarily so! In fact, not usually so, at least in a matrix organization. In a pure project organization, there is no question as to who holds the power. But in a matrix organization functional managers have powerful forces on their side. As previously pointed out, the functional manager is normally perceived by project personnel to be the real boss. Often this is inevitable, since functional management is part of the unchanging ladder in the management hierarchy and is therefore perceived to be "permanent" by the employees. After all, the functional organization represents home-base, to which project personnel expect to return after the completion of the project.

Very strong top-management support for the project manager is necessary to get the matrix to work, and even very strong support will not guarantee project success. However, the matrix will not work without it. The project manager must get the job done by any available means, even though he or she may not be perceived as the real boss. Appeal to higher authority is always possible; however, such actions must be kept to a minimum or top management may view the project manager as ineffective.

THE PROJECT/ FUNCTIONAL INTERFACE

The secret of the successfully functioning matrix can thus be seen to be not just a pure balance of power, but more a function of the type of interface relationships between the project and individual functional managers. Every project decision and action must be negotiated across this interface. This interface is a natural conflict situation since many of the goals and objectives of project and functional management are different. Depending on the personality and dedication of the respective managers, this interface relationship can be one of smooth-working cooperation or of bitter conflict. A domineering personality or power play is not the answer. The overpowering manager may win the local skirmish, but usually manages sooner or later to alienate everyone working on the project. Cooperation and negotiation are the keys to successful decision making across the project/functional interface. Arbitrary and one-sided decisions by either the project or functional manager can only lead to or intensify the potential for conflict. Unfortunately for project managers, they can accomplish little by themselves; they must depend on the cooperation and support of the functional managers. That old definition of the successful manager—"one who gets things done by working through others" —is essential for successful project management in the matrix organization.

The project manager in a matrix organization has two very important interfaces—with top management and with functional management. A good working relationship with and ready access to top management is essential for resolving big problems and removing obstacles. A good working relationship with functional management will ensure that most problems are resolved at that level and will not have to go to top management. The conventional matrix model (Figure 6-1) does not adequately emphasize these most important relationships. Obviously, neither the project manager nor the functional managers can sit in their offices and give orders. The various managers must be communicating with each other on at least a daily basis, and usually more often. Therefore a more adequate organizational model is shown in Figure 6-8, which shows the managerial relationships as double-ended arrows, indicating that the relationships are two-way streets. Consultation, cooperation, and constant support are particularly necessary on the part of the project and functional managers. These are very important relationships, keys to the success of any matrix organization, and must be carefully nurtured and actively promoted by top management and by both project and functional management.

The difficulties that occur at the project/functional interface are emphasized if the salient differences between the roles of the project manager and the traditional functional manager are analyzed. Such an analysis has been made by Cleland and indicated that "while these differences are possibly more theoretical than actual, differences do exist, and they affect the manager's modus operandi and philosophy."[16] Both project and functional management must work to achieve activity harmony in spite of these conflicting objectives and roles. The matrix organization actually is a method of deliberately utilizing conflict to get a better job done. The project team must be more concerned with solving the problem than with *who* solves it. Teamwork and problem solving must be emphasized, rather than role definition.

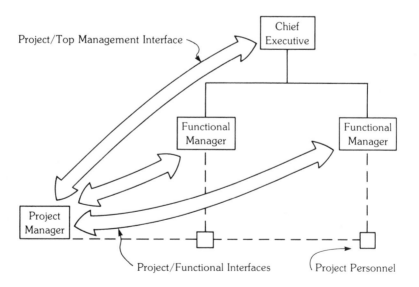

Figure 6-8. The Multiple Management Interfaces

ACHIEVING A BALANCE OF POWER

Achieving a balance of power between project and functional management may in many cases be a desirable goal. Certainly it should be a way of minimizing potential power struggles and unnecessary conflicts. There is no certain way to assure that there is a balance of power, and it is probably seldom really achieved. However, it can be approached by assuming that the project manager has the full support of top management and that he or she reports at a high enough level in the management hierarchy.

HOW HIGH SHOULD PROJECT MANAGEMENT REPORT?

It is not just a question of balance of power, but also of whether the project manager has sufficient clout to be effective. For the most part, the project manager's clout is a direct function of the level at which he or she reports in the hierarchical organization. To be effective, the project manager must be on at least an equal level with the highest level of functional management to be dealt with. As indicated in Figure 6-9, there can be a considerable difference in reporting level, depending on whether the project is confined to a single department or spreads across the entire company's activities. This optimum reporting level will change during the life of a project as the effort progresses from basic research to the manufacture of a product.

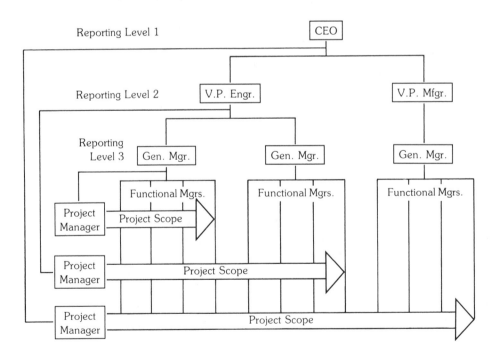

Figure 6-9. Project Management Reporting Levels

STRONG VS. WEAK MATRIX

In many situations it may not be desirable to have a balance of power. For instance, a project may be so important to the company, or the budget and schedule so tight, that top management feels that the project manager must be in a very strong position. Or perhaps the project manager feels that tilting the organizational balance of power in his or her favor will obtain better project performance. For instance, construction management has found from experience that a strong project office is often necessary to achieve good project performance.[17] On the other hand, top management may feel that functional management needs more backing. In either case, the balance of power can be tilted in either direction by changing any one or any combination of the following three factors:

1. **The Administrative Relationship** The levels at which the project and involved functional managers report, and the backing which they receive from top management.

2. **The Physical Relationship** The physical distances between the various people involved in the project.

3. **The Time Spent on the Project** The amount of time spent on the project by the respective managers.

These three factors can be used to describe whether the matrix is strong or weak. The strong matrix is one in which the balance of power is definitely on the side of project management. This can be shown by the model in Figure 6-10. A weak matrix has been described by project managers as one in which the balance of power tilts decisively in the direction of line or functional management. Many organizations have thus, for various reasons including inability to make the two-boss system work, modified the matrix by shifting the balance of power. Galbraith has described the managerial alternatives as a continuum ranging from pure project to functional (Figure 6-11).[18,19] The matrix falls in the middle of the continuum, and can range from very weak to very strong depending on the relative balance of power.

It is easy to see how the administrative relationships can be used to create a strong matrix. The higher the project manager reports in the hierarchical organization and the more visible the support given by top management, the more likelihood of the matrix being strong. The physical relationship would involve actually splitting the project personnel away from their physical reporting relationship with their functional managers. One approach would be to put the entire project team together in the same room, away from their functional bosses. This would seem to be very desirable on the part

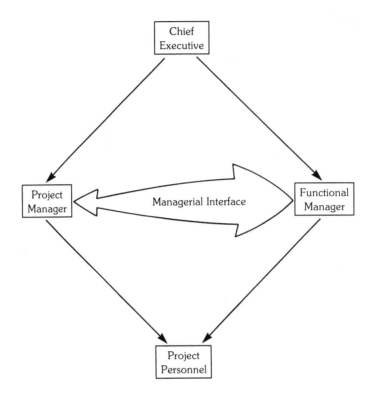

Figure 6-10. The Balance of Power in a Strong Matrix

of most project managers, but would have some disadvantages in regard to utilization of functional facilities and interaction with other functional personnel. The approach of putting all the project personnel together has been described as a tight matrix, whereas the situation of widely separated project personnel has been described as a loose matrix.

The organizational alternatives have also been described in terms of the percent of the organizational personnel who are full-time members of the project team.[20] In this manner the various organizational structures can be described as a continuum, where the three organizational forms (functional, project, and matrix) are a continuum ranging from functional on one end and pure project on the other (Figure 5-2). In a functional organization there is no one on the project team, and in a pure project organization, essentially everybody is on the project team. The matrix falls in between, and includes a variety of organizational alternatives ranging from a weak to a strong matrix. A weak matrix is described as having only a part-time coordinator, whereas a strong matrix has a project office containing such project functions as systems engineering, cost analysis, scheduling, and planning.

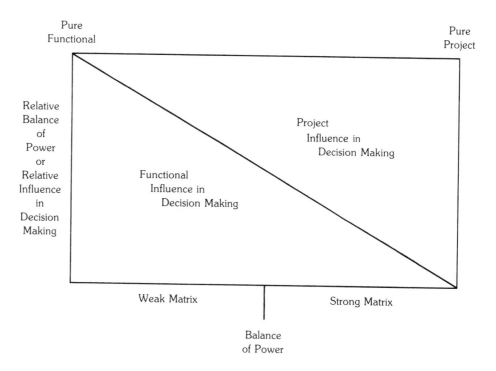

Figure 6-11. The Balance of Power in Weak and Strong Matrices

CONCLUSION The matrix organizational structure has had a great influence on project management. The matrix evolved to fill a need for an organization capable of dealing with great project size and complexity. The result was increased organizational complexity. However, it has greatly added to the versatility and effectiveness of project management. The matrix has permitted project management to be effective not only for very large projects but for small projects as well, and has been extremely valuable for solving multidisciplinary problems.

The matrix organizational form is only desirable if there is a real need for its added complexity. Not only is it not for everyone, but it also cannot be guaranteed to work. It will only work if the entire organization, from top management to the project personnel, are thoroughly sold on the matrix concept. There are many reasons why the matrix will not work, but failure to lay the groundwork and fully prepare the organization is the principal reason for failure. However, its advantages are overwhelming, and its disadvantages are not insurmountable if the matrix is really needed. The matrix will function and result in very improved project productivity if (1) top management gives its unwavering support, and (2) functional management and the project personnel accept the matrix as a "way of life" which can be of great advantage to the company in improving output and profit.

ENDNOTES

1. Russell D. Archibald, *Managing High-Technology Programs and Projects* (New York: John Wiley & Sons, 1976), pp. 14-15.

2. David I. Cleland, and William R. King, *Management: A Systems Approach* (New York: McGraw-Hill Book Co., 1972), pp. 337-362.

3. Jay R. Galbraith, *Organizational Design* (Reading, Mass.: Addison-Wesley Publishing Company, 1977), p. 167.

4. J. Wade Miller, Jr., and Robert J. Wolf, "The 'Micro-Company,' " *Personnel* (July-August 1968): 35-42.

5. Stanley M. Davis, and Paul R. Lawrence, *Matrix* (Reading, Mass.: Addison-Wesley Publishing Company, 1977), p. 3.

6. Ibid., pp. 155-192.

7. Robert B. Youker, "Organizational Alternatives for Project Management," *Project Management Quarterly* 3 (March 1977): 18-24. (Reprinted in *Management Review* (November 1967): 46-52.)

8. Stewart P. Blake, *Managing for Responsive Research and Development* (San Francisco: W. H. Freeman and Co., 1978), p. 176.

9. C. J. Middleton, "How to Set Up a Project Organization," *Harvard Business Review* (March-April 1967): 73-82.

10. Davis and Lawrence, *Matrix*, pp. 129-144.

11. John F. Mee, "Ideational Items: Matrix Organization," *Business Horizons* (Summer 1964): 70-72. (Reprinted in David I. Cleland and William R. King, *Systems, Organizations, Analysis, Management: A Book of Readings* (New York: McGraw-Hill Book Co., 1969), pp. 23-25.)

12. David I. Cleland, and William R. King, *Systems Analysis and Project Management*, 2nd ed. (New York: McGraw-Hill Book Co., 1975), p. 237.

13. Galbraith, *Organizational Design,* p. 171.

14. R. Melcher, "Roles and Relationships: Clarifying the Manager's Job," *Personnel* (May–June 1967).

15. Leonard R. Sayles, "Matrix Management: The Structure with a Future," *Organizational Dynamics* (Autumn 1976): 2-17.

16. David I. Cleland, and William R. King, *Systems Analysis and Project Management,* 2nd ed. (New York: McGraw-Hill Book Co., 1975), p. 237.

17. Marc S. Caspe, "An Overview of Project Management and Project Management Services," *Project Management Quarterly* 3 (December 1976): 30-39.

18. Jay R. Galbraith, "Matrix Organization Designs," *Business Horizons* (February 1971): 29-40.

19. Galbraith, *Organizational Design,* p. 171.

20. Youker, "Organizational Alternatives."

ADDITIONAL REFERENCES

David I. Cleland, and William R. King, *Systems, Organizations, Analysis, Management: A Book of Readings* (New York: McGraw-Hill Book Co., 1969), pp. 281-290.

David I. Cleland, and William R. King, *Systems Analysis and Project Management,* 2nd ed. (New York: McGraw-Hill Book Co., 1975), pp. 183-202.

Stanley M. Davis, "Two Models of Organization: Unity of Command versus Balance of Power," *Sloan Management Review* (Fall 1974): 29-40.

Jay R. Galbraith, ed. *Matrix Organizations: Organization Design for High Technology* (Cambridge, Mass.: MIT Press, 1971.)

Jay R. Galbraith, *Designing Complex Organizations* (Reading, Mass.: Addison-Wesley Publishing Co., 1974).

Sherman K. Grinnell, and Howard P. Apple, "When Two Bosses Are Better Than One," *Machine Design* (January 9, 1975): 84-87.

Kathryn Tytler, "Making Matrix Management Work—and When and Why It's Worth the Effort," *Training* (October 1975): 78-82.

CHAPTER SEVEN PROJECT PLANNING

Stanford B. Michael Business & Planning Analyst
Houston, Texas

Linn C. Institute of Safety & Systems Management
Stuckenbruck, University of Southern California
Ph.D. Los Angeles, California

"A good plan may be no more than a list of jobs scribbled on the back of a cigarette packet—if it is helpful as an action guide."[1]

INTRODUCTON Planning is the most basic function of management, that of determining a course of action. Logically it should precede the other management functions of organizing, staffing, directing, and controlling. However, planning is more than just setting the stage; since all the management functions intermesh, planning is an on-going process which involves continuous updating and revision. It is also very important to have a continuous communication of planning information throughout the organization to assure control of the plan. A very elaborate plan that no one knows about is worthless.

Planning is of the greatest importance since it involves focusing an organization on "an objective consideration of its future,"[2] integrating futuristic thinking with careful analysis. Therefore, in planning, an organization makes implicit assumptions about its future so that it can take action today. The pur-

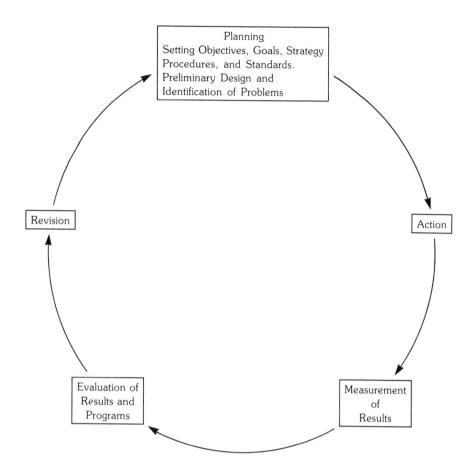

Figure 7-1. The Planning Cycle

pose of planning is thus to facilitate the accomplishment of organizational objectives, and had best be thought of as a continuously iterative process involving planning, action, measurement, evaluation, and revision (Figure 7-1).

WHY PLAN? Planning can be defined as the process of stating project objectives and then determining the most effective activities or accomplishments necessary to reach the objectives. Thus the planning process defines the actions and activities, the time and cost targets, and the performance milestones which will result in the successful achievement of project objectives. Then the plan must indicate what materials, equipment, facilities, people, and other resources are necessary. Projects, however, are seldom completed exactly in the manner originally planned.

This discussion might well be entitled "Planning in Spite of Uncertainty," because there is one certainty in planning—the plan must be capable of change. Why then is detailed planning so necessary if it is all going to change? Because the project manager needs a roadmap to guide himself or herself and the project personnel through the project. A project must have a beginning, and a projected path to the final objective. It is unusual for the project startup or the projected completion objectives to change, but what comes in between, i.e., the actions and activities, may change completely. Recognizing that change is inevitable, the plan must not be "etched in concrete"; it must be sufficiently flexible to permit changes at any point during the project life cycle. A good plan provides sufficient alternatives or detours so that it still functions as a good roadmap even when radical changes occur. A project has little chance of successfully reaching its objectives without a good roadmap.

WHO PLANS? Everybody involved with the project must plan. Planning is not done only by the project manager. However, he or she is at the heart of the planning effort. The project manager must initiate the planning process and coordinate all subordinate planning activities into the overall project master plan. Fortunate is the project manager whose project is large enough to be able to afford project planners, i.e., assistant project managers whose major duty is to coordinate and prepare project plans. On most small projects, the project manager is the only project planner.

It has been mentioned that the project plan and project control are closely linked. The amount of detail in the plan should be consistent with the level of detail to which the project is to be controlled. Acknowledging the relationship of the plan to control, the planning should be done by those responsible for the control of the project. On most projects there will be assistant project managers or line/functional managers who serve in the capacity of activity or subproject managers. These activity managers should have as their first project assignment the development of a plan for their activity. In so doing, each is required to "think through" the project, considering: staff resources, tools and/or equipment, procedures, tasks to be performed, and the checkpoints for controlling the activity. This ties the activity manager to the development of the control process. Such a relationship of responsibility is more likely to enhance the success of the project. It is particularly important that functional managers in a matrix project organization get deeply involved in project planning. The separate plans of the activities thus are brought together in the overall project master plan. Discrepancies are worked out between the activity managers, the functional managers, and the project manager.

Once the project plan has been developed, responsibility for it is assigned to the designated project planner. This could be a full-time key position within the project or an extension of the project manager's duties, or it may be assigned to a line planner of the company on a part-time basis. This individual is responsible for seeing that all aspects of the project requirements are met in the plan and that those with task responsibilities are afforded documentation instructing them of their contribution within the project. Whoever gets the "nod" as the project planner must have superstar characteristics of flexibility, creativity, analytical ability, responsiveness, and communication skills (Figure 7-2).

TYPES OF PLANS

There are many types of plans. It can be said that anything that affects future thought and action is a plan; therefore, policies, strategies, procedures, schedules, and budgets are all plans. It has been pointed out that plans form a hierarchy, or a "system of plans."[3] This hierarchy has been described as having three critical levels—policy, strategic, and operational.[4] The different organizational levels produce plans which are greatly different in type and scope (Figure 7-3).

Company or organization policy planning is a function of the very highest management levels. Strategic planning is also a top management function; however, it extends further down into the organization. The director

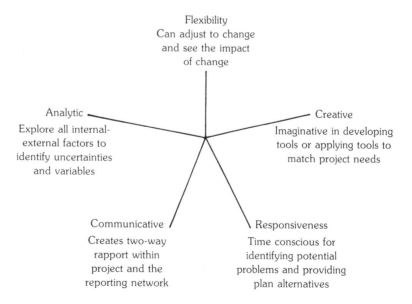

Figure 7-2. Project Planning Characteristics

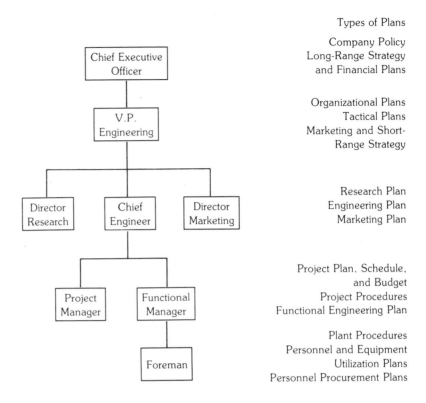

Figure 7-3. A Hierarchy of Plans

of research, the chief engineer, and the director of marketing (among others) must all do strategic planning, because strategic planning is the process of spelling out their general approach for reaching their goals. It is this strategic planning which results in the initiation of projects. Planning for the project organizational structure is also a function of top management (see Chapter 5). Most of the planning at the managerial level and below can be classified as operational planning, and consists of detailed plans for getting the job done.

Often another step in the planning process is the preparation of a proposal to a government agency or other customer to carry out a particular project. A proposal is a more-or-less detailed plan to carry out a project. After the contract has been received and the project has been initiated, then the real detail planning begins. Much of the planning accomplished during the proposal phase will be found to be inadequate or deficient in detail. Vague statements may be satisfactory in a proposal, but they will not result in a successful project. Now is the time to concentrate specifically on how you get the job done.

During the implementation of project management, the project manager must first accomplish the various actions discussed in Chapter 4. These actions are necessary parts of the overall project plan. Individual project plans may be thought of as "basic building blocks of the system of plans."[5] The system of plans then becomes the overall project plan, the program plan, the master plan, or whatever it is convenient to call it. It is this overall project plan which will be the subject of this chapter. How do you put it together, and what elements should it contain?

PROJECT PLANNING

Project planning, which is of critical importance in the project environment, is a system of analyses and decisions for the purpose of:

1. Directing the intent of the project

2. Identifying actions, risks, and responsibilities within the project

3. Guiding the ongoing activities of the project

4. Preparing the project for changes.

The extent of planning is dictated by the objectives of the project and the resources to be applied to it. Many elements of the project are established during the conceptual/feasibility analysis and preliminary planning and design phases. It is during these activities that the parameters of the project are established, which form the basis for the "go-ahead" and the creation of the project.

Armed with the general objectives of the project, the resource constraints and goals to be achieved, a general requirement concept is formulated for the project and the project plan begins to take shape. The single most important decision at this point is the depth of planning detail necessary on *this* project. In some instances, where the control is at one place and vested in a single individual, a job list is all that is necessary. Should this job list become time-dependent and interrelated, more planning detail may be required. As the work becomes more complicated, with dependency on outside support and with jobs at different sites and divisions of responsibility, further information is required in the plan. In most cases, the plan involves a number of interrelationships with functional operations, and these interfaces of activities must be detailed within the project plan.

The planning detail should be limited to the level of control expected to be exercised within the project. Detail beyond this level results in the collection of unused data which has no bearing on success or failure in achieving the project objective. An often sighted case is the desire within some companies to collect cost information for developing a data bank for future estimates. If this can be compiled as a by-product of the project information system, it may be acceptable—however, if it requires additional planning detail that does not contribute to the guidance and control of the project, it should be eliminated.

In *directing the intent* of the project, the plan must clearly identify the project objectives, goals, and any special influences or constraints on the project scope. The objectives are the end results of the project, whereas the goals are those desired operational specifications, or cost-time relationships. Special influences or constraints would include such impacts upon the project as environment, local customs, governmental policies, and corporate practices. Combined, these features of the project give it form and are prerequisites to establishing project requirements.

The *identification of actions, risks, and responsibilities* provides the substance of the project plan. These requirements are translated into the determination of activities and the allocation of resources for the project. This element of the project plan serves the purpose of breaking the project into controllable segments understandable to those responsible for the project's successful execution. The actions and responsibilities are self-explanatory; however, the identification of risk or problem areas creates a basis for consideration of alternatives.

Another cornerstone to creating purpose in the project is the guiding of *on-going activities*, through the proper identification of all required activities for meeting the goals and objectives, and in establishing workable procedures to generate project dynamics. This element sets the stage for uniformity and "oar-beat" of the project, from which all activities can have meaning.

A final purpose in project planning is *preparing for project changes*. The plan must have enough flexibility to adapt to changes but still retain the qualities of integrity and durability. Having set activities into motion, the plan must be alert to danger signals and be responsive in a positive manner.

A project plan must fulfill each of these purposes. In effect, a complete project plan will answer all the questions of Why, What, Where, When, Who, together with the How To and How Much, leaving as little as possible to the guesswork of those responsible for the project execution.

PLANNING IN THE MATRIX ORGANIZATION

Planning is infinitely more complex in a matrix organization than in a pure project organization. Planning is done to assure good communications among all portions of the project, and early planning provides the means for developing these communication links. In a matrix, planning cannot be solely a function performed by the project manager, but must be participated in by all members of the project team, including the key functional managers and their principal investigators. There are many types of plans, depending on the level in the organization. The problem is complex because each organizational unit has its own planning needs completely separate from project plans. In every organization there exists a hierarchy of plans, from top to bottom of the organization. These various plans become interrelated in the matrix organization, as shown in Figure 7-4. Project plans must intermesh with all other plans at all levels of management in the matrix organization. The project manager of a pure project organization has considerably more latitude and flexibility in planning, since most of the people working on the project report only to her or him. The life of a matrix project manager can become very complicated.

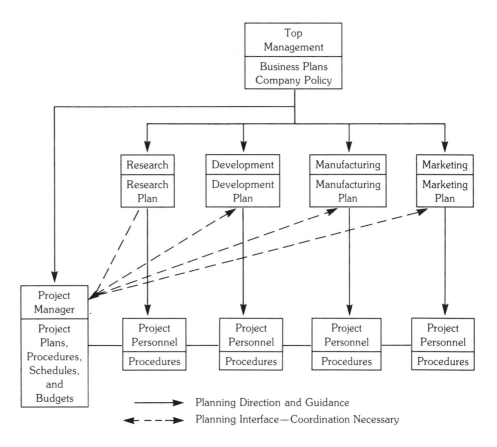

Figure 7-4. Planning Complexity in the Matrix Organization

WHAT'S SPECIAL ABOUT PROJECT PLANS? Project plans are subsets of a business plan, and although each is tailored to meet a single objective, it must conform to the requirements of the larger plan. As such, the project plan is subject to abrupt changes that may impact on the entire project-business plan interface. Project plans differ from general business plans in that there are limited objectives with well-defined sets of parameters. Project plans must be tight, providing a manageable guide to controlling the project. Business plans tend to be looser in that there can be alternative "tradeoffs" in meeting the company objectives.

Once the parameters are defined, it is much easier to chart task requirements with time-cost references. Putting the task building blocks together in the most effective way is the assignment of the project planner. In this respect, the planner is working with a number of known parts, as opposed to a business planner with an extensive list of interdependent unknowns.

Another feature of the project plan is that it can be tailored to meet special needs of the project. It can be made very simple with manual controls and a minimum of documentation, or it can involve upwards of 20,000 tasks spread over several countries with differing regulations and requiring sophisticated computer information systems to keep "tabs" on all the project activities.

PLANNING THE PLAN It may be elementary to say that the planning process starts with "planning the plan," but this is the key to the entire development of the project plan. Planners are normally given a good start in this, as much of the information generated in selling management on a project commitment is available from the proposal effort; the study team that compiled the information is also available. Although certain parameters will change as the project progresses, the basic objectives, goals, and constraints will provide the foundation for the master plan.

When the scope of the project and its objectives have been provided, the requirements of the project and control should be examined. At this point there must be agreement among those responsible as to how much detail is required to effectively execute and control the project.

In planning the plan it is well to recognize that the planning effort is a continuous process going through several phases, from concept to implementation and operation. This is appropriately displayed in Figure 7-5.

Project activities are here considered as the key elements needed for the execution of the project. This could be administration, personnel, accounting, documentation, planning, estimating, scheduling, engineering de-

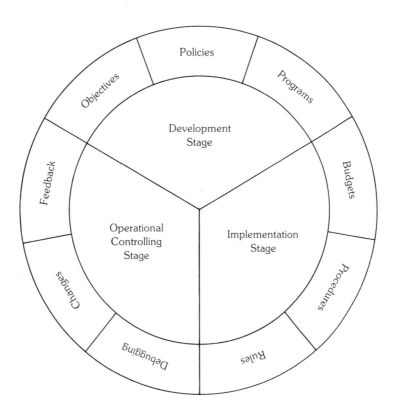

Figure 7-5. Planning Evolution

Peter M. Mears, "Integrated Planning and Controlling." *Managerial Planning* (March/April, 1978). Reprinted with permission of *Managerial Planning*. Copyright Planning Executives Institute, Oxford, Ohio 45056.

sign, field engineering, contract administration, procurement, logistics, operation, construction, inspection, and training. Activities can be combined when desired in the smaller projects, be only part time in the very small projects, or be divided where multisite requirements are in the project scope. Normally the determination of the number of activities within the project is a "fall-out" of the conceptual study and the control necessary to the project. Many companies are approaching the planning process with a modular concept, in which the project manager can select the primary units to be included or choose different layers of detail in a pyramiding effect (Figure 7-6).

In this manner each project can be tailored to the level of documentation and control required of the project. Such detail requirements are nearly always dictated by the developer/manager responsible for the project and the governmental institutions having jurisdiction over the project.

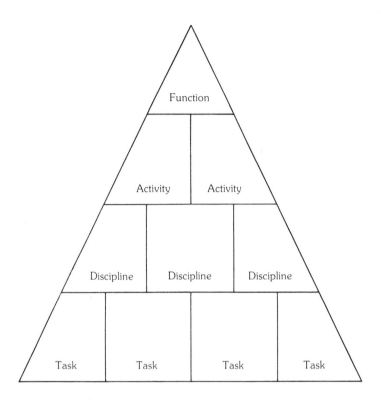

Figure 7-6. Project Module Pyramid

THE PLANNING PROCESS

The process of planning does not have any mysticism about it, requiring some sort of special "mumbo-jumbo." The person who makes a shopping list for the supermarket and selects a route for traversing the aisles with a minimum of effort, has executed a simple project plan. Such a plan fulfills all the requirements of the shopping undertaken.

The more complex the objectives and the constraints, the greater the degree of planning required. A decision as to the activities necessary for the performance of the project, the level of control required, and the technical methods of planning and control are essential for legal, financial, technical, and operational commitments of the project. Each project is unique and must be carefully assessed according to its special planning needs. It is good to remember that the more elaborate the plan, the greater the feedback. Too often the planner gets carried away in developing an elaborate plan, causing the project to serve the plan rather than the plan serving the project. If feedback is not needed in a particular area, then that area does not need to be in the plan. A logical sequence for a planning cycle is shown in Figure 7-7.

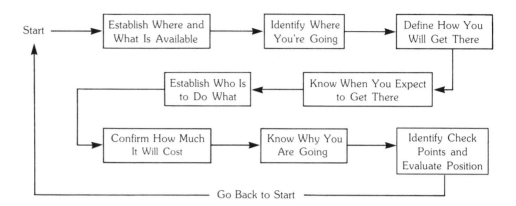

Figure 7-7. Simplified Planning Cycle

William S. Royce, "The Problems With Planning." *Managerial Planning* (November/December, 1978).

THE WORK BREAKDOWN STRUCTURE

The project Work Breakdown Structure (WBS) is the heart of the project planning effort. It is more than just an element of the project plan, it is the framework on which the project is built. No realistic overall project plan is possible without first developing a WBS that is detailed enough to provide meaningful identification of *all* project tasks that must be accomplished. The process of creating the WBS is very important in that during the process of breaking down the project, the project manager, the staff, and all involved functional managers are forced to think through all aspects of the project.

A WBS is a technique for breaking down a total project into its component elements. It is a graphic picture of the hierarchy of the project broken down level by level into subprojects and finally into tasks. It serves to organize the project by defining all the tasks that must be performed in the conception, design, development, fabrication, and test of the project hardware, software, or service. As the levels become lower, the scope, complexity, and cost of each subproject become smaller, until tasks which are completely capable of accomplishment are reached. These smallest tasks, called Work Packages, must be identified as manageable units which can be planned, budgeted, scheduled, and controlled. Appendix B is an actual WBS. The WBS indicates the relationship of the organizational structure to the project objectives and tasks, and so provides a firm basis for planning and control of the project.

There are no hard-and-fast rules for preparing a WBS; good judgment is the only criterion. However, the size of these Work Packages is very important since they must be small enough in terms of cost and manpower to permit realistic estimates to be made and to simplify control. The "eighty-hour rule" can be of tremendous help in formulating the WBS and keeping it under control.[6] This rule states that each task should be broken down into Work Packages that require *no more than eighty hours of work for completion*. At the end of each eighty-hour-or-less period, the Work Package is reported simply as either completed or not completed. By means of such periodic check-ins, drifting of a project can be controlled early.[7]

THE ELEMENTS OF THE PROJECT PLAN With the guidelines for the project plan thus established, the next step should be to identify the essential elements that need to be included in the plan. No list of essential elements can be all-inclusive, since every project is different and may have different needs. However, the following list of elements of a project plan provides a starting point for a planning checklist, and these elements can be combined, changed, and amended to suit special requirements:

1. Project Summary

2. Specifications

3. Work Statement

4. Master Schedule

5. Procedures Guide

6. Budgets and Cost Control System

7. Activity/Event Network Plan

8. Materials and Equipment Forecast

9. Cross-Impact Matrix

10. Project Organization Plan

11. Management Plan

12. Project Personnel Plan

13. Reporting and Review Procedure

This list of project plan elements is quite extensive since it is a compilation of the types of elements found in a number of different types of plans (from different industries). The project manager can pick from this list those elements which are essential to the project plan, discarding others or combining them as desired. It is not surprising that these headings appear similar to the parts of a proposal, since a proposal is a plan to carry out a particular project. The project plan will differ from a proposal only in having more detail and, possibly, additional elements that would not be of interest to a customer.

It is expected that each of these project plan elements will be prepared in a preliminary form so as to provide rough guidance early in the project. As an example, a project personnel staffing plan needs to be developed as one of the first priorities, to identify key positions within the project so that hiring of the project team can proceed without delay. This information can be converted into a project labor requirements plan in more detail as the scope of the project takes shape. Certainly this early plan for personnel would define areas of responsibility for each position.

Where the project relies on using personnel from the functional line operations, the availability of individuals must be worked out with the line managers. In these cases it is important that the person responsible for project planning work with the functional managers in developing the job descriptions and establish tentative assignments by the manager.

Development of the plan requires a great deal of effort in the front end of the project. Once the plan is agreed upon by those with project responsibility, the progress of the project must be routinely monitored and adjustments made to the plan to accommodate circumstances. The individual elements of the project plan will now be discussed in more detail.

Project Summary

The Project Summary should be essentially an executive summary that can be easily absorbed by a high-level executive in a few minutes. It should identify the objectives, the goals, and the constraints of the project. An objective is the stated result of and purpose for the project. This can be a general statement of purpose, as: divert Colorado River water to Los Angeles, get the army across the Alps, build a secure burial vault befitting my station, create a vehicle providing fuel economy.

A statement of goals gives the size and shape of the project from which the technical work requirements may be devised. The goal applies some quantitative factors to the results to be achieved in the project. Examples of these would be: build a dam across the Colorado River and a 400-mile pipeline connecting the dam to Los Angeles; move 10,000 troops across the Alps within thirty days using available transportation; build a pyramid of 1,000 cubits containing a secret self-sealing vault to be completed by my thirtieth birthday; design an experimental car that will achieve 100 mpg and carry eight people.

Finally, the Project Summary should specify the constraints. This can be the environment in which the project objectives are to exist (if applicable), the financial resources available, time limitations, local customs, and the governmental restrictions. These constraints further shape the project and set the parameters for procedures, location of project staff, type of project personnel, technical requirements, budgets, and schedules.

Specifications This element of the project plan should define the characteristics and the performance goals for the final end product. This may be an extensive document or it may be very small, depending on the needs of the project and the customer. In a contractual project the specifications are very important.

Work Statement Every proposal writer is familiar with the Work Statement. This is the part of a proposal request that tells the contractor what is desired, or the part of a proposal that tells the customer exactly what the contractor proposes to do. The Work Statement is an essential part of every technical proposal, and should be one of the basic documents on which the project plan is built. Every project plan should have a Work Statement, even a very simple one, because it specifies the path by which the project goals and objectives will be reached.

Master Schedule The project Master Schedule interrelates all tasks on a common time scale. For a simple project the project Master Schedule may consist of a simple bar or Gantt chart; a complex project may necessitate the use of elaborate critical path or PERT techniques to fix the details of the schedule. A Master Schedule should contain the following information:[8]

1. The names of the tasks (and Work Packages) listed on the WBS

2. The names of the persons responsible for each task

3. The starting date of each task

4. The expected duration of each task

5. The due date of each task.

An excerpt from a Project Master Schedule of this type is shown in Appendix C. Many types of subschedules may be necessary for large and complex projects. A particularly troublesome schedule problem is encountered with governmental regulatory agencies. Appendix D is an example of a Project Authorizations and Agreements Schedule for a construction project.

Procedures Guide Early in the development of the plan, there is a need for establishing a Procedures Guide or Project Practices Guide which covers the rules and practices to be observed during the project. Care should be taken that such procedures do not violate those of the company. Regardless of the uniqueness of the project, it will be necessary to use company systems already in existence. It may be necessary to embellish them at times, but it is prudent to use tools that are available rather than build new ones.

The purpose of the Procedures Guide is to set down project guidelines and standards for the conduct of the project. These procedures are mostly administrative practices relating to the various functions of the project. Such a guide will provide procedures for hiring staff, restrictions on offsite labor, pay differentials, travel routines, style of engineering drawing to be used, who has the authority to sign various types of correspondence and drawings, what type of project coordination is required, and even how to write a new procedure.

This Procedures Guide comes from the principal people involved in the project. Each activity is responsible for those procedures that fall within its responsibility, although some procedures will take the collaboration of two or more activities. It will be necessary to review all legal documents and regulations and the company and developer practices guides, and to reexamine the needs of the project. Even though each activity is responsible in its own area, it is imperative that a single person be responsible for the editing and publishing of this document. The elements of the Procedures Guide are shown in Figure 7-8.

Each project will have its own requirements for a "how to" guidebook. Seeing that the Procedures Guide is liberally available to the project staff will save a number of headaches in the routine matters of the project.

Budgets and Cost Inherent in any planning process is the creation of a budget and cost control
Control System system to provide the project manager with cost, schedule, and performance status. A brief version of the budget was most likely prepared in the economic analysis that supported the decisions in favor of the project. Budgets will be set up in a manner that is suitable for control. The simplest approach is to use the WBS individual tasks, relating them to the activity, component, or location of the activity. Budgets should be simple to ensure understanding of the line-item dollar-time relation. The project itself will dictate the primary budget identification. Establishing a code of accounts could then identify the segments of the project assigned to individuals of responsibility. Subcodes can be used to define costs in much more detail; however, it is advisable to avoid more paper work than is necessary to control the project.

PERSONNEL PLANNING	ADMINISTRATIVE PLANNING	ACCOUNTING PLANNING
• locale work restrictions • hiring practices & permits • rotation schedule (if needed) • work practices • special benefits • use of temporary help • project position requirement class codes	• project authorizations (who signs what) • communications use • distribution levels • travel practices • supplies & furnishings • meeting practices/ schedules • public information guide	• code of accounts (use) • time records • pay practices • insurances • expense reports • cost records • accounts payable

ENGINEERING PLANNING	MATERIAL PLANNING	INSTALLATION PLANNING
• work authorizations • drafting room practices • change order procedures • drawing control • design progress standards • installation manual • start-up procedures	• vendor survey-qualification • identify long lead time items • material control practices • inspection procedures • shipping procedures/ marketing • special handling authority • disposition & surplus	• contractor/subcontractor responsibilities/liabilities • offsite business licenses • local construction permits (as available) • bid procedures • work monitoring practices • field change orders • systems checks and work approvals

Figure 7-8. Project Procedures Guide Elements

Budget information must be obtained from those responsible for the individual activities. A budget estimate will be submitted by the activity manager at the time the WBS is submitted. The coding of the project budget should be made according to the needs of each project activity. Preestablished codes can be so inflexible that they force the project to fit the plan rather than allowing the plan to support the project. Cost control is tied to the budget through the work-task coding. Programmed control systems provide information on "line-items," including budget, weekly/monthly expenditures, accumulative expenditures, percentage of budget expended, and costs estimates to completion.

Activity/Event Network Plan

An Activity/Event Network Plan is an essential tool for the planning of complex projects. An activity/event network is a representation of how project activities and events progress. For very simple projects a bar or Gantt chart is adequate; however, as projects become more complex, some form of

CPM/PERT is necessary. The PERT chart uses a graphic display or network to depict the relationships and interdependencies among the project tasks. In addition, it identifies critical paths and permits consideration of schedule uncertainties. In major projects computer scheduling is essential because the size and complexity of the network defies manual updating of the system. There are a number of commercial programs for developing such networks (see Chapter 8). Hillier and Lieberman,[9] and Mulvaney[10] present in-depth discussions of CPM/PERT networking.

Materials and Equipment Forecast

In those projects where the procurement and movement of materials and equipment is required, it is essential to develop a system of managing these activities. This forecast will consist of the procedures and tools for managing the complete material cycle. A very important ingredient in the development of the Material and Equipment Forecast is the element of time. Since all material is time-related, it must be ordered, delivered, and disposed of in a timely manner. Of course, the Master Project Schedule provides an integration of material deliveries and their important progress events, but for the specific control of individual orders, a time-referral process is a beneficial aid.

The preparation of this forecast begins with the documentation of material classes to be included in the project. This is a rough preliminary list, used basically for the purpose of vendor qualification evaluations and for initiating purchases of long lead-time items. It also provides a reference list for surveying stocks on hand.

The forecast then follows the order from requisition through bid packages, vendor selection, purchase order, inspection, delivery, transportation, receiving, warehousing, and disposition. At the point of requisition writing, a tentative schedule is established, noting the checkpoints within the cycle. This schedule will be updated as each checkpoint occurs. It is important to include on the material schedule the date that delivery becomes critical to the project, at which time alternatives must be evaluated.

The forecast will specify the material forms to be used and the document distribution. Much of the material control can be computer-programmed, since many of the commercially available project control systems include a material control option. The purpose of the material forecast is to set the extent of control necessary for the project to assure compliance with the Master Schedule. A Project Materials and Equipment Forecast is shown in Appendix E.

Cross-Impact Matrix

A Cross-Impact Matrix indicates which organizational units and which key personnel are involved in the process of completing each task of a project. The list of tasks are taken from the WBS and the major task responsibilities are indicated in the matrix. It is important that the matrix identify not only the person responsible for the completion of the task but also what key personnel are involved and who has to be consulted or who should give approval. A representative project Cross-Impact Matrix is shown in Appendix F.

Project Organization Plan

The project organization need not be complex, it should only indicate the breakdown of the major project responsibilities. It should indicate specifically who is responsible for each project subsystem and task. An example of a project organization in a public utility is shown in Appendix G.

The Project Organization Plan is primarily for the purpose of establishing key responsibilities. For this reason it is well to include a brief statement of the responsibilities. Some organizations go another step with the identification of those having certain signature authority, those with committee assignments, and the substitute responsibility in case of absence. Special committees, such as the Design Review Board or the Quality Verification Committee, are usually necessary in big projects. Such committees should be established in the Project Organization Plan.

Management Plan

The Management Plan should describe how management will conduct and monitor the project, i.e., how the project will be organized and administered. This element of the project plan often contains the project organization; however, it should concentrate on the relationships of the project team with the rest of the organization, particularly with top management. The relationship of the project to top management is very important to the customers or clients since they want assurances that top management attention can be instantly and effectively focused on their project. This is particularly important in a proposal or contract effort where the customer is worried that the project may not receive adequate attention.

The Management Plan contains such items as: (1) corporate organization charts, (2) statements of authority and responsibility, (3) a description and an analysis of the effectiveness of the information and control system to be used, and (4) a top management plan of attack in case the project runs into difficulties.

Project Personnel Plan

The labor resource requirements and organization should be determined as early as possible in the planning cycle. This will establish key responsibilities, numbers, and qualifications.

Often a great deal of waste occurs early in the project: people are hired without assignments, there is confusion over responsibilities, and people are assigned without regard to their qualifications. This waste can be minimized by preparation of a Project Personnel Plan. It should contain a listing of every position in the project, regardless of classification, and its period of assignment. Each position should be identified by title, job class, start date, end date, and reassignment position (if any). The Project Personnel Plan needs to be sufficiently flexible to allow for frequent assignment changes.

Reporting and Review Procedure

Without a good reporting and review process, there is no control over the project. This process must be adequate to keep everyone on the project and in top management informed as to progress, problems, modifications, and other factors.

The key word in any managerial effort is *communications*. Good communications give the motivation and control required for a smoothly functional operation.[11] Among the ingredients essential to a successful project is a reliable communications network and a conscientious documentation effort. Not including these in the project plan could cause a great deal of confusion and a very bad beginning for the project.

The communication plan does not refer to telephone or telex, but to the practice of keeping project personnel informed. This requires that an early assessment of the required reports, meetings, presentations, and project documents is made to determine those contributing to the overall or individual activity performance. The tendency in projects is to generate more paper than is essential for maintaining the progress of the project. Most project managers agree that it is safer to err on the side of too much paper than get the project into trouble because someone did not get the word.

The Reporting and Review Procedure will list all documents and communications materials essential to the project. It will state the purpose and content of the document, its schedule of issuance and distribution, and the person responsible for its preparation. Should a document require approval and/or sign-off it will be noted in the plan. Project document control can be implemented by a Project Documents Matrix as shown in Appendix H.

Other Elements of the Project Plan

In addition to the very important project plan elements which have just been discussed, there are a large number of other possible elements of a more specialized nature. These elements may be an extremely important part of many project plans, or they may be individual plans for a specific part of a project. Many of the following plan elements would be unnecessary on a small project; as projects become large, more of them would be necessary:

1. Financial Plan

2. Contingency Analysis

3. Logistics Support Plan

4. Facilities Requirements Plan

5. Market Intelligence Plan

6. Quality Assurance Plan

7. Configuration Management Plan

8. Security Plan

9. Test Plan

10. Production Plan

11. Make-or-Buy Plan

12. Procurement Plan

13. Training Plan

PROVISIONS FOR CHANGE

The final plan must be flexible and dynamic. It first establishes a project guide so that all work can begin in harmony. Later, as the details of the project requirements are unveiled, a more careful evaluation of the plan is needed when all the key positions are filled. At this time the plan is refined to a point of perhaps 70 percent firm. The plan will never be completely firm, as changes in the scope, work circumstances, and technical approach tend to obsolete portions of the project. Therefore, the plan must be constantly revised to reflect the latest status and conditions.

How the planner provides for project change will depend on the size and complexity of the project. For the more complex projects much of the plan should be placed into the computer so that adjustments can be readily implemented. With the advent of the minicomputer, project management can control their own programming and in some instances be able to manipulate format.

As long as the planner does not restrict the flexibility of the records established by the plan, the opening for changes will exist. The plan itself is not a firm commitment, but a guide to direct and control. When necessary, it will reflect the latest thinking of those responsible for the project.

PLANNING TOOLS

Throughout this discussion reference has been made to the use of the computer as an aid to project planning. Because of its unique qualities the computer has become a formidable partner in the planning and control of projects. However, before rushing to the computer department to line up a stable of programs to help with the project, the project manager should consider what help is needed from the computer. Computers should fill a project need and not become a showcase for computer technology. If uncontrolled, the computer can "spit" out volumes of paper which project leaders do not have time to digest or use effectively.

There are many commercial programs that provide the format for budget control, schedules, material control, and staff load data. Most of these programs are adequate for managing a project and, where required, computer experts can modify these or develop specifically tailored programs to suit the project. It is enough that the planner be aware that such programs do exist and can be of great help if applied wisely.

There are available a number of excellent project management systems manuals which provide usable forms and instructions for developing project plans. The planner should check with the company's systems and procedures group to see what is available that can be used in the project without setting up new forms.

The basic tools for the project are in the heads of those selected for their special expertise in the activities of the project. These provide the thinking that prepares the WBS and estimates the cost-time relationships. If the planner is able to develop a manageable WBS, together with a Reporting and Review Procedure and a Procedures Guide, the control of the project becomes routine.

The significant input/output ingredients of the project plan are shown in Figure 7-9. This planning documentation is necessary to direct the intent of the project and identify the actions necessary to accomplish the project objectives. Information in the form of plans, schedules, budgets, and reports is the key medium for integrating a project and functional organization. The degree of detail for each of these documents is dependent upon the complexity of the project and the requirements set by the developer or company. Close attention to these input/output ingredients will provide the project with a good start on the road to success.

CONCLUSION

Effective planning is an essential ingredient for project success. Planning is extremely important because it focuses the attention of an organization on its future. A good plan is flexible in that it provides a sufficient number of alternative paths to function as a good roadmap even when radical changes occur. Since the future is unknown and changes will occur even with the best of plans, planning must always be made "in spite of uncertainty."

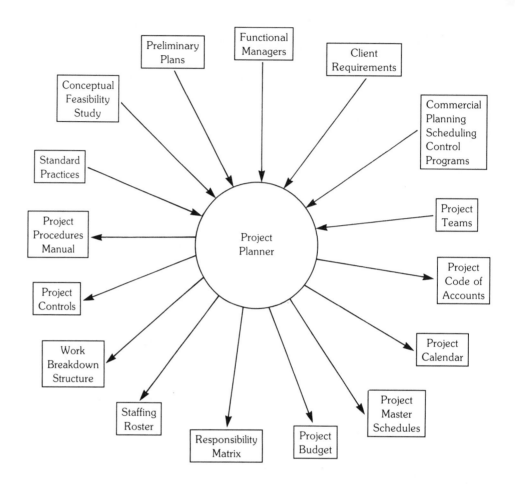

Figure 7-9. Project Plan Input/Output

The planning effort is the responsibility of the project manager, although all members of the project team must participate. This is particularly important in a matrix organization, where the functional managers, who actually supervise their project tasks, must contribute their portion of project planning. The project team produces an overall project plan which is actually made up of a number of elements or subplans. The first step in planning is the preparation of the WBS; more than an element of the project plan, it is the framework on which the project is built. The elements of the project plan are then produced, based on the WBS. The most important of these elements or subplans are the project specifications, the work statement, the master schedule, the cross-impact matrix, and the management plan. Most project plans need these elements; however, there are many others which must be included as the project becomes more complex.

ENDNOTES

1. G. H. A. Morton, "A Practical Approach to Project Management," *Project Management Quarterly* (June 1977).

2. David I. Cleland, and William R. King, *Systems Analysis and Project Management,* 2nd ed. (New York: McGraw-Hill Book Co., 1975), p. 27.

3. Ibid., pp. 41-42.

4. Charles C. Martin, *Project Management: How to Make It Work* (New York: Amacom, 1976).

5. Cleland and King, *Systems Analysis.*

6. Harold B. Einstein, *The Management of Project Uncertainties in Banking* (Los Angeles: Security Pacific National Bank, 1978), pp. 30-35.

7. Cleland and King, *Systems Analysis,* pp. 41-42.

8. Einstein, *Management of Project Uncertainties.*

9. Frederick S. Hillier, and Gerald J. Lieberman, *Introduction to Operations Research,* 2nd ed. (San Francisco: Holden-Day, Inc., 1974).

10. John Mulvaney, *Analysis Bar Charting—A Simplified Critical Path Analysis Technique* (Washington, D.C.: Management Planning and Control Systems, 1969).

11. John G. Simpkin, "Management of Construction Projects," *Project Management Quarterly* (December 1977).

CHAPTER EIGHT
TOOLS OF PROJECT MANAGEMENT

Wilfred Charette, Ph.D. — President, Systonetics, Inc. Anaheim, California

Walter S. Halverson — Halverson & Associates Brea, California

INTRODUCTION

Project success is completely dependent on adequate planning, direction, scheduling, monitoring, and control. These project functions must be closely bound together by an adequate information and control system if project performance is to be adequately measured and controlled. For efficient project operation, a single information and control system should be used, not separate project and functional department cost control systems. The information and control system should be compatible to the needs of project and functional managers. When such systems are being considered for a new project, consideration should be first given as to whether an existing system could be modified to meet project requirements. Maximum use should be made of existing accounting systems.

However, projects have special requirements which must be met by the information and control system. These requirements make use of such tools as PERT/CPM, PERT/cost, precedence diagramming method (PDM), work breakdown structure (WBS), resource allocation, and cost/schedule integration. Many of these tools and methods date back to the 1950s, and their extensive automation was developed during the 1960s. Their modern implementation depends upon the wide availability of economical computing power and display devices. There are many commercially available software packages that can be used to implement either all or parts of an information and control system very efficiently and at a reasonable cost.

Project control tools should be selected and implemented as early in the project life cycle as possible. Such decisions must be made: (1) To what detail and how often should program cost and schedule status be provided to project, functional, and top management? (2) What graphic displays should be utilized? (3) Should critical path networking be incorporated in the system?

THE PROJECT MANAGEMENT PROCESS

As shown in Figure 8-1, the project management process is a closed-loop system. The project management problem is to accomplish a given task (defined by specific deliverable items and/or performance criteria), by a certain time, within a certain budget, usually within a specific set of organization, manpower, and resource constraints, and always in the presence of noise (unpredictable outside disturbances). This feedback control system model yields valuable insights into appropriate design criteria for project information systems and management responses to correct inadequate project performance progress. However, the purpose of the model used here is to place

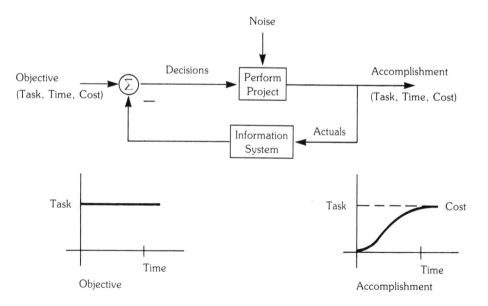

Figure 8-1. The Project Management Process

project information systems in perspective from which we will review the development of modern project management practices and the use of computers in implementing them.

PROJECT MANAGEMENT PRACTICES

Barcharts

Modern management planning and control can be dated from the development of the barchart by Henry L. Gantt during World War I (see Figure 8-2). The bar or Gantt chart represented a tremendous improvement over prior practices, and Gantt charts are still in very wide use to report project status especially among top management. However, the increasing size, complexity, and risk associated with modern, technically sophisticated projects motivated the development of new methods. These methods are superior to Gantt charts for planning (by showing task interdependencies), for scheduling (by highlighting the critical path), and for control (by providing insights into time vs. resources tradeoffs).

Barcharts are a weak planning tool, but a simple and effective progress reporting tool.

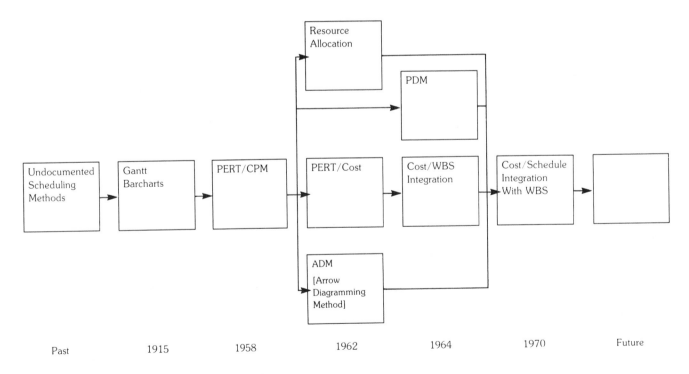

Figure 8-2. Evolution of Project Control Methods

PERT/CPM The British added logical relationships to Gantt charts in the early 1940s. The DuPont Company together with Remington Rand (Univac) developed CPM (Critical Path Method) in 1957-1958 for planning and scheduling plant maintenance and construction programs where the dominant emphasis was on controlling cost and leaving the schedule flexible. The essentially identical method of PERT (Program Evaluation and Review Technique) was conceived by the Special Projects Office of the U.S. Navy in 1957-1958, and developed by Booz, Allen, and Hamilton in conjuncton with Lockheed Missiles Systems Division on the Polaris Fleet Ballistic Missile Program where the dominant emphasis was on meeting stringent schedules for internationally strategic reasons and taking a rather flexible view of cost control. Today, PERT and CPM are identical methods with slight variations in network format.

Resource Allocation Resource allocation or leveling (i.e., the distribution of resources over a given time span) attracted attention beginning in the early 1960s. By using positive float available on noncritical paths through the project, the project planner can arrange a schedule of work that accomplishes the same result in the same time while smoothing or leveling the peaks and valleys in the resources to be consumed. This process is not new, but it is much more easily accomplished from a framework of a PERT or CPM project network.

PERT/COST Following PERT/CPM, systems for tracking project cost by activity were developed in the early 1960s. Cost estimating by activity compares with the traditional method of take off of material quantities from drawings and specifications, estimates of material, unit costs, labor costs, and indirect costs. Theoretically, PERT/COST as a technique provides a tool for measuring project progress and for forecasting completion cost. However, great care is required in implementation to avoid tracking of costs in too much detail. The basic problem in implementing project-oriented cost accounting is in properly breaking down and allocating costs logically and in detail.

PDM The Precedence Diagramming Method was introduced at Stanford University during 1962-1964. PDM is essentially the same method expressed in a new format. In PERT/CPM networks all relationships among tasks are "finish-to-start" relationships and constraints must be depicted by so-called "dummy" activities. PDM adds "start-to-start" and "finish-to-finish" relationships. This offers certain efficiencies in modeling concurrent tasks.

WBS An important addition to the rapidly expanding body of modern project management methods also occurred in the early 1960s known as WBS (Work Breakdown Structure). A WBS is a diagram of the work to be done, expressed in detail from the top down in a tree structure. Originally, WBS was functionally oriented. The currently used product or project orientation facilitates cost and schedule integration. A WBS establishes how the work will be performed and how cost and schedule data will be tracked and reported. As shown in Figure 8-3, it identifies specific management responsibility with various tasks or groups of tasks. And, it facilitates the proper summarization of cost and schedule status to provide a measure of project progress.

Network Formats Figure 8-4 illustrates the most widely accepted project network formats in use today. While considerable debate on the relative merits of PERT networks, arrow diagrams, and precedence diagrams has occurred in the past, differences are largely subjective. The network format used by a particular organization or entire industry usually is determined by historical precedent. The

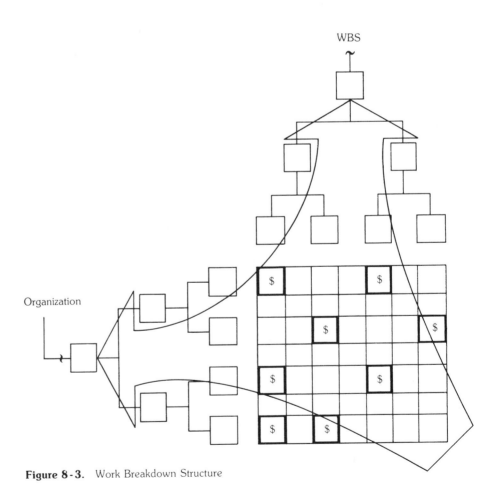

Figure 8-3. Work Breakdown Structure

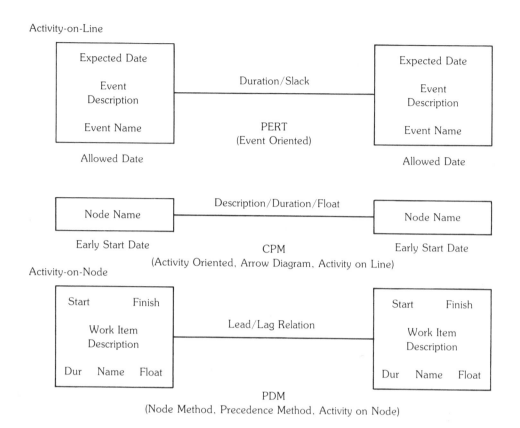

Figure 8-4. Project Network Formats

construction industry seems to prefer arrow diagrams with a linear time scale or precedence diagrams. PERT networks are preferred in the electronics, aerospace, and R&D industries. The merits of a particular network format over another are insignificant compared to the major benefits of using the network planning and scheduling method itself.

Schedule/Cost/WBS Integration of schedule, cost, and WBS in project management had been an elusive goal until the early 1970s. It is probably best achieved in certain methods and systems applied to government defense contracts. Fundamental to this integration is cost tracking by activity and reporting of cost based on the schedule of planned work. It is felt that accurate status of the project can be determined from the cost and time consumed of completed activities, then comparing these figures with the remaining project duration and budget. These comparisons yield cost and time estimates to complete the project. Figure 8-5 summarizes these concepts and depicts the key role played by the

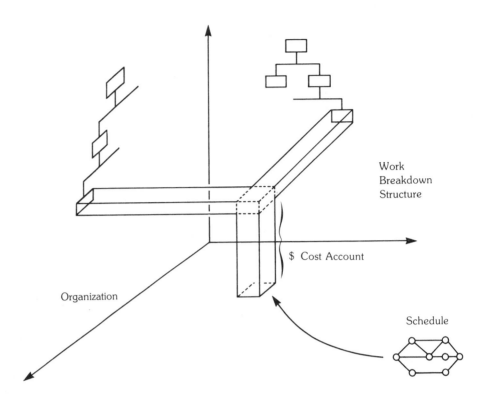

Work
Breakdown
Structure

$ Cost Account

Organization

Schedule

Figure 8-5. Cost/Schedule/WBS Integration

WBS in achieving an integrated cost and schedule control system. The cost account is defined by the intersection of the WBS at a given level with the organization at a given level at the lowest point in the WBS where actual costs are collected for performance measurement purposes. The cost account manager is normally the individual who prepares, plans, and manages lower-level work assignments. Hence cost control, schedule control, and performance monitoring are operationally integrated at the cost account level.

Defense Contracts Currently, nearly all Department of Defense (DOD) contracts require detailed scheduling and reporting, most Department of Energy (DOE) contracts require similar information of their contractors as does the National Aeronautics and Space Administration (NASA). These requirements are variously named: Cost/Schedule Control System Criteria (C/SCSC) in DOD, Performance Measurement System (PMS) in DOE, and 533 System in NASA. These criteria all require WBS, activity cost accounting, and network-based planning (PERT/CPM, PDM). These project management criteria are applied to various types of projects by DOD depending upon project type and project cost

TABLE 8-1. GOVERNMENT CONTROL SYSTEM CRITERIA

	Program	Contract	Subcontract
R&D	$ 75M	$ 25M	$15M
Production	$300M	$100M	$35M
Modification	$300M	$100M	$35M

DOD Thresholds

Contract Size	Requirement
$2M-$50M	Mini-PMS
Over $50M	PMS

DOE Thresholds

(see Table 8-1). As expected, the riskier the project, the more likely the criteria are to be applied at a lower cost threshold. DOE applies less detailed but just as stringent criteria to contracts down to $2M in size. Basically all these systems require the contractor to assign baseline budgets, properly evaluate work in process, properly assess cost and schedule variances, calculate current costs to complete, perform proper analysis, and periodically report costs sustained and schedule status.

Performance Measurement

Exactly how progress on a project should be measured is anything but obvious. The criterion used by various government agencies is that of earned value which makes the cost account critical to performance measurement (see Figure 8-6). Each increment of work has a budget which represents its planned cost (or perceived value) in terms of the total project. As the work is accomplished, the actual costs incurred are compared to the budget or planned cost to determine whether more or less money has been spent than was planned for that work. Variances are analyzed to determine reasons for deviations and corrective actions initiated if necessary.

The budgeted cost of work scheduled (BCWS) is the performance measurement baseline, i.e., the originally scheduled project cost. The budgeted cost of work performed (BCWP) is the originally estimated cost of work that has been completed. The actual cost of work performed (ACWP) is the incurred cost for completed items. The estimate at completion (EAC) is the projected project completion cost. Since ACWP is "actual cost," BCWP is "actual work," and BCWS is "work plan," two variances (Actual Cost − Actual Work = Cost Variance, and Planned Work − Actual Work = Schedule Variance) make it possible to predict project overruns and/or project slippage at any given point in the project. While these tech-

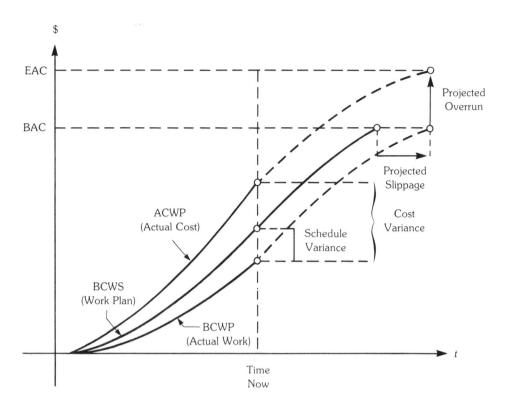

Figure 8-6. Project Performance Measures

niques are primarily used on government projects today, they are also valid for projects in the private sector and more companies are voluntarily implementing such methods for project control.

MODERN PROJECT MANAGEMENT

Basis

The basic premise of the project network planning method is that a network can be used to reasonably represent the performance sequence of a project. The key to success is to logically apply knowledge, experience, and instincts to plan, then to schedule the project as shown in Figure 8-7. A project network is nothing more than a graphic model of a project in the form of a flow chart. Network rules of logic are simple, but the network method exposes poor planning.

Experience indicates that it does not take longer to plan a project using network techniques than with traditional methods, but the network method yields more accurate and detailed plans. For monitoring, network techniques

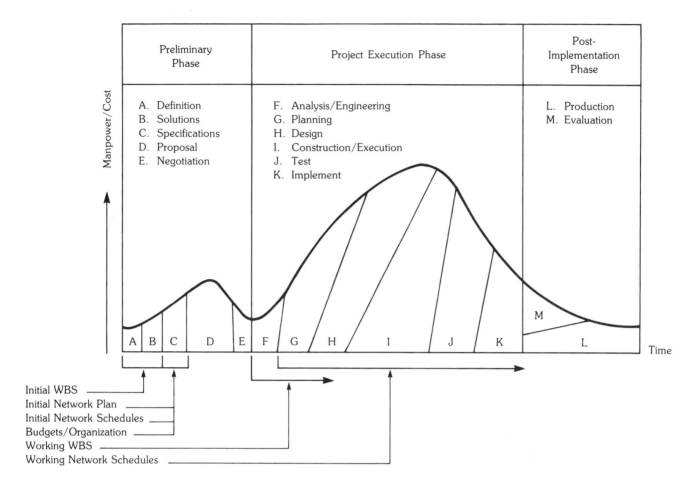

Figure 8-7. Project Network Planning Sequence

far exceed traditional methods in speed, accuracy, and reliability. For replanning or evaluating new factors, the network method has no equal among traditional planning tools.

Experience also indicates the cost of applying network methods is small, perhaps no more than 0.5 percent of the project cost. Project time and cost savings return this investment several fold when these methods are successfully applied.

Applications Some of the major reasons for using modern project control methods include factors related to the project itself (e.g., size, complexity, and risk). Other reasons include more subjective factors (e.g., customer requirements, management requirements, and company image). The more costly or time consuming a project, the more frequently project control is applied and the more detailed is the project planning. The great number of things to be done, the amount of money involved, and the resources to be applied necessitate the use of sophisticated project management techniques.

Unusual project complexities often dictate the use of modern network methods for adequate project control. For example, if the project is located in a physically remote area, the staging, delivery, and assembly become significantly complex. If a project requires many independent subcontracting companies to interact, coordination becomes very complex. Research and development projects, and projects at the leading edge of known technology, are particularly susceptible to poor cost and schedule estimates.

For internal projects the financial risk can be enormous. For projects containing chances of post-project litigation, revised requirements and schedules add additional elements of risk. Customers frequently require detailed plans and reports of progress throughout the duration of the project. Frequently these ongoing project status reports are contractual requirements. Some managements require modern project methods and central control of all projects in all areas within the company. Other companies allow projects greater autonomy. There is also some prestige in being the first company in an industry with "something new."

Today modern project methods are used in virtually all industries; consequently, there is a negative prestige if a company does not use these methods. Also, there is greater prestige in being the best at using the methods available. Customers examine closely project management capabilities in the contractor's organization. Often a project is awarded not to the lowest bidder, but to the one with expertise in the field who demonstrates superior project management capability.

Techniques

Accurate project plans and schedules depend upon the competence and experience of the planner. Accurate project costs depend upon the competence and experience of the estimator. Experience shows that total project duration derived by breaking the project down into discrete activities and basing each activity estimate on the planner/estimator's judgment, experience, and historical data is valid and useful. Planners and estimators should be thoroughly familiar with field realities.

Which projects should be networked? Usually any project of $1M in cost or greater can benefit from applying network methods. The detail to be included in the average activity is a matter of judgment. The type, duration, cost, and risk in the project are all factors to be considered. One rule of thumb is to limit the maximum time per activity to a maximum of ten working days. One way to control project risk and reduce uncertainty is to establish a target detail level, e.g., with a variation of 10:1 in activity cost, a 1,000 activity project has no activity worth more than 1 percent of the project value, and the average activity is worth 0.1 percent of the total project. Level of detail planned and monitored varies by industry.

Acceptance   The power, utility, simplicity, and validity of modern project control methods have been proven in thousands of situations; yet paradoxically, the use of these methods still is only in its infancy. While modern project control methods are generally accepted as necessary, they are not universally applied to all projects, and frequently they fail to deliver the expected benefits. Some of the main reasons for failure are a lack of top management commitment, untrained or unprofessional project control personnel, and schedules which are unrelated to field realities. The definition of project activities must relate to performance realities and the degree of the risks involved. Such efforts require a high degree of knowledge and competence among planners. When properly done, successful implementation of project control methods involves assessment of risk in defining project responsibilities, selective application of controls, relevant management reporting, and compatible transaction systems.

PROJECT CONTROL AUTOMATION

Computations

PERT/CPM/PDM computations are very simple: with project start, scheduled completion, activity durations, and a calendar given, a forward and backward pass yield activity early and late starts and finishes, total float, free float, and the critical path. A small network of 50 activities easily can be calculated by hand, but larger networks, of say 800 to 2,000 activities and up, require automation.

An appreciation of the data processing problem can be obtained (see Figure 8-8) by considering a typical project and the size of the data base which is required to apply modern project control methods. Assuming a project of 1,000 activities, with 166 characters of information per activity for the project schedule; add 175,000 total for the WBS; then add 182,000 total for associated cost data, for a total of 523,000 characters of project data which must be maintained, stored, processed, summarized, and reported. While the computations involved are easy, the magnitude of the data manipulation problem is not. Significant computation resources are required to perform an adequate job in the typical situation involving thousands of activities.

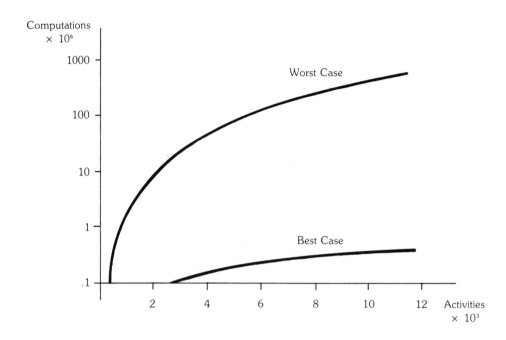

Figure 8-8. Schedule Computations vs. Project Network Size

Project Control
Automation

As illustrated in Figure 8-9, the hardware development of computers and plotters in the 1950s and 1960s respectively were followed by the software developments of Network Analysis Processors (NAP's) and Graphics in the 1960s and 1970s respectively.

The application and use of automated project control has proceeded along two main lines. The first line, computation, followed large computer availability. The second main line, graphics, followed digital plotter availability. Now, with the wide availability of minicomputers, these two lines of development can merge to yield fully integrated project planning and control systems.

Network Analysis
Processor

The availability of large-scale computers in the 1950s led to the development of PERT/CPM/PDM Network Analysis Programs, or NAP's as they became known, to perform project network calculations. These early NAP's included: IBM PCS and PMS, CDC PERT/TIME, Univac PERT/TIME, AF PERT, NASA PERT, and GE PERT. Computers such as the IBM 1401, 1130, 7094, and 360, GE 225 and 635, CDC 3000 and 6000 series, Univac 1100, and Honeywell 600 were used for processing. These early NAP's vastly improved the speed and economy with which schedule calculations

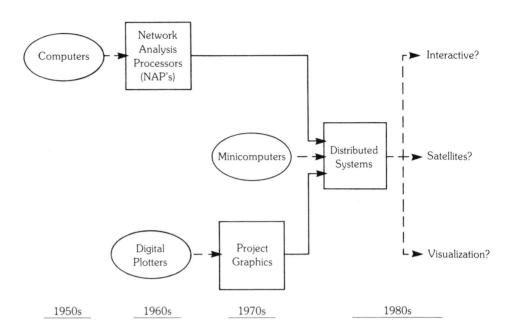

Figure 8-9. Project Control Automation

could be performed, but they were limited in the size and duration of project which they could accommodate. Outputs were often limited to a few fixed-format reports.

Through the 1960s, various NAP's were created for all the commonly available large computers. These programs were developed by computer manufacturers, government agencies, users, and independent suppliers of software. Today in the USA the majority (60 percent) of project management packages run on IBM 360-370 computers. The remaining 40 percent are fairly evenly distributed among CDC, Honeywell, and Univac computers. Sources of currently used NAP's are:

Source of NAP	Percent of Users
Computer Manufacturer	55%
Independent Software Supplier	20%
User	20%
Government Agency	5%

Modern NAP's

Modern NAP's can accommodate very large projects, e.g., 15,000 to 50,000 or more activities. A comparison test of five large NAP's using a 2,000 activity network was recently run on an IBM 370/155 computer. Core requirements ranged from a low of 120K bytes to a high of 356K bytes and execution times ranged from 1.5 CPU minutes to 22 minutes. Interestingly, the fastest system required the least core. Commercial prices of these systems ranged from $350/Mo. to $3,250/Mo., or $30,000 to $42,000 on a purchase basis. Maintenance ranged from $175/Mo. to $210/Mo.

Features of the NAP's tested as well as other modern NAP's include the ability to do both PERT/CPM and precedence networks; resource allocation; compute project and task estimates for labor, capital, and other resources; and accept inputs on actual costs and resource commitments. Some provide for summarization by the project work breakdown structure, by the organization functional structure, and by financial account. Estimates, budgets, and actuals are available to compute current and cumulative variances between plan and actual cost/schedule. Reporting packages bring together both the cost and the schedule information for integrated presentation and also enable selection, processing, and display.

Leveling

The resource allocation or leveling ability of modern automated NAP's permits the user to specify the priority rules to be used. The computer then develops an optimum schedule, saving the user considerable time since only the result has to be fine tuned. In addition, an activity may be assigned multiple resources, and the user may define activities that require varying levels of resources to be specified for allocation to an activity when the first choice of resource is not available. Resource leveling systems make "what-if" simulation feasible and facilitate the scheduler's and project manager's job of project planning.

Resource allocation or leveling is of critical importance to multiproject scheduling, e.g., for maintenance operations in the petrochemical industry. Multiproject scheduling is one of the best uses of project planning and scheduling since often a special skill or resource is mobilized and utilized across many projects simultaneously. In spite of the substantial amount of concurrency among activities, there often is enough flexibility in the schedules of individual projects that resource allocation yields substantial savings.

PERT/COST

Automation makes the search for cost alternatives more feasible. If each activity has a normal as well as a crash time and cost estimate, and work must be expedited to meet or compress the schedule, analysis is required to select the optimum strategy of increasing cost to save time. This problem is ideal for the computer which can be programmed to search for the minimum cost solution on the critical path.

Project Data Display Since PERT/CPM and PDM are graphical management techniques, the main problem in the effective use of PERT/CPM has been an inability to generate graphical displays in a timely fashion. If graphical displays were available within hours of each data base update, management would have the opportunity to review the current problem and take effective actions. Such a capability could improve management's response to unexpected situations. With increasingly complex projects and rapidly changing external conditions, the ability to respond quickly to sudden changes is often critical. The impact of strikes, changes in project scope, material shortages, etc., can quickly be assessed with the aid of timely project graphics reflecting the current situation.

Automated Graphics After NAP's, the second main application of computers to modern project management methods was automated project graphics. This was dependent first upon the development of automatic digital plotting devices, and second, upon the development of appropriate graphics software for project networks. The widespread use of computers for project network calculations preceded automated graphics by a decade. In an attempt to avoid graphical displays, NAP's generated vast amounts of project status reports with various sorts, extractions, etc. However, the fundamental problem of reducing these reports to readily understandable graphics persisted. Manual project graphics methods were and are slow, error prone, and very costly.

With the introduction of the EZPERT Project Graphics System in 1969 by Systonetics, project graphics was automated on an efficient and reliable basis. The process of automating project graphics is shown in Figure 8-10. Typical computing and plotting speeds of EZPERT are shown in Tables 8-2 and 8-3 for all major computer and plotter makes and models.

Computer Mfg.	Computer Model	Activities/ CPU-Hour
IBM	360/65	9,000
	370/155	12,000
CDC	6600	12,000
	CYBER 175	30,000
Honeywell	6080	6,700
	66/80	8,700
Univac	1108	11,000
Burroughs	7700	8,500
DEC	PDP-10	2,000

TABLE 8-2. EZPERT PROCESSING SPEEDS

TABLE 8-3. EZPERT PLOTTING SPEEDS	Type	Plotter Mfg.	Plotter Model	Activities/ Hour
	Electro-Mechanical	CALCOMP	1136	350
		GERBER	62	400
		XYNETICS	2000	500
	Microfilm	STROMBERG	4060	7,500
		III	FR80	10,000
		SINGER	5000	10,000
	Electro-Static	VARIAN	STRATOS	15,000
		GOULD	5000	20,000
		VERSATEC	8136	36,000

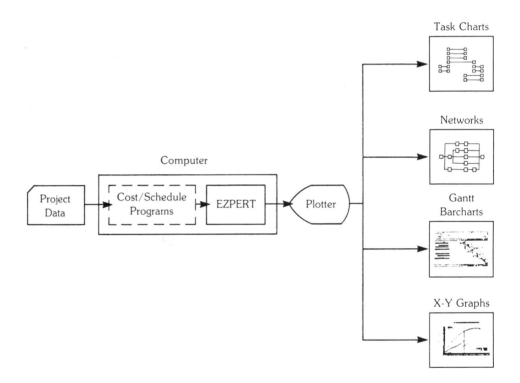

Figure 8-10. Automated Project Graphics

Time and motion studies show that original fully annotated project networks can be manually produced at an average speed of ten activities per hour. Assuming a fully burdened drafting hour cost of $20.00, the average cost is $2.00 per activity. A comparison of manual to automated project net-

TABLE 8-4. MANUAL VS. AUTOMATED PROJECT GRAPHICS

	Manual		EZPERT With	
	Original Drafting @ $20/Hr.	Each Update @ $20/Hr.	COMPUTER IBM 370/155 @ $300/Hr.	PLOTTER VERSATEC 8136 @ $100/Hr.
Time (Activities/Hr.)	10	25	12,600	36,000
Cost ($/Activity)	$2.00	$0.80	$0.024	$0.003

work production using EZPERT is shown in Table 8-4. A comparison for a one-year history on a 1,000 activity project is shown in Table 8-5. The savings for this example project, in time and cost provided by automation, are impressive: automation takes 0.3 percent of the time and 3.0 percent the cost of manual methods.

Automated project graphics should include networks, barcharts, and cost/resource graphs to provide managers with complete information. Reliable graphics automation affords project visibility that was previously lacking in manual approaches. Many circumstances call for graphs and charts of parts of the project data to highlight areas of immediate interest or importance. Data manipulation, extraction, and relevant presentation are facilitated with an automated graphics system capable of generating a wide variety of graphical reports. Specifically these can be designed for the area of interest or responsibility of the recipient. Trouble spots highlighted on top-level summary charts can be traced to the level of detail required to isolate the cause of the problem and its resolution.

TABLE 8-5. 1,000 ACTIVITY PROJECT

	Manual		EZPERT IBM 370/155 VERSATEC 8136	
	Original	23 Updates	24 Computer Runs	24 Plotter Runs
Time	100 Hrs.	920 Hrs.	1.90 Hrs.	0.67 Hrs.
Cost	$2,000	$18,400	$570	$67

Automation: 0.3% the Time of Manual
3.0% the Cost of Manual

Improving Project Management

The quantitative benefits of project graphics automation are impressive both in time savings and in cost savings. However, the qualitative benefits of improved performance of project managers and the accuracy of their decisions can far exceed the quantitative savings of automating a previously manual process. The quality of project management is directly related to the availability of clear, concise, and timely project status information as the basis for good decisions.

For small projects, approximately 5 percent of the project cost is consumed by planning, scheduling, monitoring and control. Approximately half of the amount is spent for project control. A very small improvement in overall project management performance can justify automation. Just 1 percent cost savings due to project management improvement on a relatively small $10 million in cost project, or a savings of $100,000 will buy project management automation technology that can be repeatedly applied to projects ten or hundreds of times larger to yield similar savings.

CURRENT AND FUTURE TRENDS

Distributed Processing

The use of PERT today is nearly always automated on a large scale computer either internally or at a service bureau. An increasing trend is toward distributed processing and widespread use of minicomputers either as department satellites, or remote stations within large companies, or as the central data processing unit for smaller companies. The authors think this trend will include project management automation at the department level with dedicated minicomputer systems.

Minicomputer Based Systems

As illustrated in Figure 8-11, modern minicomputer based project information systems are characterized by automatic prompting to decrease demands upon operator sophistication; inclusion of a Data Base Management System to accomplish Cost/Schedule/WBS integration; standard processing modules for all important project management methods plus other modules for special requirements; a flexible report writer for management reports; and automated graphics for bar charts, networks, and two-dimensional graphs.

The wide availability of economical computing power and display devices is nowhere made as apparent as in today's minicomputers and their peripherals. A "micro" or very small "mini" computer today will commonly have a processing speed hundreds of times faster than a major mainframe of the 1950s or early 1960s, and a core size tens of times larger. A modern

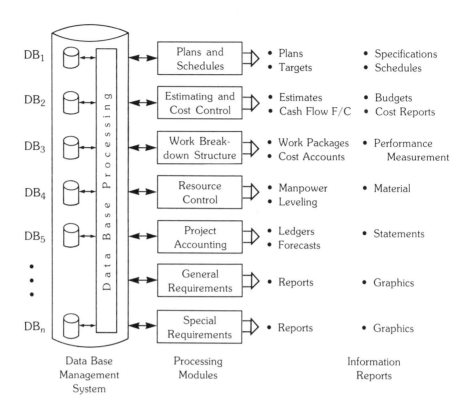

Figure 8-11. Modern Project Information System

minicomputer is capable of handling many sophisticated programs inter-
actively and simultaneously, and is very modestly priced.

Because of this progress, a minicomputer system principally dedicated
to project management is now technically and economically feasible. Three
important reasons for using a minicomputer system for project management
include: (1) a physically remote project, (2) a remote project by manage-
ment/customer decision, and (3) a smaller company principally engaged in
project management without another general purpose computer, wishing to
avoid service bureau costs and planning to use the system for other processing.

Remote Sites A physically remote project can use manual project management methods, a
service bureau (if available), or tie into the headquarters system, if communications links are available. If the project is sizable and if the service bureau
costs or headquarters tie-in costs are significant, a minicomputer system may
be feasible. The hardware must be portable, inexpensive, have few environmental requirements, and have the potential to support a wide range of

needs. The project management software must be easy to learn, easy to use, and include network calculations, resource allocation, cost tracking, and graphics. With these capabilities, the benefits of on-site control and cost savings over other methods could justify the dedicated remote minicomputer based project management system.

A project remote by company/customer decision could be one which is secret in nature or consequence and must receive special treatment. In these situations, a satisfactory large computer may be available, but inadequate for security reasons. The project would be considered to be on its own, and a nuisance or inconvenience to normal data processing. A minicomputer system, dedicated to the problems of managing the project, would improve the acceptance and approval of its management methods.

Small- to
Medium-Sized
Companies

Small- to medium-sized companies are less likely to have the requisite expertise, staff, equipment, resources, and experience in automated project management methods. Today's minicomputer system dedicated to project management requires significantly less technical skill as shown in Figure 8-12. They need conversational interaction with a prompted project management system, and a system which can accommodate their functional accounting needs. A minicomputer with wide ranging capabilities but easy to learn to use and oriented to the principal project management needs of the company would appear to be feasible.

Future Trends

With the tremendous improvements made in computing hardware and software in the past few years, and the wider acceptance of modern project management methods, it is interesting to speculate on the possible trends that will emerge in the 1980s.

Distribution

The use of fully integrated minicomputer based project management systems will become more widespread both as a dedicated capability and as a satellite to a central DP facility. Sophisticated project management methods will thereby become more broadly accepted in industry and greater competence will be shown throughout all levels of an organization. Such systems will become as common in project management as word processing systems are today.

Prompting

These systems will be capable of "prompting" the user through a CRT terminal in correct and appropriate use, thereby decreasing the level of expertise in either data processing or planning and scheduling to the bare minimum on the part of the system operator. This feature will be conducive to the acceptance of these systems by managers and smaller companies. Modern project management methods will make smaller companies more competitive and/or profitable.

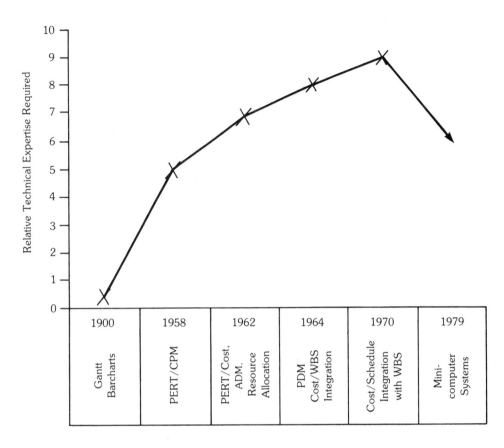

Figure 8-12. Required Technical Expertise for Computer Operation

Interactive The systems will contain increasingly sophisticated interactive graphics and data base capability. The improvements that will follow in project simulation, consideration of alternatives in planning and scheduling, impact assessment, risk analysis, and crisis management will be substantial.

Visualization It is possible to conceive of integrating Computer Aided Design techniques with Cost/Schedule/WBS methods to link reported schedule progress with a computer-generated visualization of actual project progress on projects such as a high-rise office building, bridges, tunnels, roadways, and similar constructions.

CONCLUSIONS A great variety of information and control system hardware and software packages are available for the prospective implementer of project management. The project can choose from such tools as PERT/CPM, PERT/COST, PDM, WBS, resource allocation and cost/schedule integration. In many cases the use of a particular tool will be a contractual requirement. The use of a WBS and one of the networking planning and scheduling tools are almost a necessity for every project. The WBS is made even more effective if it is made a part of an integrated cost/schedule control system.

Project performance measures are also available which allow comparisons of planned vs. actual work and cost. Schedule variances make it possible to predict schedule overruns and/or project slippage at any point in the project.

Modern project control methods are based on the premise that project network planning can be used to reasonably represent the performance sequence of a project. Therefore, it is not only an excellent control and evaluation tool, but it has no equal as a planning tool. Modern project control methods are most successful when automated as has been found necessary to handle today's very complex and rapidly changing projects. Project control automation has reached a high level of sophistication, and a large variety of computers, plotters, and other graphic aids are available. Now, with the availability of microcomputers and advanced graphics, fully integrated project planning and control systems are a reality. Such developments in hardware were followed by the software developments of Network Analysis Processors (NAP's) and graphics. Modern NAP's can handle very large projects and can integrate networking, resource allocation, computation of estimates for labor, capital, and other resources, and accept inputs for actual costs and resources commitments. Automated graphics systems can then provide a wide variety of clear, concise, and timely project status information as a basis for decision making. A compatible system is available for all potential users, large or small, and at any level of sophistication.

CHAPTER NINE

THE JOB OF THE PROJECT MANAGER: SYSTEMS INTEGRATION

Linn C. Stuckenbruck, Ph.D.

Institute of Safety and Systems Management
University of Southern California
Los Angeles, California

INTRODUCTION The project manager responsible for the department or construction of a large, complex system has all the responsibilities and functions of any other manager. However, the job has aspects and problems which go beyond those of the usual line or functional manager. The major difference between line and project management can be found in the project manager's necessary preoccupation with the integration of her or his project. However, a review of the literature provides remarkably little useful information indicating exactly how this important process of systems integration is conducted. This chapter will investigate the integration process and indicate to prospective project managers how they can initiate the process.

WHAT IS PROJECT MANAGEMENT?

It is a management axiom that the overall job of every manager is to create within the organization an environment which will facilitate the accomplishment of its objectives.[1] Certainly the job of the project manager fits this role very well. In addition, every manager is responsible for the generally accepted managerial functions of planning, organizing, staffing, directing, and controlling. Since every manager has these functions, how does the job of the project manager differ from that of the line or discipline manager?

The project management concept is based on vesting in a single individual the sole authority for the planning, resource allocation, direction and control for the accomplishment of a single, time-, and budget-limited enterprise. But this statement does not indicate any major difference between the job of the project manager and the line or discipline manager.

THE PROJECT MANAGER'S PROBLEM

The project manager has one particular problem which is intensified in comparison with the similar problem of the line or discipline manager. Any complex project must be subdivided into tasks that are capable of accomplishment. The result is a multitude of separate tasks. These tasks are then performed by specialized functional- or discipline-oriented organizations as appropriate. The resulting complex matrix organization gives the project manager many more organizational and project interfaces to manage. Archibald indicates that "the basic concept of interface management is that the project manager plans and controls (manages) the points of interaction between various elements of the project, the product, and the organizations involved."[2]

These interfaces are a problem for the project manager, since whatever obstacles are encountered are usually the result of two organizational units going in different directions. An old management cliché says that all the really difficult problems occur at organizational interfaces. The problem is complicated by the fact that the organizational units are usually not under direct management, and some of the important interfaces may be outside of the company or enterprise.

INTERFACE MANAGEMENT

Interface management consists of identifying, documenting, scheduling, communicating, and monitoring interfaces related to both the product and the project.[3] Interfaces are of many kinds. Archibald divides them into two types—product and project, and then further divides them into subgroups, of which management interfaces are a major division.[4] The problem of the overall project/functional interface is thoroughly discussed by Cleland and King who point out the complementary nature of the project and the functional or discipline-oriented organizations. "They are inseparable and one cannot survive without the other."[5]

Project management, however, is more than just this management interface, it involves three types of interfaces which the project manager must continually monitor for potential problems: (1) personal interfaces, (2) organizational interfaces, and (3) system interfaces.

Personal Interfaces These are the "people" interfaces within the organization which are working to carry out the project. Whenever two people are working on the same project we have a potential for personal problems and even conflict. If the people are both within the same line or discipline organization, the project manager has limited authority, but can demand that the line supervision resolve the personal problem or conflict. If the people are not in the same line or discipline organization, the project manager enters into the role of a mediator, with the ultimate alternative of insisting that line management resolve the problem or remove one or both of the individuals from the project team. Personal interface problems become even more troublesome and difficult to solve when they involve two or more managers.

Organizational Interfaces Organizational interfaces are the most troublesome since they involve not only people, but also varied organizational goals and conflicting managerial styles and aspirations. Each organizational unit has its own objectives, its own disciplines or specialties, and its own functions. As a result of these differences in organizational units, each has its own jargon, often difficult for other groups to understand or appreciate. It is thus apparent that misunderstanding and conflict can easily occur at the interfaces. These interfaces are more than purely management interfaces since much day-to-day contact is at the working level. Purely management interfaces exist when important management decisions, approvals, or other actions will affect the project. Organizational interfaces also involve units outside the immediate company or project organizations such as the customer, subcontractors, or other contractors on the same or related systems.

System Interfaces System interfaces are the product, hardware, facility, construction, or other types of nonpeople interfaces inherent in the system being developed or constructed by the project. These will be interfaces between the various subsystems in the project. The problem is intensified because the various subsystems will usually be developed by different organizational units. As pointed out by Archibald,[6] these system interfaces can be actual physical interfaces existing between interconnecting parts of the system, or performance interfaces existing between various subsystems or components of the system. System interfaces may actually be schedule milestones involving the transmission of information developed in one task to another task by a specific time, or the completion of a subsystem on schedule.

The project manager's problem is that of interface management. What is done to solve this problem can be described by the more general term—*systems integration.*

THE INTEGRATION PROCESS

Systems integration is related to what Koontz and O'Donnell call "the essense of management-coordination, or the purpose of management is the achievement of harmony of individual effort toward the accomplishment of group goals."[7] However, doesn't every manager have this function? Yes, but the project manager has to be preoccupied with it. The project manager's major responsibility is for assuring that a particular system or activity is assembled so that all of the components, parts, subsystems, and organizational units fit together as a functioning, integrated whole according to plan. Carrying out this responsibility comprises the function of systems integration. Integration is an action that is important to the success of any project whether hardware is involved or not. Any project involving many people, many organizational units, and many subsystems must be carefully and thoroughly integrated if the system is going to fit together as projected.

The management function of integration was identified and described by Lawrence and Lorsch. They pointed out that with the rapid advances in technology and the increased complexity of systems to be managed, there is an increased need both for greater specialization (differentiation) and for tighter coordination (integration). An effective manager has a need for both; however, since these two needs are essentially antagonistic, one can usually be achieved only at the expense of the other.[8, 9] It can be described as a tradeoff between these two needs as shown in Figure 9-1.

It has been suggested that the ideal high-performance manager falls on the arrow midway between differentiation and integration, and probably is typical of high-performance top management. It is also true that line or discipline management usually falls closer to the differentiation arrow, and that the project manager falls closer to the integration arrow. This model illustrates the need for the project manager as integrator.

The role of the project manager in the matrix organization has been analyzed by Galbraith,[10, 11] Lawrence and Lorsch,[12, 13, 14] Lorsch and Morse,[15] and Davis and Lawrence.[16] They point out that the horizontal communication in a matrix organization requires an open, problem-solving climate. However,

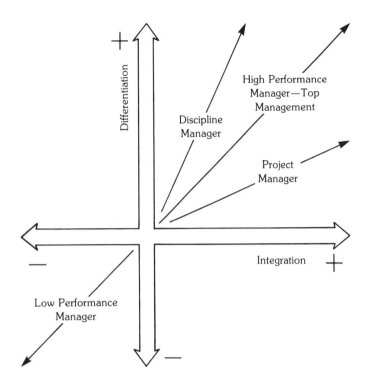

Figure 9-1. Measuring Managerial Performance

as pointed out by Galbraith,[17, 18] when the subtasks in an organization are greatly differentiated, a matrix structure may be required to achieve integration. The integrator coordinates the decision processes across the interfaces of differentiation. The project manager as the integrator is necessary to make the matrix organization work.

Problem solving and decision making are critical to the integration process since most project problems occur at subsystem or organizational interfaces. The project manager is the only person in the key position to solve such interface problems. The project manager provides "(1) a single point of integrative responsibility, and (2) integrative planning and control."[19] The project manager is faced with three general types of problems and the subsequent necessity for decision making:

1. Administrative problems usually involving the removal of road blocks or the setting of priorities. A major effort is usually necessary to resolve organizational conflicts involving people, resources, or facilities.

2. Technical problems which necessitate making key decisions, deciding on scope changes, and making key tradeoffs among cost, schedule, or performance. Decisions are necessary to select between technical alternatives which impact project performance.

3. Customer or client problems which involve interpretation of and conformance to specifications and regulatory agency documents.

It is just the first step for the project manager to recognize that his or her primary job is that of integrator. It is then important that the project manager has a good idea as to how to accomplish the total process of integration. What exactly should be done to assure that the process of integration takes place?

THE CRITICAL ACTIONS OF INTEGRATION

The integration process is difficult to separate from general good management practice. However, the integration process consists of a number of critical actions which the project manager must initiate and continually monitor. In most cases the project manager is the single point of integrative responsibility, and is the only person who can initiate these actions. Among the most important of these actions are:

1. Plan for integration.

2. Develop integrated work-breakdown structure, schedule, and budget.

3. Continually review and update project plan.

4. Assure project control and adherence to project plan.

5. Assure design for an integrated system.

6. Resolve conflict situations.

7. Remove roadblocks.

8. Set priorities.

9. Make administrative and technical decisions across interfaces.

10. Solve customer or client problems.

11. Assure that project transfer takes place.

12. Maintain communication links across interfaces.

Plan for Integration Integration doesn't just happen—it must be planned. The project manager must develop a detailed planning document that can be used to get the project initiated, and to assure that all project participants understand their roles and responsibilities in the project organization.

The project manager is the only person in that key position having an overview of the entire system, hopefully from its inception, and can foresee potential interface or other integration problems. After identifying the interfaces the project manager can keep a close surveillance on them to catch and correct any integration problems when they first occur. Particularly important in the project plan is a clear delineation of the project requirements for reporting, hardware delivery, completion of tests, facility construction, and other important milestones.

An important part of the project plan should be the integration plan. This plan may even be a separate document if a single department or even a separate contractor is responsible for project integration. In any case, the integration plan should define and identify all interface problems, interface events, and interrelationships between tasks and hardware subsystems. The integration plan should then analyze the interrelationships between tasks and the scheduled sequence of events in the project.

Develop Integrated Work-Breakdown Structure, Schedule, and Budget The most important part of a project plan is an integrated work-breakdown structure, schedule, and budget. Whatever type of planning and control technique is used, all the important interfaces and interface events must be identified. Interface events such as hardware or facility completions will be important project milestones. The project network plan must be based on the interface events in order to facilitate analysis of the entire project on an integrated basis. Resource allocation and reporting periods can then be coordinated with interface events, and schedules and budgets can be designed on an integrated basis.

Continually Review and Update Project Plan The project manager must continually review and update both the administrative and technical portions of the project plan to provide for changes in scope and direction of the project. She or he must assure that budget and resource requirements are continually reviewed and revised so that project resources are utilized in the most effective manner to produce an integrated system.

Assure Project Control and Adherence to Project Plan The most complete and well integrated project plan is worthless if no one uses it. Only the project manager can assure that all task managers are aware of their role and responsibilities in project success. But continuous follow-up by the project manager is necessary to assure adherence to the project plan, and awareness of any necessary revisions.

Assure Design For An Integrated System

The design step is extremely critical since integration must be designed into the system. Therefore the project manager must exercise considerable influence during the design phase to assure that interfaces are recognized and that the system is designed as an integrated whole. Subsystem designers must work closely with other subsystem designers and the overall system designers to assure complete integration.

Large aerospace projects have often been fortunate enough to afford the luxury of an integrating contractor. This contractor would plan the design and hardware development phases so as to assure effective systems integration. They would prepare an integration plan which would serve as a guide for the other system contractors in designing, developing, testing, and manufacturing the subsystems. The integrating contractor would have responsibility for assembling the overall system. An example would be the development by separate contractors of three separate stages and a warhead by a fourth contractor. A fifth contractor would serve as the systems integrator, guiding the four contractors throughout the development project.

Resolve Conflict Situations

It is inevitable that problems occur at organizational and subsystem interfaces. These problems may or may not result in actual open conflict between individuals or organizations. A common situation is personal conflict between the two managers involved at the interface. Conflict situations result primarily from the concerned groups or managers losing sight of the overall project goals or having differing interpretations of how to get the job accomplished. The project manager must continually be on the lookout for potential and real conflict situations and resolve them immediately.

Remove Roadblocks

Roadblocks are inevitable in a complex organization, and the inevitable result of conflict situations. Resolving the conflict situation will eliminate many roadblocks, but there are always other roadblocks set up intentionally or unintentionally by managers and other personnel not directly involved with the project. These roadblocks may be the result of conflicting needs for resources and personnel, or conflicting priorities for the use of facilities and equipment. Administrative roadblocks often occur because managers outside the project do not understand or sympathize with the project manager's urgency. Such roadblocks are difficult to deal with, and the project manager may be forced to go to top management to get a satisfactory resolution.

Set Priorities

In order to resolve or prevent conflict situations, the project manager is continually faced with the problem of setting priorities. There are two types of priorities that concern the project manager: (1) the overall company or organizational priorities which rate project needs in relation to other projects within the organization, and (2) the priorities within the project for the utilization of personnel, equipment, and facilities.

The first type of priority may be beyond the control of the project manager, but it is a problem with which one must be continually concerned. Pity the poor project manager who is so busy getting the job done that he or she forgets to cement relationships with top management. The result may be a low project priority that dooms the project to failure. The second type of priority is within the project organization and therefore within the control of the project manager. These priority problems must be handled on a day-to-day basis, but in a manner that will promote the integration of the system.

Make Administrative and Technical Decisions Across Interfaces

The project manager must recognize and solve the critical technical and administrative problems and make the critical decisions that arise during the course of a project.

Solve Customer or Client Problems

It is obviously very important to assure that the customer or client be kept happy. To do this, the project manager must keep the client thoroughly informed both as to the technical status and the schedule/budget status of the project. Top management looks to the project manager as the primary contact with the customer or client, and expects that these relationships be open, honest, and on a friendly basis. The project manager is a very real representative of top management.

Assure That Project Transfer Takes Place

Project transfer is the movement of a project through the project organizations from the conceptual phase to final delivery to the customer. Project transfer does not just happen, it must be carefully planned and provided for in the scheduling and budgeting of the project. The project manager has the responsibility of assuring that project transfer takes place without wasteful effort and on schedule. The steps in a typical project are shown in Figure 9-2.

The movement of the project from block to block involves crossing organizational interfaces, an action which must be forced if it is to happen on schedule. The basic problem is that of making certain that the project is transferred quickly, without organizational conflict, without unnecessary redesign or rework, and without loss of relevant technology or other information. Experience has shown that the best method of assuring effective project transfer is to utilize people who can move with the project across organizational interfaces. The project manager has two alternatives to facilitate project transfer: (1) the designation of suitably qualified personnel who can move forward with the project, i.e., change their role as indicated by the left to right dashed arrows; or (2) the utilization of personnel who can move backward in the

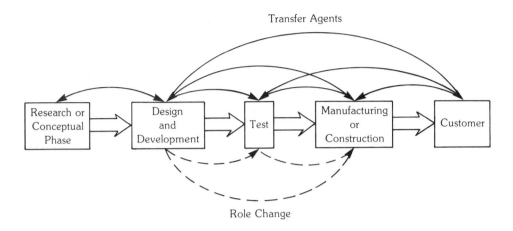

Figure 9-2. Project Transfer

organization and serve as consultants or active working members of the project team. When the project moves forward they serve as transfer agents in moving the project forward in the organization. Various possible personnel transfers are shown by the right to left solid arrows in Figure 9-2. Great importance must be placed in having customer, manufacturing, and/or construction representatives take part in the design phase.

Maintain Communication Links Across Interfaces

The last of the integration actions, that of constantly maintaining communication links, is perhaps the most difficult and troublesome because it involves the necessity for considerable "people" skill on the part of the project managers. Most project managers find that they spend at least half of their time talking to people—getting information, clarifying directives, and resolving conflict and misunderstanding. Much of this time is involved with the critical responsibility for maintaining all communication links both within and outside the project in order to assure project integration. Internal communication links must be maintained between each subdivision of the project, and the project manager must make sure that all the team members talk with each other. In addition, the project manager is personally responsible for maintaining communication linkages outside the project. Many of the external communication links can be personally expedited by the project manager, and in most cases the communication consists of written documents.

Communication linkages internal to the project, however, must function continuously, with or without documentation, and whether the project manager is personally involved or not. These internal communication linkages are most important to the health of the project since they involve the technical integration of the subsystems of the product or project. However, there are usually very real barriers to effective communications across any two such subsystem interfaces. In order to assure that problems do not accumulate and build up at these interfaces, the project manager must act as a transfer agent or a communications expediter. The model shown in Figure 9-3 illustrates the interface problem.

The project manager must serve as the bridge to make sure that communication barriers do not occur. Communication barriers can be caused by a variety of circumstances and occurrences which the project manager must watch for. A communication barrier may or may not result in actual conflict depending upon the individuals involved.

The project manager is the one person always in a position to expedite communication linkages. He or she can be considered to be a transfer agent by assuring that the communication link is completed by transferring information and project requirements across the interface. Considering the number of interfaces in a complex, multidisciplinary matrix-organized project, this process becomes a major effort for the project manager. The only saving grace is that many of these interfaces will be trouble free with good communications, at least the problems will not all occur at the same time.

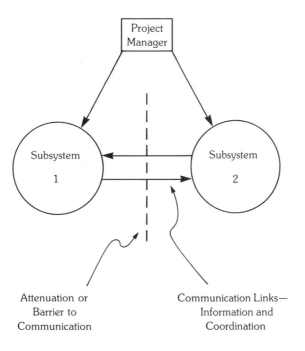

Figure 9-3. The Project Manager As Communications Expediter

Communication barriers may be caused by a variety of circumstances and occurrences. Some of the causes of communication barriers are:

1. Differing perceptions as to the goals and objectives of the overall system will cause problems. Lack of understanding of project objectives is one of the most frequent and troublesome causes of misunderstanding. It can be directly attributed to insufficient action on the part of the project manager, since defining project objectives is a major responsibility. Even when these objectives are clearly stated by the project manager, they may be perceived differently by various project team members.

2. Differing perceptions of the scope and goals of the individual subsystem organizations can likewise restrict communication. Again it is the responsibility of the project manager to clarify these problems, at least as to how they impact the project.

3. Competition for facilities, equipment, materials, manpower, and other resources can not only clog communication routes, but can eventually lead to conflict.

4. Personal antagonisms or actual personality conflicts between managers and/or other personnel will block communications flow. There may also be antagonism toward the project manager by line managers who perceive a threat to their authority or their empire.

5. Resistance to change or the NIH (not invented here) attitude may also detrimentally affect communication links between organizational units.

As indicated in Figure 9-4, the project manager has four important communication links: (1) upward to top management, (2) downward to the people working on the project, (3) outward to line managers and other projects at the same level in management, and (4) outward to the customer or client. The project manager has a major responsibility for maintaining communications with the chief executives in the organization. They must be provided with timely, up-to-date progress reports on the technical and financial status of the project. Similar reports must be provided the client or customer, particularly if the customer is outside the company (i.e., the government).

The other important communication link is with the people working on the project. The project manager must keep them informed by means of project directives and personal communications. In addition, there is a continual

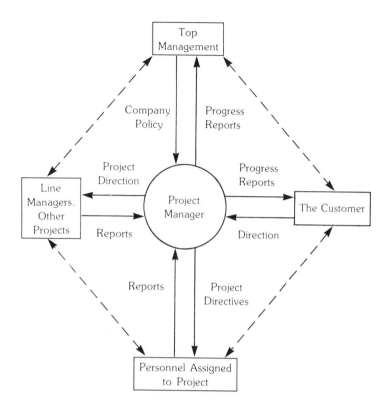

Figure 9-4. The Project Manager's Communication Links

stream of reports from the discipline/line-organization managers and specialists working on the project. Many of these reports concern details that can be evaluated by administrators and assistant project managers. However, the ultimate decisions as to the worth of the report, and as to whether it should be included in progress reports to the customer and/or top management, is in the hands of the project manager. Communication skills therefore must include the ability to accurately and rapidly evaluate, condense, and act on information from many sources.

Attenuation in these communication links at the organizational interfaces must be minimized. This means that the project manager must have an open line to top management. Conversely too many line managers cannot be interpreting instructions and project goals to the people working on the project. Without open communication links, the project manager will surely fail. There are also a number of important communication links outside the scope of the project, but which may be very important to the health of the project. The four most important such links are shown by the dashed arrows in Figure

9-4. The project manager has to recognize the existence and the necessity for these communication links. Rather than fight them, the project manager should endeavor to make use of these relationships.

CONCLUSION Systems integration consists of assuring that the pieces of a project come together at the right time and that it then functions as an integrated unit. However, to accomplish the integration process, all the various types of interfaces must be monitored and controlled, because integration, for the most part, is just another way of saying interface management. In addition, the number of interfaces can increase exponentially as the number of organizational units increase. The life of the project manager can become very complex.

It makes little difference whether "the system" is a missile, a nuclear power plant, a petroleum refinery, or a transportation system, the principles of systems integration are applicable. Similarly, it makes little difference whether the project manager has a pure project organization or is in a matrix organization, the integration function is the same (although interface problems are greatly intensified in a matrix organization).

A number of positive actions that the project manager must make to assure that integration takes place have been suggested. The most important of these actions is that of maintaining communication links across the organizational interfaces. This once again proves that the principal function of the project manager is to serve as a catalyst to motivate the project team.

ENDNOTES

1. Harold Koontz, and Cyril O'Donnell, *Principles of Management: An Analysis of Managerial Functions* (New York: McGraw-Hill Book Co., 1972), p. 46.

2. Russell D. Archibald, *Managing High-Technology Programs and Projects* (New York: John Wiley and Sons, 1977), p. 66.

3. Ibid.

4. Koontz and O'Donnell, *Principles of Management.*

5. David I. Cleland, and William R. King, *Systems Analysis and Project Management,* 2nd ed. (New York: McGraw-Hill Book Co., 1975), p. 237.

6. Archibald, *Managing High-Technology.*

7. Koontz and O'Donnell, *Principles of Management,* p. 50.

8. Paul R. Lawrence, and Jay W. Lorsch, *Organization and Environment: Managing Differentiation and Integration* (Boston: Division of Research, Graduate School of Business Administration, Harvard University, 1967).

9. Paul R. Lawrence, and Jay W. Lorsch, "New Management Job: The Integrator." *Harvard Business Review* (November-December, 1967): pp. 142-151.

10. Jay Galbraith, *Designing Complex Organizations* (Reading, Mass.: Addison-Wesley Publishing Co., 1973).

11. Jay Galbraith, *Organization Design* (Reading, Mass.: Addison-Wesley Publishing Co., 1977).

12. Lawrence and Lorsch, *Organization and Environment.*

13. Lawrence and Lorsch, "New Management Job."

14. Paul R. Lawrence, and Jay W. Lorsch, *Developing Organizations: Diagnosis and Action* (Reading, Mass.: Addison-Wesley Publishing Co., 1969).

15. Jay W. Lorsch, and John J. Morse, *Organizations and their Members: A Contingency Approach* (New York: Harper and Row, 1974), pp. 79-80.

16. Stanley M. Davis, and Paul R. Lawrence, *Matrix* (Reading, Mass.: Addison-Wesley Publishing Co., 1977).

17. Galbraith, *Designing Complex Organizations.*

18. Galbraith, *Organization Design.*

19. Archibald, *Managing High-Technology,* p. 5.

CHAPTER TEN THE USE OF MANAGEMENT BY OBJECTIVES IN PROJECT MANAGEMENT

David H. Morton Construction Manager
Construction Division
Houston Center Corporation
Houston, Texas

Eric Jennet Vice President
Brown & Root, Inc.
Houston, Texas

John F. Murphy Project Planner
Brown & Root, Inc.
Houston, Texas

Fred Peters Chief—Programs, Scheduling & Analysis
NASA
Johnson Space Center
Houston, Texas

INTRODUCTION The process of managing covers a spectrum of operating styles between two extremes, management by objectives and management by activity. At the one extreme, effectiveness is measured by the flurry of activity that takes place and the effort put forth, rather than by the results produced. At the other end is management by objectives (MBO), which defines in advance the results that are to be achieved and the program steps needed to achieve these results. MBO shifts the focus to goals and the purpose of the activity rather than the activity itself. Under this concept, managers are held responsible for results rather than for activities. No longer is it a matter of how well they understand the machinery, or how many meetings they hold, or what volume of correspondence they are able to turn out, but how their activities pay off in terms of objectives of the organization.

The environment of a project is an ideal place to utilize MBO, since all projects should be strongly goal- and objective-oriented. In fact, the reaction of most active project managers is to say, "Isn't that what I've been doing all along?" They are right, that is what all good project managers do, but MBO formalizes the process and makes it a part of the entire organization's activities. MBO has the great advantage of providing top management and the project manager with objectives, goals, and results, which can be used as yardsticks in evaluating performance. The organization's merit review and reward system should be an integral part of MBO.

WHAT IS MBO? MBO is a commonsense, systematic approach to getting things done, and is based on principles and techniques that good project managers have been practicing for decades. In spite of the new jargon that has come into vogue, there is nothing mysterious about it. It does not require a project manager to stop those activities that have been successfully performed for years and learn a whole new approach. It simply requires the project manager to focus on results rather than activities.

MBO is a system of managerial leadership that defines individual managerial responsibilities in terms of corporate objectives.[1] It has been described as a technique for promoting better plans and performance. It has also been defined as a means of applying our knowledge of motivation.[2] There are as many definitions of MBO as there are authors on the subject, with very little agreement as to exactly how it is accomplished.

The philosophy behind MBO was first put forward in 1954 by Peter Drucker in his book, *The Practice of Management*,[3] and since that time it has undergone an evolution. The key word in the term *management by objec-*

tives is not *objectives*, but *management*. Drucker also emphasized "management by objectives and self-control,"[4] that is, the ability of a manager to control personal performance through self-control or stronger motivation. In addition, he stressed the management aspects of MBO and the need for top-down objectives. Later interpretations of MBO have dropped Drucker's "self-control" and have tended to emphasize the bottom-up aspect.[5]

Today's MBO experience, particularly with project management, indicates that the setting of objectives should be a process of tradeoffs between management and their subordinates. Policy and top management goals should come down through the management hierarchy. These goals will be interpreted by all lower levels of management and their subordinates in preparing their own objective statements, which will go back up the hierarchy for criticism and approval. A process of iteration will result in common agreement.

WHAT OBJECTIVES? An objective is a specific description of an end result to be achieved. The objective should indicate *what* (the end result is), *who* (is accountable), and *when* (the objective is to be completed). A specific objective is not described by such "weasel words" as *shortest possible, maximum, minimum, justifiable, allowable, desirable, reasonable, lowest, highest,* or *optimum*. In addition, each job-related objective should be simple, understandable, challenging, job related, achievable, measurable, and above all, verifiable. Setting verifiable objectives is often extremely difficult. Therefore, the manager or subordinate should be asked simple questions such as, "At the end of the year, how will you know whether this objective has been accomplished?" or "How will your subordinates know when they are accomplishing an objective?"[6] A little thought on these questions should lead to the development of better objectives.

Every business, corporation, or governmental organization has objectives. As pointed out by Peter F. Drucker,[7] no business has only a single objective, such as profit; there are many other areas in which it should have objectives. An emphasis only on profit, for instance, could lead management to miss growth opportunities or even endanger the survival of the enterprise. Obviously, then, an organization needs multiple objectives. Drucker indicates that, "objectives are needed in every area where performance and results directly and vitally affect the survival and prosperity of the business."[8]

The question then becomes: what specific objectives? Drucker lists eight areas in which objectives of performance and results have to be set: market standing, innovation, productivity, physical and financial resources, profitability, manager performance and development, worker performance and attitude, and public responsibility.[9] Many of these are corporate or top management objectives, and may not be as specific as those of middle management. Top management objectives must answer such questions as: What is the nature of our business? What market place are we aiming at? How much and what kind of growth do we need? How much profit should we expect?

A lower-level manager or employee has more specific objectives, of which there are four types: (1) innovative, (2) problem solving, (3) routine, and (4) personal development. Innovative or creative objectives describe something that has never been done before. Such an objective is a challenge to move into an area in response to new needs or new opportunities. Problems that must be solved can be made a personal challenge, and a target date set for completion. Routine tasks or activities must be completed; therefore, they should be indicated as managerial or employee objectives. MBO is also applied in helping the manager or employees manage themselves and aid in their personal and career growth. These objectives will indicate what can be done to make a person more valuable to the organization, and will state specific things that can be done in preparing for more responsibility.

Middle- and lower-level management objectives and goals should be sufficiently specific and sufficiently measurable (verifiable) to serve as performance indicators at the end of the period. Such management objectives should consist of statements such as, "To reduce air pollution at the plant by 15 percent, as measured electrostatically at the stack, by January 1." In other words, an objective should be a written statement that states the results to be achieved by a certain date.

THE PROCESS OF MBO

The process of an MBO program has been described as the development of understanding between every superior-subordinate pair about the subordinate's continuing objectives and specific goals.[10] The process thus consists of joint negotiation and agreement upon mutual goals and objectives, followed by evaluation of the results. The best way to understand how MBO works is to look at the steps involved in the actual practice of implementing it.

SETTING OF OBJECTIVES BY TOP MANAGEMENT

It is first necessary for top management to establish all corporate or organizational goals and objectives. Top management must determine where they want the organization to go and what they want it to achieve during a particular period. MBO is seldom completely satisfactory unless it starts at the very top of an organization. It also must have top management's continuing active and unqualified support, and top management must have realistic and verifiable organizational objectives. Project managers can implement MBO for use only in their own organizations; however, it will be relatively ineffective without top management support. No subordinate manager can be asked to establish realistic objectives without very clear guidelines from top management. Vague or inconsistent corporate goals will result in equally vague and inconsistent objectives from subordinate managers.

SETTING OF SUBORDINATES' OBJECTIVES

After top management's goals, strategies, and objectives have been thoroughly disseminated throughout the organization, every superior-subordinate pair must work out the subordinate's objectives. The first step is for the superior to ask the subordinate for a written statement of his or her objectives and specific goals for the coming year. This statement should contain both personal career objectives and objectives for the department or organization he or she manages. The objectives should indicate what can be accomplished, in what time frame, and with what resources.

JOINT NEGOTIATION AND AGREEMENT

The superior should then meet with the subordinate to discuss the practicality of these objectives. These objectives must be fully attainable, fully supportive of top management objectives, and consistent with the long-term objectives of the department and the whole organization. The superior must determine if these criteria can be met. This can be done by asking some very important questions such as: Can this objective really be completed in a year? How can we tell when this objective is complete? What can we do to improve your operation? How does this objective interface with department X? What can I do to help?

Goal-setting by subordinates does not mean that they can do whatever they want to do. Superiors must remember that in the end they have the responsibility for ensuring that all objectives are consistent, and for approving their subordinates' objectives. Superiors must continually be on the watch for impossible goals, because it's very easy to promise the moon if it's a whole year away. However, subordinates must be allowed to exercise a major influence on their objectives, since improved motivation can result if they are allowed to help in determining the criteria by which their performance will be evaluated. As a result of joint negotiation and review, the superior-subordinate pair agrees *in writing* on the subordinate's final objectives and goals for the coming year.

PERIODIC COUNSELING AND REVIEW

The written statement of objectives should be flexible so that it can be changed whenever necessary to fit changing conditions. It should be a working document in that it is used as a basis for periodic counseling and review by each superior-subordinate pair. Informal counseling and review meetings should be frequent, and everything should not be saved for a formal performance review at the end of the review period. The meetings should provide subordinates with feedback on how they are progressing, based on specific criteria from their objectives. The frequency of the meetings should be based on need and opportunity, not on a rigorous schedule. Too frequent or too formal meetings take away some of the subordinate's feeling of autonomy and self-determination as a result of too-close surveillance by the superior.

THE PERFORMANCE REVIEW

A formal performance review should be held at the end of the review period (usually one year), when employee performance will be evaluated in respect to predetermined objectives. MBO thus becomes an integral part of the organization's merit review and reward system. In fact, MBO will not work unless it is tied to the real reward system of the whole organization.

In applying an MBO program it is usually desirable to have subordinates propose a written appraisal of their own performance that can be jointly reviewed with their superiors. This is a valuable tool in keeping the subordinate involved and motivated; however, neither the written appraisal nor the discussion should result in any surprises. Every aspect of the subordinate's job and objectives should have been thoroughly discussed and actions taken during the preceding review period.

MBO AND THE PROJECT MANAGER

As indicated in previous chapters, successful project management is heavily dependent on having clear and unambiguous project goals and objectives. Clear cost, schedule, and product performance goals are necessary. The question then becomes: how can MBO be of most use to the project manager?

The project manager will interface with MBO in a number of ways depending on whether it is implemented: (1) by the organization's top management, (2) by the project manager, or (3) by and in a separate functional department.

MBO works best when it is implemented and fully supported by top management. MBO would thus be utilized by the whole organization, including the project managers. This works because the line/functional managers receive their orders for implementation of MBO from top management; therefore the project manager can expect full cooperation throughout the organization.

In the absence of an organization-wide MBO program, project managers can initiate their own programs within the project organization. This is very satisfactory within a pure project organization, where every member of the project team reports directly to the project manager. It is far less satisfactory in a matrix, where project-implemented MBO may only increase the potential for conflict between the project and functional managers. Matrix functional managers are often very reluctant to accept project-initiated MBO, and will not push it within their own organizations.

PROJECT MANAGER'S OBJECTIVES

Just as project management is the formalization of the process for doing non-routine work, MBO is the formalization of the process of goal-setting and establishment of measures that will indicate goal accomplishment. The project's and the project manager's goals and objectives should reflect corporate and top management goals, as well as the customer's or client's goals. There may even be some conflict of interest as the project manager weighs corporate goals against the interests of the customer. Both corporation and client are the bosses when it comes to evaluating the success or failure of the project.

Project managers face a built-in conflict of interest between their two bosses. The customer as client wants the best possible product (highest performance, long life, easily maintained, reliable, etc.) at the lowest possible cost, whether the product is an aircraft or a new power plant, and therefore will want great emphasis on such tools as quality control, configuration management, life cycle cost, etc. Top management, on the other hand, wants the highest possible profit with minimum disruption of their facilities, resources, or management structure. They also want a producible product that will lead to follow-on or new business. Project managers cannot forget that they have two bosses and become so preoccupied with the problems of one that they forget the other in developing objectives. It is particularly easy to so relate to the customer's problems that top management is forgotten.

The project manager's objectives will obviously be a combination of the objectives of top management and customer, plus his or her own personal development goals.

PROJECT OBJECTIVES

Overall project objectives are usually very clear since they have been carefully negotiated with a customer or a client. Therefore, the most important use of MBO is with subsystems and individual parts of the project. The project work breakdown structure (WBS) is the best place to start since it results in the project being broken down into readily accomplishable subdivisions. Managers or specialists can then be made responsible for every such subdivision (work package), and their objective statements made to reflect this responsibility.

It is often asked, "Isn't a good schedule and budget sufficient to pinpoint all project objectives?" Yes, if they are sufficiently clear and detailed, but the mere existence of a schedule and a budget doesn't by itself ensure agreement and conformance among all project personnel. However, a formalized MBO program can result in the preparation of meaningful, verifiable project objectives from every member of the project team, thus making life a lot easier for the project manager.

The writing of project objectives should be based on the following guidelines, and although all objectives may not conform to these criteria, they should still be used as a check and should not be bypassed unless a conscientious determination has been made that they do not apply.

An objective should:

1. Be consistent with basic company and organizational policy and practice.

2. Be measurable and verifiable.

3. Specify only the *what* and *when*, and avoid the *how* and *why*.

4. Start with the word *To*, followed by an action verb.

5. Specify a completion date for its accomplishment.

6. Specify a single key result to be accomplished.

7. Provide a maximum payoff on the required investment in time and resources as compared to other objectives that might be considered for obtaining the same results.

8. Specify cost factors, including labor hours or materials needed for its accomplishment.

9. Be consistent with resources available or anticipated.

10. Relate directly to the subordinate and his or her job requirements.

11. Be understandable by those who will be contributing to the attainment of the results required.

12. Be realistic and attainable and still represent a challenge to the subordinates.

13. Be willingly agreed to by both the project manager and subordinates without undue pressure.

14. Avoid or minimize dual accountability for the achievement when joint effort is required.

15. Be recorded in writing with a copy kept and periodically reviewed by both the project manager and subordinates.

16. Be communicated not only in writing, but also in face-to-face discussion between the subordinate and the project manager.

MBO IN THE MATRIX

In a matrix organization MBO provides the project manager with an ideal tool to direct, motivate, and assess the performance of the functional manager and specialists working on the project. The project manager needs every bit of help available in reaching clear and unambiguous understanding with the functional people who do not work directly for her or him. Since the process of MBO requires that the functional personnel submit their objectives (including project objectives) in writing, the project manager can use it as a tool in obtaining positive commitments, which then become valuable yardsticks in evaluating performance. Not only can performance be measured (was the desired result effectively achieved?), but one can also determine how efficiently the job was done (within budget). Project objectives submitted by functional managers should resemble the following statements:

1. To write a ground support service manual for missile X and obtain project approval by January 1.

2. To complete the wiring layout drawings for the Rio Hondo power plant and obtain project and client approval by January 1.

3. To complete the design, fabrication, and functional testing of the prototype turbopump for the X-engine in order to meet contract performance specifications by January 1.

PITFALLS OF MBO

One of the most frequent comments voiced by managers who have been involved in implementing MBO is that "it sounds better than it works." Unfortunately this is true, because, as with project management, there are a lot of things that can go wrong. This accounts for its rather limited acceptance in industry. A 1974 survey of *Fortune* magazine's list of the 500 largest American industrial companies indicated that less than 10 percent of these companies had MBO programs which they rated as successful.[11] The following pitfalls account for most of the problems encountered in implementing MBO:

1. The philosophy of MBO may not have been sufficiently sold throughout the organization so that all levels of management understand, approve, and support the concept.

2. The concept may receive inadequate top management support. Adequate guidelines on top management and corporate policy must be given to the whole organization.

3. Preparing truly verifiable objectives and goals is hard work, and takes considerable effort on the part of both subordinates and superiors. Without considerable motivation (and pressure from top management), objective- and goal-setting can yield to the pressure of less arduous duties.

4. Objectives may become inflexible or "etched in stone" to the point where they are a hindrance to organizational progress.

5. Since objectives are set for the short-term period of review, there is considerable danger that the needs for long-term planning and goals may be lost.

6. MBO may not be equally applicable to all phases of a project such as mobilization, conception, and past production.

7. MBO may suffer when management expects results before the project achieves maturity.

8. Personnel must be capable of planning their own work—an activity in which not everyone is comfortable or skilled in accomplishing.

9. The MBO program may not be integrated into the other management systems (i.e., budgeting, personnel, etc.).

CONCLUSION

MBO is a simple concept, but very difficult to put into practice. It can be very effective, however, in the project environment, as an aid to the project manager in motivating and working with the members of the project team. The greatest benefit to top management, project managers, and functional managers is that MBO provides yardsticks for performance evaluation. The process functions well only if it is an integral part of the organization's merit review and reward system. In addition, it will only work if great care is taken to ensure that objectives and goals are achievable and verifiable. If these precautions are taken, MBO can help take some of the load off the project manager's shoulders.

ENDNOTES

1. George S. Odiorne, *Management by Objectives* (New York: Pitman Publishing Co., 1965), pp. 54-67.

2. Herbert G. Hicks, and C. Ray Gullett, *Modern Business Management* (New York: McGraw-Hill Book Co., 1974), p. 165.

3. Peter F. Drucker, *The Practice of Management* (New York: Harper and Brothers, 1954).

4. Ibid., pp. 121-136.

5. Ross A. Webber, *Management* (Homewood, Illinois: Richard D. Irwin, Inc., 1975), pp. 346-360.

6. Harold Koontz, and Cyril O'Donnell, *Management—A System and Contingency Analysis of Managerial Functions*, 5th ed. (New York: McGraw-Hill Book Co., 1976), p. 166.

7. Drucker, *The Practice of Management*, p. 62.

8. Ibid., p. 63.

9. Ibid.

10. Stephen J. Carrol; Henry L. Tosi; and J. Rizzo, "Setting Goals in MBO," *California Management Review* 12 (1970): 70-78.

11. Fred E. Schuster, and Alva F. Kindall, "Management by Objectives—Where We Stand—A Survey of the *Fortune* 500," *Human Resource Management* 13 (Spring 1974): 8-11.

CHAPTER ELEVEN KEEPING YOUR BOSSES HAPPY WHILE IMPLEMENTING PROJECT MANAGEMENT—A MANAGEMENT VIEW

John M. Tettemer Assistant Chief Deputy Engineer
Los Angeles County Flood Control District
Los Angeles, California

INTRODUCTION Project management is one of several organizational management styles. It is often championed first by middle management in a functional organization that is under pressure to get results that require high levels of intraorganizational cooperation on a complex project or on large volumes of dissimilar work. Both situations clearly need close coordination and scheduling. Neither of these usually exists to the extent required to get top quality project performance.

The enlightened middle manager sees the need and starts to find ways to assemble the power to create changes toward project management. Middle management may criticize top management's reaction to a proposed project management system as stodgy, overly restrictive, slow, and nonrational. Understandably, these criticisms focus on items which cause frustration for the evolving project management organization. The pressure for change brought by middle management can be very unnerving to top executives. Project management requires changes in the role of top management that, in the beginning, may be seen by top management as threatening and inappropriate.

Since change in top management style is required, it is important that we understand top management's background, needs, and probable reactions to this new role being pressed on it from below. With this understanding, we can identify some clear objectives for project managers. These objectives are particularly useful during the evolutionary period when the style of the organization is changing from the traditional style to one characterized by a matrix of functional and project orientations.

TOP MANAGEMENT VIEWS ITSELF

The following examples are typical causes of top management anxiety about the conversion to project management. Readers should place themselves in the role of top management as they consider the ideas.

1. **Why Change?**

From a top management standpoint, it is fair to say that most of us got where we are by doing something right. In most cases, we were more effective than others in perceiving the complexities of the administrative job while carrying out the functions of middle- or upper-level management. Most of us were chosen because we appeared to have the social, organizational, and managerial skills required to succeed and to further the organization's objectives at a higher level. If we have been promoted and rewarded for a certain style of management, what could be a better strategy than to continue the style that succeeded in the past?

2. **Balance of Power.**

Top executives, keenly aware that their strength, success, and personal worth depend on their power in the organization, spend years developing a power base through daily, conscious actions. The resulting balance of power among top executives remains fragile and tenuous. Any change that could adjust this fragile balance is viewed with alarm.

3. Loss of Control.

To top managers with successful careers at stake, the specter of change being controlled outside the top management group, by project managers whose career risks are minimal, is alarming. Major adjustments in organizational style will be viewed negatively by top management since the adjustments will reduce the functional manager's ability to control subordinates' activity. Project management advocates see this negative reaction as irrational, motivated by fear, ignorance, and jealousy.

4. Need for Contact with Projects.

As administrators, we hear the burden of steering organizations successfully from day to day and year to year, using a combination of experience and good judgment. Since a significant portion of our decision making is not purely analytical or supported by factual information, we have succeeded as functional managers largely by becoming extensively involved in our projects. The project management team approach, by integrating the various disciplines, meeting tight schedules, controlling costs, and effectively completing complicated projects, reduces the need for extensive involvement of top management. Without full-time involvement, we feel out of touch with some of our most important traditional sources of information, and are fearful that our understanding of the organization and its problems and policies will suffer.

5. Excessive Delegation.

Project management involves a planned and controlled delegation of responsibility (and commensurate authority) for important corporate end products to staff with whom we do not have frequent direct contact. Until we understand the extent of and need for delegation, we are very apt to feel that we will be cut off from control; consequently we will be extremely negative to the idea.

6. Coordina-tion.	Most organizations have grown through functional hierarchies that place great but often ineffective emphasis on interfunction cooperation, stimulated as necessary by top-level management. Settling of disputes among functional elements is a traditional top management role and one of the major points at which top management interjects itself. Through this interjection, management becomes aware of problems. These problems are often the genesis of new policy. Loss of the role of coordinator-problem solver again cuts off information and functional management involvement in interfunctional problems. This creates additional discomfort for top-level managers.

In summary, administrators are apt to resist change because of unspoken and personal concerns expressed by:

1. Why Change?	I must be doing something right to get where I am. I may have to start working differently. Can I succeed?
2. Balance of Power.	I understand the balance of power and my role within top management. Why change it? I might lose my present power.
3. Loss of Control.	I presently generate change on projects and in policy areas. Why change it? I won't be able to control recommended changes.
4. Need for Contact with Projects.	I will lose my ability to perceive appropriate adjustments in organization policies when I lose detail involvement in projects. Why change it?
5. Excessive Delegation.	It is not good practice to have key decisions delegated below the top man. Why change?
6. Coordina-tion.	Coordination responsibility is a key management job. Why delegate it to project managers?

A STRATEGY FOR SUCCESS The few unspoken personal concerns of top management previously itemized suggest why many of you receive a mixed reception from top management about your recommendations to convert to project management. Since serious top management opposition will absolutely prevent change, it is in your interest to be sensitive to the concerns of all members of the top management team and to deal with them as best you can.

The question might be asked, "How, then, do we make progress?" The answer is, "Through a strategy which allows the displacement of traditional relationships and practices with new ones while placing great emphasis on comforting top administrators during the period of change."

The strategy must help top management consider and allow the implementation of a project approach, rather than fight it. It must provide top management with comfort, not only about the validity of the project management process, but above all with the validity of the outcome.

The following concepts have proven useful in providing comfort, reducing opposition, and oiling the wheels of change.

CONCEPT 1— BREAKTHROUGH PROJECT

During the early stages of project management evolution, it is common for a top administrator to compare the results obtained with the results which may have obtained on the same projects through the normal functional organization. The degree of comfort required by top administrators in allowing change varies from organization to organization. At any point in time, it also varies as a function of experience with the process. Since experience is gained only through the actual application of the process, and since few administrations are willing to bless an overnight conversion to project management or a matrix organization, it is obviously useful to:

▶ Start with a "breakthrough" project which the administration can keep pace with in the new project management format.

The choice of the specific project for initial application is important to both the project manager and the top management. It may have problems that top management wants help with, or it may be a project which top management feels is trivial in terms of impact in the event of failure. It is often best to choose a brand new application of the organization's work, since the existing functional organization has not yet established a traditional approach. It is best to choose a small- to medium-sized project so top management can easily observe the process without undue complexity; and finally, the project must not involve issues having serious internal political implications to the organization.

CONCEPT 2—
TRADITIONAL
INFORMATION FOR
TOP MANAGEMENT

There is a tremendous need, from an administrative standpoint, to be provided with information about special problems on special projects. In addition, for the administration to be comfortable they must receive information about problems in a timely manner, in order that the problems may be dealt with through timely decisions or adjustment in policies. Any experiment with project management in a new environment must be sensitive to the administration's need to know and the timeliness of its need. Therefore:

> ▶ The new project manager must be sure that traditional types of functional and project information are available to top management for traditional problem solving. The project manager should take this information forward voluntarily, ahead of top management's knowledge of the problem, preferably more quickly than the traditional line of communication.

During the early stages, large changes in information should be avoided and timely identification of project problems should be strengthened. Top management will seek help from the project management organization in solving the problems once it is found that the project organization is, in fact, dealing with the "product reality," both inside and outside the organization. This suggests a very mature project management philosophy and therefore a mature manager even for the very first project.

CONCEPT 3—
RETENTION OF
POWER

Another early objective is to:

> ▶ Allow every administrator to retain traditional power within the hierarchy during the implementation phase.

It is mandatory for successful project management that major power adjustments take place in the organization. These, however, should not be forced on top management in the first two or three years. Power adjustments should be allowed to evolve as a result of project successes. Specific attention must be paid to the needs of those administrators who have opportunities to sandbag project management efforts. This sandbagging becomes a frustrating problem to project managers and to top administration, since it ultimately will become the top administration's job to discipline members of the top administrative team to prevent further problems. In other words, if project managers create friction or polarization within top management, project managers stand the risk of becoming problem creators themselves at a time when their stock has experimental value only.

CONCEPT 4— POLICY RECOMMENDATIONS

Policy adjustments in most functional organizations are the result of top management's reaction to the need for adjustments. They are at least symbols of executive decision making. As such, administrative policy setting must be viewed as a sensitive matter. A project manager often becomes aware of the need for adjustments in policy before top management has become aware of the problem. Another important strategy during the early implementation stage, then, is:

▶ Project managers should carefully and thoughtfully develop only policy recommendations which can be *easily accepted* by the administration as being in concert with the organization's goals and objectives and which are easy to implement and readily accepted by those outside the organization.

These early policy adjustments should obviously be winners and set the stage for the more complicated policy clarification that is required during the development of many projects within a complicated matrix organization. It must be remembered that by taking the "action" to the administration in a project format, not only are you dealing with the administration's wariness about project management, but you also are inserting the new ingredient of bringing the "action" to the administration in policy form rather than as a traditional organizational problem. Most administrators are more used to dealing with project problems than with policy recommendations from subordinates who traditionally "do not have sufficient overview to structure comprehensive policy statements." Recognizing the need to judiciously select policy issues to present to management may require compromising project goals and objectives and requires maturity, patience, and a firm grasp of the "big picture" by the project manager.

CONCEPT 5— SLOW DOWN

From an administrative standpoint it is difficult to justify the transition from one form of organizational style to another as being an emergency. The hazard with project management advocates is that they consider the style change an extremely urgent organizational matter. This perspective is useful to project management trainees since it creates the right attitude about a results-oriented process and clears up the struggles with the functional organization. It must be understood, however, that most administrative personnel have long ago learned to pace organizational change in an attempt to reduce friction and conflict and hopefully allow time to improve the results. Therefore:

> ▶ It is necessary for project managers to push for change, but not at a rate that in itself builds opposition.

Administrators recognize that a slower rate of change may carry with it added expense. Divisive conflict in an administrative organization can be so detrimental that it negates the potential benefits of project management.

CONCEPT 6— SCHEDULES AREN'T THE END OF THE WORLD

It is common for overzealous project managers to view their scheduling and cost control activities and reports as being as important as organizational policies and other matters over which they have no control. From an administrative standpoint, organizational policies are traditionally viewed as being far more important than a schedule. Therefore:

> ▶ Project managers should keep schedules and other tools in the background of their involvement with top management. (The tools of project management are of far less interest to top management than the results obtained through them.)

CONCEPT 7— DECODE ALL INFORMATION

The interest and focus on scheduling and cost control analyses by project managers have often led to the development of management reports, much as those developed during the "drunken sailor" days of data processing where the reports had no sensitivity to the style of the top manager. As either the early data processor or the modern neophyte project manager would tell you, it is important that top management learn to understand where project managers are in their world and get acquainted with *their* information. Organizational realities, however, suggest just the opposite. Therefore:

> ▶ It is extremely important that project managers decode all their reporting documents to meet the style of the executive with whom they are trying to communicate.

Sending any data processing information into front offices is a mistake if it can be avoided, unless of course the front office personnel have grown up with the style and type of information with which you are expecting them to deal. Success in project management requires a form of communication that is in the style of the top administrator and that does not force him or her to change any more than necessary, particularly initially, personal views of the types of information that is going to have to be used. The same concept is true in dealing with mid-level management. The overlay of networks and schedules, starts and stops, specifications, etc., requires a great deal of extra energy, much like learning a foreign language. A good project manager provides project-type communication through traditional means.

CONCEPT 8— USE BROAD PERSPECTIVE

It is common for those close to project activities to see the problems and solutions in terms of their projects. Often there is a feeling that organizational policies and practices should deal directly with the problem related to the manager's current projects. In reality, solutions that are appropriate to a specific project may be inappropriate as organization-wide policy and should therefore be treated as exceptions. Therefore:

▶ Project managers should be sure to recommend as general policy changes only those items that are applicable to a broad range of projects. Exceptions should be clearly indicated as exceptions to meet clearly defined project objectives.

The recommendations received from project managers that demonstrate a clear understanding of the present organizational policy will be well received and will build confidence in the project management organization.

CONCLUSION

The preceding are some specific examples of how a project management organization should be cognizant of the needs of top management as it evolves. Fancy rational arguments about benefits are not enough. Interpersonal sensitivity in communications and a project management attitude of "we are willing to try this to show you that it works" is an appropriate approach. You must allow time for the human beings involved to evolve. Top management has a good basis in its own mind for its performance. The adjustments required in the evolution of a matrix organization from an administrative standpoint require time and study and, most of all, actual experience.

It is also important to remember that the delegation required for good project management substantially adjusts the job of the top executives. It appropriately removes the detailed involvement in coordination, controls, schedules, budgets, etc., from top managers. This void is felt by top managers as a blow to what they believe to be some of their most important functions.

The evolution to a full matrix organization is inevitable in most organizations dealing with complicated projects unless there is a very specific strong-willed administrative view against it. It does makes sense and it is rational. The project manager's enthusiasm must be developed in top management through judicious care and feeding and not through hard-nosed rhetoric and logic. It requires patience from those installing a project management system and a great deal of interpersonal wisdom, good timing, and good luck.

CHAPTER TWELVE PROJECT MANAGEMENT: HOW MUCH IS ENOUGH?

James N. Salapatas Manager, Project Control Services
Florida Power and Light
Miami, Florida

INTRODUCTION How much project management is enough? The answer to this question depends on a variety of complex issues involving the project itself, the organizational climate in which the project will be carried out, and the management philosophy of the company sponsoring the project.

While not a simple task, analyzing and categorizing any project by objectives, size, scope, and other individual characteristics can be accomplished using a predetermined framework. Furthermore, organization theory provides the ability to assess organizational character and idiosyncracies. In determining how much is enough, a dilemma occurs in matching the project, the organization, and the value system of the sponsoring company.

What is the value of the project to the company? What constitutes project success? What is lost if the project fails? What constitutes failure? What is the operating strategy of the company, and what types of management actions should be taken to reduce the chances of project failure? The answers to most of these questions are highly subjective, and filled with value judgments.

This chapter reviews the criteria most companies use for initially considering project management. The important concepts which make project management distinctive from other management forms are summarized for the reader. Management involvement in project work is categorized and unfolds into a new concept for measuring project management effectiveness. But it is stated that, while this new idea has potential, there is not enough empirical data to formulate explicit results. The chapter concludes by developing some value guidelines, from the author's experience, to help the reader in determining "how much is enough."

REVIEWING THE CONCEPTS

Project management is said to improve the efficiency of a project. In some organizations, however, the contention is that it is just an insurance policy against risks of skyrocketing costs and impossible schedules, as opposed to an effective management method. Large-scale projects still get done in spite of all the problems and conflicts that project management evokes in these organizations. Some claim it is the only solution to manage the myriad of complex tasks in a multidisciplinary environment. Despite contradictions, both the public and private sectors are spending vast sums of money for this so-called project "insurance policy."

The project management field is very broad and encompasses a variety of specialized skills and knowledge in management and technical areas. If a group of executives were asked to describe project management, each description would be different. An accurate description of project management depends on the project and its magnitude, project complexity, the sponsoring company in which the project exists, and the strategy to be used for achieving results. Project management is based on three key concepts:[1]

1. Central responsibility for the job to be done, held by a single individual usually designated as a project manager.

2. Central planning and control of the total effort, accomplished by several project control functions which use specialized tools, techniques, and systems.

3. Decentralized performance of the work by various people from different functional organizations, who receive project direction from a single individual who is responsible for the project.

Fundamentally, the concepts have universal application. However, caution should be used in arbitrarily applying any one of the project management concepts across the board.

One important distinction that should be made is between organizations whose core operating strategy is to manage project-type work and those whose primary mission is to make and sell a product or provide a service. In a project-type organization, project management concepts may be taken for granted because that's the only way company personnel have been trained to do their work. Project-type organizations are architect-engineers, construction and petrochemical companies, aerospace and computer software firms, and government agencies that are involved with them.

In nonproject-type companies, such as manufacturing, retailing, and utilities, the introduction of project management is often viewed with disdain and as an intrusion into functional department responsibilities. This occurs because the project organization is essentially superimposed over the normal operating company's organization. While operating personnel may understand the project management concepts, acceptance of new working relationships is difficult even in the best organizational climates. Furthermore, despite their project knowledge and experience, project-type organizations are not totally immune to cross-functional problems. Overcoming these obstacles is a key factor in assessing project management effectiveness. However, quantitative methods for measuring project management results do not seem to exist. What does exist are some sound principles of management and tested project management concepts supported by experience and literature accumulated over the past two decades.

Obviously, project management is necessary only when there are projects to be managed. The literature is filled with descriptions of projects and tasks, using different words to say the same thing. For the purpose of this discussion, a project shall be defined as a complex effort to achieve a specific objective within a schedule and budget, which typically cuts across organizational and functional lines, is unique, and is not completely repetitious of some previous effort.

With the existing state-of-the-art, combining what is known about a project and the organization, it should be possible to expand the Project Definition Model (Chapter Five) so that any nonproject company can follow the process to manage their projects. However, this is not practical. Managing projects is not the same as implementing project management in a company. Unfortunately, semantics have confused this important distinction. According to project management concepts, *project management should be considered only if the characteristics of a potential project warrant a change to the organization and the information systems of the company.* Otherwise, the project can be assigned to liaison personnel and handled within the existing organization.

MANAGEMENT INVOLVEMENT AND VALUES

While the project organization structure is directly related to size and complexity of the project, the key to recognizing how much is enough is based on how confident management feels about obtaining the expected results and how much effort they are willing to expend to reduce uncertainty.

Normally, the management of project work follows a continuum which begins with observation and ends with complete control. This is called the Project Control Sequence (PCS) and is shown in Figure 12-1. This PCS curve, developed from empirical data, describes the extent of management involvement in project work, in relation to total project effort. It remains for top management to select the desired degree of management involvement, based on some operating strategy, associated costs, and expected payback. A measure of effectiveness in project-related work is important for making such decisions. In its absence, an independent cost benefit analysis is helpful.

Equally important, but more difficult to measure, is the evolving pattern of the communication links and lateral relationships. These are governed by the project dimensions.

Since there are no universally accepted quantitative methods that can be used to measure project management success, the extent of its use to accomplish a desired objective depends on management's belief in project management concepts and their willingness to spend funds to reduce the risk of project failure. Among the reasons given for lack of measurement of project management success are that (1) the unique character of a project normally precludes meaningful critique for the next project, and (2) study of a project to improve performance is sometimes as costly as the project itself because of its unique and complex characteristics. These are merely excuses.

The primary reason behind the lack of uniform project management effectiveness criteria is that each company places different values on their projects. The value of a project to the sponsoring company may be assessed in economic terms—intangible benefits such as image, prestige, external and in-

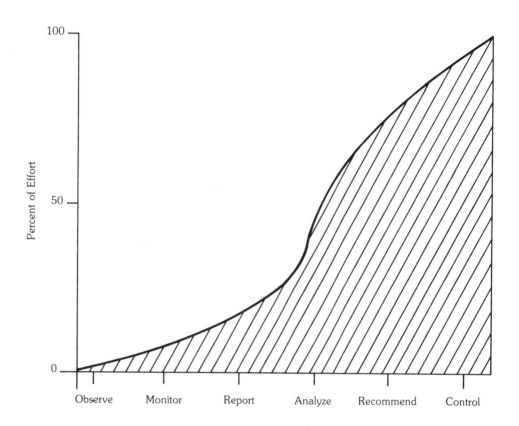

Figure 12-1. Project Control Sequence—Theoretical

ternal politics, etc., or some combination of all of these. For example, creating a new product line for a manufacturing firm may be expected to increase sales and bring new profit; conversion of an old computer system is perceived to improve inventory control and save money; construction of a new generating station for a utility is planned to meet future customer load requirements.

In each case, project success normally implies achievement of all project objectives. This means schedule, cost, and quality. If so, what constitutes failure? Obviously, total failure is an aborted project—no results, no new product line; no computer conversion, no new generating station. Possible? Yes. Probable? No. More than likely, failure will not be total, but in degrees.

Perhaps the market potential for the new product was overestimated and sales are lagging. The company's image as a market leader becomes tarnished. Maybe the cost of the new sophisticated computer system consumed all the savings gained from the improved inventory control process. The computer division's prestige drops and requests for new programs go to outside vendors. It's very possible that the completion of the new generating station was late due to regulatory problems and construction delays and the project ended up costing almost twice as much as the original estimate. The customers protest the higher rates, and the state regulatory commission orders a management audit for the utility.

Could these situations have been predicted and prevented from happening? Forecasted? Yes. Prevented? Maybe. Forecasting depends on how well project management interprets the information from the internal control systems that track progress. Preventing depends on how well the information is used to make timely project decisions whose actions change unfavorable conditions into positive situations.

If these are the considerations, then, in order to reduce the extent of project failure, what price tag shall management place on (1) the tracking mechanism, i.e., the internal control system; and (2) the decision facilitators, i.e., the project organization.

Today, some costs attributed to using project management run between 1 to 5 percent of the total project cost. This percentage may vary depending upon magnitude and complexity, but is usually larger on smaller or more complex projects. Management appears willing to accept this apparent cost increment because the total project costs in most cases would have been higher or much more than the 5 percent if project management had not been used.[2] This is merely conjecture, because there is no special formula for cost analysis that can accurately measure or explicitly justify the benefits of project management.

There are those who insist that we need project management—it will cost what it will cost to get the job done! For project-type organizations it's their cost of business. It's the bottom line—they do what they have to do to survive in the market place. Why should they share their secrets with the competition? But where does that leave the others, the occasional users—the "two projects a year" firm or the multitude of companies who devote only a part of their resources to projects? How much project management is enough to do their project work? In most situations, it is based on some opportunity cost or top management's personal interest in the project—the sponsoring company's value system!

Thus, while project management is clearly a useful management form and growing in popularity, its use among practitioners is based mostly on sound management principles as opposed to hard proof and justification. The question is whether tomorrow's business will accept project management in this way. Today, there are increasing pressures on private business for regulatory agencies, consumer advocates, the stockholders, and customers. The government also is not immune to these pressures. Taxes and social security are rising and there appears to be no relief in sight. Inflation continues in the market place, and national productivity is on the decline. The intent here is not to portray a picture of gloom and despair, but to emphasize the urgency for action. Project management is not a panacea, but its contributions for improving productivity in the public and private sectors have been significant.

MEASURING EFFECTIVENESS— A NEW CONCEPT Assume, however, that a correlation could be established between a project's life cycle and the Project Control Sequence; then this might serve as a basis for decision making to determine the degree of project management for that particular project. Correlation studies of this type would require extensive research to develop a reliable data base. Figure 12-2 shows a PCS curve developed from a study of several execution stages of major construction projects and a corresponding project life cycle. While results could prove beneficial for all, it may not be practical for most, except those companies with extensive project work.

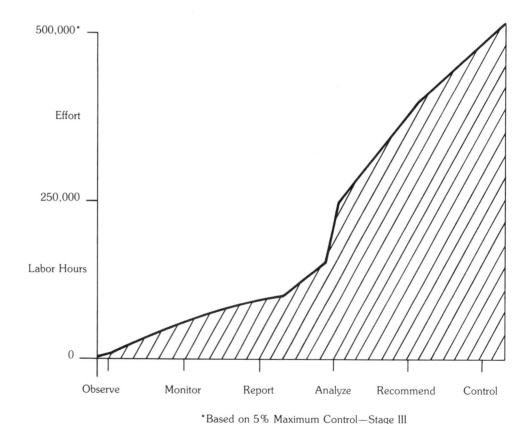

*Based on 5% Maximum Control—Stage III

Figure 12-2. Project Control Sequence—Actual

For example, the estimate for a plant construction stage was ten million labor hours. The choices for management of project work could be calculated using the PCS curve. While this still does not measure project management effectiveness, it does quantify the degree of project management for each stage of the project and translates it into cost. Management then has the option to decide how much it can afford to spend to minimize risk of project failure, based on some values dictated by corporate strategy.

By using the PCS curve, each project stage may be evaluated on its own merits and handled separately from the other stages. However, there is a potential weakness in this process. Because there is less effort involved during the first few stages of a project, management may choose to deemphasize initial involvement while expecting to concentrate effort at the execution stage, which contains 60 percent of the work. This is risky. Each stage should be evaluated in relation to the others.

Experience has shown that increased management involvement in the design stage has had a greater effect on the project outcome than all other stages put together. This occurs because the design stage is where the major decisions are made that result in work specifications and commitments for resources in the subsequent stages. While this may be true for all projects regardless of size, it is most critical in large-scale efforts.

For example, utility industry construction projects normally have 70 to 80 percent of the costs committed almost immediately after completion of the design stage. Contracts have been signed for major equipment, engineering services, site development, and placement of facilities. These commitments are normally binding, subject to cancellation clauses in the contracts. Thus, the influence management has over cost during the project life cycle is drastically reduced beginning with the execution stage. Conversely, management's decision to exercise full control in the design stage and only monitor the rest of the project can also have an adverse effect on the schedule and cost of the project. While only 20 to 30 percent of the expected project cost remains to be controlled, its fluctuation or increase might have a significant impact on the company's cash flow and profit picture.

Thus, even with the PCS curve, without more explicit measures of effectiveness, there is really no simple way to determine how much project management is enough. There is no single solution—only an "approach."

As additional research is undertaken on project management, theorists may eventually construct a "general theory of project management" which, along with its concepts, will include effectiveness formulas and value-system guidelines. Perhaps these guidelines might look like the actuarial tables from an insurance company or financial modeling curves which plot expected rate of return against risk. Whatever the situation, the PCS curve will most likely be used as the formula base.

HOW MUCH IS ENOUGH? – INTERIM GUIDELINES

Meanwhile, if you're thinking about implementing project management, or if you are already a project management user and are wondering how much is enough, consider these guidelines:[3]

1. Put a fence around your project work by defining each project's characteristics and determining what project success means to you.

2. Fix the objectives, where practical, and develop a project plan and timetable for the decisions needed to meet them.

3. Determine the different functional departments that will be involved in the project work and the extent of their participation in decision making to achieve the project objectives.

4. Review the existing management information and control systems to see whether they support the project's decision-making process.

5. Design a project organization and information system according to the most efficient and effective decision-making activity at the lowest possible level in the organization.

6. Determine the type of management involvement along the Project Control Sequence Continuum that will support the project decision-making process in time to take corrective action and guide the project to a successful conclusion.

If you have done all this and the project organization is not much different from the existing functional lines of authority and decision making, then you do not need project management.

However, if your project organization looks like a montage of functional departments, your new information systems a patchwork of criss-cross communication lines, decision making is split between several levels of hierarchy, and the common boss for resolving conflict turns out to be the president of the company most of the time, then project management is a must for you. How much is enough? The minimum project organization and information systems needed to support the decision-making process.

CONCLUSION

Project management is distinct from other management forms because of its departure in organizational structure but not in strategy. Among the most important features is project management dependence on lateral communications for decision making supported by a centralized internal control system and direction from a single accountable individual. Because of these features, any complex effort can be managed effectively despite obstacles created by people from different functional groups and time and monetary constraints. But not all complex efforts need project management. It is only when project dimensions outgrow a company's existing information system and organization that project management is really necessary.

However, since there are no universally accepted project management measures, the extent to which companies employ it depends primarily on their management's belief in the concepts. Management involvement in projects ranges from a minimum of monitoring activities to a maximum of complete control. While there is sufficient evidence to develop a correlation between management involvement in project activities and cost-benefits, there are no existing formulae which explicitly tie management involvement to project management effectiveness.

This does not mean that project management use is without justification. Many companies perform some type of cost-benefit analysis. Ultimately, however, it is the company's value system which dictates how much is spent to achieve project success.

To further complicate matters, although many successful projects have been documented in the literature, most project failures are perceived in degrees, at least in the eyes of the sponsoring company.

The common denominator seems to be the value a company places on its project and the corresponding risks which are taken to achieve results. If values and risks could be measured uniformly, then project management effectiveness criteria could be established to determine how much is enough.

Activities concerned with assessing values and making risks are inherent in the nature of business. However, until recently, value and risk analyses were more of an art than a science. These sophisticated techniques are being used extensively in the fields of finance and insurance. Project management application of these techniques will be necessary if project management is to mature into a recognized management science.

Until then, project management practitioners are urged to use the decision-making process as the key to effective project management, and to strive for the minimum project organization and information system that will get results.

ENDNOTES

1. R. B. Archibald, *Project Management Seminar Report,* Tres Utilities System, June 1973.

2. Charles C. Martin, *Project Management: How To Make It Work* (New York: Amacon, 1976), p. 272.

3. J. N. Salapatas, "Project Management: How Much Is Enough?" *Project Management Institute Proceedings,* Anaheim, California, 1978, II-D.

CHAPTER THIRTEEN

THE IMPLEMENTATION OF PROJECT MANAGEMENT: THREE CASE HISTORIES

Dr. Linn C. Stuckenbruck — Institute of Safety and Systems Management
University of Southern California
Los Angeles, California

Harold B. Einstein — V.P., Manager, Program Management Division
Security Pacific National Bank
Los Angeles, California

Robert L. Day — Project Engineer
Southern California Edison
Rosemead, California

James N. Salapatas — Manager, Project Control Services
Florida Power and Light
Miami, Florida

INTRODUCTION This chapter presents three case histories of the implementation of project management in organizations having very different activities and types of projects—a bank and two public utilities. The steps taken by each organization in implementing project management are discussed to emphasize that every organization has different problems and must plan an implementation process tailored to its specific needs. The case histories also emphasize the types of problems that were encountered and the specific ways in which the problems were solved. All of the examples resulted in the successful implementation of project management, but could have just as easily resulted in failure. The case histories emphasize that there is a very fine line separating success from failure. The cases differed in their approach to implementing project management in that the utilities converted all their projects at one time, while the bank converted only a single project and used it as a trial of the concept. However, in spite of the great difference in the organizations, a remarkable similarity in the problems encountered was apparent.

A number of generalizations which can be used as criteria for successful implementation of project management can be drawn from these case histories. Project management is most likely to succeed if the following conditions exist:

1. There is a great need in the organization for a better way of handling complex jobs.

2. The need is recognized by top management, even if they don't know what to do about it.

3. The jobs are multidisciplinary or multidepartmental.

4. Both top management and line or functional management are thoroughly sold on the need for project management and are ready for it before it is implemented.

5. There is one dedicated person (or more) who is a firm believer in project management and will shepherd it through the critical implementation phase.

6. The process of implementing project management is carefully planned and carried out according to plan.

7. The first project is chosen with great care because it must be successful; if the first project is a failure, project management is doomed.

It can be seen from the following case histories that there is no such thing as a standard form of project management; it may take an infinite variety of forms depending upon the characteristics and idiosyncracies of the existing organization. In order to minimize organizational disruption, it is desirable to utilize as much of the existing organization as possible when implementing project management. The case histories illustrate several unusual modifications of project management resulting from the necessity to adapt to the organizational structure as it existed prior to implementation of project management.

CASE HISTORY NUMBER 1: THE IMPLEMENTATION OF PROJECT MANAGEMENT AT SECURITY PACIFIC NATIONAL BANK (SPNB)

BACKGROUND   Banking today is facing a set of unprecedented problems and opportunities. These are caused by a continuous flow of technological, regulatory, and competitive impacts which are altering the manner in which banks are managed. The most significant of these impacts is the new competitive environment in which banks must operate. Now there are credit unions, savings and loan associations, mutual funds, investment houses, and even retailers (e.g., Sears and Roebuck) who offer services which used to be the sole responsibility of banks. In addition, banks are proliferating like mushrooms because every bank (including foreign banks) feels that it must be physically represented in every location. Competition is so severe that banks are forced to cut costs in order to be able to offer services competitively. Since banks are very paper-oriented the obvious way to cut costs is to automate.

Automation forced SPNB to become deeply involved in complex data processing and computer systems technology. Prior to 1977, SPNB had initiated a number of such projects which were carried out by task forces. A task force consisted of four or five people from different parts of the organization, each responsible for a particular part of the project. In general, there was no single person in charge, and there were no standards indicating how projects should be run. In most cases the final results of the project were not what top management expected; either cost, schedule, or performance was out of line. As a rule, they did not get the expected output: the performance. Top management did not know what to do about it, but they realized that there must be a better way to handle these major technological projects; they had to get them completed faster.

TYPES OF PROJECTS

The types of projects that SPNB was having difficulty with were all multidisciplinary in that they crossed most of the bank's functional organizational units. Projects that were limited to a single department (such as Data Processing or Industrial Engineering) were not candidates for project management. The projects considered for project management involved advanced automation technology to provide such systems as automatic tellers, an automated retail leasing system, an automated collection system, and an automated mortgage loan closing system. For the most part, these systems used to be completely manual, involving a great deal of paper work and expense. Another major project involves solving SPNB's space problem; they are running out of space for data processing. (This five-year project involves determining what kind of facility is needed, where it should be located, and what kinds of hardware and software would need to be procured.)

IMPLEMENTATION PROCESS

The bank's top management recognized that project management was a possible solution to their problems, and that the following forces were pushing them toward project management:

1. The new systems which were under development were extremely complex from the point of view of the new technology required and the systems concepts involved.

2. The projects had a high degree of interdependency; that is, within a rigid time frame, they not only crossed organizational lines within the bank, but also required concurrent interactions in many instances with computer network vendors, large corporate accounts, government regulations, and operations.

3. In order to launch a major project, they needed highly trained manpower which is difficult to find.

4. Large capital investments (some of which were in the eight-digit dollar range) were needed for these major projects.

5. Management foresaw that it may take years to complete the projects; and during this long time span they will undoubtedly have to deal with technological obsolescence.

Having recognized these forces, top management hired Harold B. Einstein, a consultant with extensive project management experience in the aerospace industry. His background was well-known by a SPNB Vice President who approached him about working with the bank. It was indicated that SPNB wanted to determine if aerospace project management experience was applicable to the bank's environment and problems. Mr. Einstein joined the bank as a full-time employee. He was asked to bring project management to the bank with the job of selling the feasibility of the concept to the entire organization. Fortunately, the bank's top management knew that there had to be a better way of handling projects, and they were behind Mr. Einstein 100 percent. However, he had to prove to them that project management was the better way.

SELLING PROJECT MANAGEMENT

When Mr. Einstein joined the bank in April 1977, he recognized that he could not immediately set up a game plan for selling project management until he had thoroughly understood the workings of the bank. He had to get a feel for management's problems and the types of projects in which they were involved. But he also recognized that by successfully completing the projects he undertook, he would prove the desirability of the project management system.

Therefore, he first set out to educate himself on the bank's problems, and then to give presentations on project management to the various top management groups within the organization. For his first presentation he used key word charts; however, he realized that this technique was not effective. He next tried some diagrams, but became convinced that he needed some highly visual, informative art work that would leave a picture in the viewer's mind. As a result, he prepared a series of colored slides which were also reproduced in a fifty-four-page primer on project management which accompanied the presentations and amplified his explanation of how banks should use project management.

A slow, low-pressure sell was felt to be necessary in order not to make management feel that project management was being thrust down their throats.

The process of selling to top management, which took approximately four months, was relatively uneventful since they were very receptive to the need for a better method of managing projects. At the end of this period, top management was 100 percent behind the project management concept, and subsequently key executive members of the bank have either written about or given presentations on the use of project management at SPNB. Mr. Einstein found that the most effective orientation process was a series of short, concise (forty-five minutes to one hour) seminars utilizing his slide presentation to about ten invited members of top management.

The same orientation process was utilized with middle- and lower-level management, in that the same slide presentation was utilized. However, to avoid any appearance of talking down, Mr. Einstein spent considerable time before each presentation in getting to understand his audience. As a result, every presentation was different in that it was tailored to his audience, and the selling process was very effective.

PROJECT LIFE CYCLE

It was recognized that projects typical of those in SPNB should pass through four distinct phases, each with a beginning and an end, and with a minimum of overlap. It was decided that at SPNB a project life cycle would consist of the following phases:

1. **Conceptual phase.** The initial period when identification of need is established.

2. **Preliminary study.** The period when the technical, operational, and economic bases for the project is established through a thirty-day broad-outline feasibility study costing from $15,000 to $30,000.

3. **In-depth study.** The period when project characteristics are defined. This phase includes:
   a. extensive study and analysis
   b. a detailed design of product(s) or service(s)
   c. prototype hardware development, testing, and evaluation,
   d. evaluation of alternate solutions.

4. Product development and implementation phase.	The period that includes development, procurement, and development of required resources. The objective is to produce and deliver, in an efficient manner, an effective and supportable project to the operating unit(s).

At the completion of the preliminary study and before the in-depth study can begin, a detailed plan for continuing the program must be developed by the project manager and approved by Administrative Planning Committee. At the completion of the in-depth study phase, a development and implementation plan must be prepared by the project manager and approved by the Administrative Planning Committee. One to two years after the implementation of a project, the Program Management Division submits to the Administrative Planning Committee a written comparison between planned and actual results which is called a post project evaluation.

PROJECT ORGANIZATION

The original plan proposed by Mr. Einstein for the implementation of project management at SPNB proposed to have a project manager putting 100 percent of her or his time on the project. This proved to be impractical in the bank environment since top management wanted a high-level executive to be the project manager. As a result, a Senior V.P. from corporate banking was picked to have sole responsibility for the first project. Since this Senior V.P. had other daily responsibilities in addition to the project, a modification to the usual project management structure was made in that a project director was appointed. (The project director was supposed to put 100 percent of his or her time on the project and had the day-to-day responsibilities for the actual operation of the project.) The Senior V.P. project manager was primarily involved in longer range planning and policy, in handling any political situations that came up, in decision making, and in opening doors to top management when higher level decisions were necessary. The first project manager took a very "hard-nosed" attitude and indicated to Mr. Einstein that it must be proven that project management would work.

Mr. Einstein personally functioned as project director (in addition to his other assignments) to ensure the success of this first project. After two months, the project was well into its in-depth study phase, and it was evident to all that the project was going to be very successful Since it was then proposed to put other projects under project management, the project organizational structure (a modified matrix) was adopted (Figure 13-1).

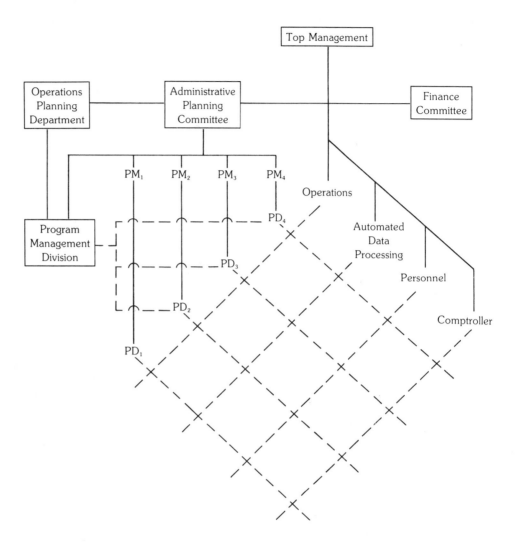

Figure 13-1. Matrix Organization at SPNB

The project managers report to the Administrative Planning Committee (APC) for their project function. The APC is one of several major decision-making bodies at SPNB. The APC authorizes projects, sets project goals and objectives, approves project budgets and schedules, establishes project priorities, reviews project progress, and takes corrective action whenever necessary. Anyone who has an idea (the Concept Phase) can present it to the APC, and if the APC approves the project it goes into the Preliminary Study Phase and the project is on its way.

The new function of program management was created with Mr. Einstein at its head, also reporting to the APC through a member of top management who sits on the committee. The Program Management Division is a project planning and control function for the APC, and has the following duties:

1. It provides guidance and assistance to project managers by helping them plan, manage, and control their projects.

2. It coordinates the activities among the various departments of the bank.

3. It initiates actions for the resolution of problems.

4. It prepares and submits progress reports to the APC.

5. It establishes and conducts educational programs that will improve the understanding of project management concepts, methodologies, and practices at all levels of the organization.

The project directors report directly to the project manager and in a dotted-line relationship to the Program Management Division, so they are also in a matrix situation, although their tie to the project manager is somewhat stronger. The project directors actually run the day-to-day operations of the projects, including budget responsibility. The project directors could have been called assistant project managers, however the title was unacceptable to most candidates for the position. Success was assured by the development of a clear working relationship and clear-cut division of responsibilities among the project manager, project director, and the Program Management Division. Much of the success can be attributed to Mr. Einstein's skill on coordinating the project efforts.

FIRST PROJECT

Mr. Einstein's previous experience had convinced him that the choice of the first project was very critical since it could rapidly indicate whether project management really works. As a result of discussions with top management the first project was put under project management in May 1977, two months after Mr. Einstein joined SPNB. It was decided to start with a single project and to evaluate its progress. The project was large enough to be a good test of project management, and to provide top management with a convincing case for continuing to use project management.

The first project was entitled "The Real Estate Loan and Escrow Operations Project." Its goal was to reduce present operating expenses, stop spiraling expense growth, take advantage of revenue-generating opportunities, standardize compliance with regulatory agencies, control credit procedures, establish management control, and eliminate present operating problems by the centralization of all real estate activities at the bank. The concept phase of this project had been completed, therefore the first phase under project management was a preliminary study. This thirty-day study was completed within schedule and cost a budgeted $15,000. The project report recommended a continuing in-depth study to look at three alternatives. These recommendations were approved by the Administrative Planning Committee and the in-depth study was initiated in July and completed in March 1978. The project then entered the development and implementation phase, which consisted of developing two computer systems, software and hardware, and locating the entire real estate organization at a single center in Santa Ana, California. The total cost of the project was $2 million, and everything that was planned during the in-depth study phase was accomplished within budget and on schedule by the end of 1979.

Top management has been extremely satisfied with the real estate project and considered it to be highly successful. They see the project as saving the bank over $5 million per year. It also has proven to be a good selling tool for the bank, and top management makes a big point in their writing and other presentations that the bank operates under project management. SPNB now has eight projects under project management, and any new project where there is considerable risk involved is a candidate for project management.

PROBLEMS ENCOUNTERED

The only serious problems encountered in implementing project management at SPNB were concerned with convincing the various levels of management that project management was the way to go. As previously indicated, there were few problems encountered in obtaining the full support of top management, however middle management was a different story. It took approximately two years of concentrated effort to eliminate the last areas of resistance.

During this implementation period there were a number of instances of conflict characterized by foot-dragging and/or haggling over authority. This conflict was almost entirely due to the unfamiliarity of the line/functional managers with the matrix and their failure to accept the multiple-boss situation. The conflict was accentuated when the functional manager and the project manager were on the same level, which sometimes led to a power struggle over who really controlled the efforts of the project personnel. Project management insisted that project personnel live by tight schedule, budget, and performance deadlines, which functional managers were not used to.

Another problem encountered, and one that still remains somewhat of a problem, is caused by the high visibility inherent in major projects under project management. This proved to be a major problem at SPNB because they were not used to high visibility in their organizational units. High visibility was particularly disturbing to project personnel since they could no longer hide in anonymity or blame others for project failure.

An occasional problem resulted from the appointment of a project manager who turned out to be very weak. The project would have been doomed, had the project director not been strong and willing to make decisions.

The final problem in the bank environment involved getting people to be project managers, project directors, and full-time project personnel. Accepting a project management job in addition to a regular full-time position was not appealing to a vice president. For project personnel, there were (and are) few incentives and no rewards for serving on a project team. In fact, there were the usual disincentives such as the loss of a "permanent home" for project personnel to return to, and the uncertainty as to who makes project team member performance valuations. The problem of a bonus or other incentive for project personnel is still a topic of discussion at SPNB.

CONCLUSION

Looking back on the implementation of project management at SPNB, the following conclusions were apparent to management:

1. All levels of management must be in favor of project management. It is very important that top management be 100 percent supportive of project management, but it is equally important (or even more important) that lower levels of management be sold. This is particularly important with the operating levels, the users of the results of the project. If the user is not on the side of project management, the project is dead. The operating levels can be very difficult to sell unless all presentations are made in their operating language.

2. There must be one person totally responsible. In many organizations such as SPNB, both management and working levels are just not used to being held accountable for their actions and performance; they are used to having someone else to blame. Project management must hold functional management as well as project team members accountable whenever necessary. Project management must begin with total accountability, starting with the project manager and continuing down through the organization.

3. The first project must be an outstanding success. Everyone in the organization from top management to the operating levels has "fingers-crossed" until that first project is a success. At this point, everyone jumps on the bandwagon and fully supports project management; but if the first project fails, project management is doomed.

4. Each project must have a workable control system. Whatever existing control systems the organization has may be used or modified for project use. However, each project has its own unique control problems, and it is essential that each project be individually evaluated. Each project will have individual control problems and will need its own control system, specifically designed for project needs. For example, if PERT is not needed, it should not be forced on the project. The project control system should be kept as simple as possible.

5. Every project must have a complete and workable project plan. However, every project plan must be designed specifically for each particular project. A standard planning format is a good place to start, but the actual elements of the plan should be carefully chosen for relevancy to the needs of each particular project.

CASE HISTORY NUMBER 2: IMPLEMENTATION OF PROJECT MANAGEMENT AT SOUTHERN CALIFORNIA EDISON (SCE)

BACKGROUND

Southern California Edison (SCE) is the major power generating electrical utility in the greater Los Angeles area. It is involved in the design, development, construction, and contracting for the construction of coal- or oil-fired power plants and nuclear power plants. It is also involved in hydroelectric power generation, high voltage power transmission, extra high voltage power transmission (EHV), and new energy alternatives such as solar power.

Until their original initiation of project management in 1972, SCE was a typical line/discipline organization. This organization evolved through the years, but always had a power supply department (responsible for operation), and always had an engineering department, although the manpower levels went up and down with business cycles. However, just prior to the reorganization, they had a very strong engineering department which was organized by discipline. The major divisions were mechanical engineering, civil engineering, electrical engineering, and, more recently, nuclear engineering. Each division of the line organization had its own supervisor who reported to the manager of engineering.

SCE had some very significant projects during the 1950s and 1960s prior to the implementation of project management. The largest of these were fossil-fueled steam power plants, which were handled by a lead-discipline management concept. Take, for example, a major generating project which was oil fired. This project was led by a hand-picked key mechanical engineer inside the mechanical engineering division who was primarily a planner and coordinator. He had some limited budget responsibility, but had no control over how the money was spent. In making estimates of how many labor hours should be spent to do the engineering or the coordinating with an engineer constructor, he indicated how much help he would need and which discipline would provide it. The lead-discipline concept had some of the functions of project management, but without the responsibility and authority and without even title or recognition. For example, a lead-discipline engineer would come to civil engineering and indicate what was needed. A person would be assigned to the project, but this person had other jobs to do and did not always accomplish the project work on time. And if the work did not get done, the lead-discipline engineer had no recourse to mandate that the work be done. If no response was received, if the work didn't get done, and if it was impossible to go to top management, all the lead-discipline engineer could do was complain to his or her immediate supervisor who sometimes could negotiate with the other disciplines.

The lead-discipline concept worked, after a fashion. However, many things were overlooked and some terrible things happened in terms of deficiencies, particularly in inadequate design criteria. In fact, certain disciplines within the company were overlooked altogether. Many of the projects were primarily coordinated with an engineer-constructor who did the actual work. On other projects, usually smaller but sometimes very significant, SCE did their own design. These kinds of projects were particularly troublesome. For instance, SCE developed an extra high voltage transmission system (EHV). They embarked on new systems design, led by an electrical engineer under the guidance of the Electrical Engineering Division. They decided they didn't need help from inside the company, and went to the outside for consulting help. They then proceeded to do all of the original design work. All kinds of problems developed, resulting in the project being considerably over cost and schedule.

Power generation plants, particularly coal and nuclear, were becoming bigger and far more complex, particularly in the involvement with regulatory agencies. These factors were greatly affecting SCE's ability to manage projects within cost and schedule, and management was coming to the realization that there must be a better way.

THE REORGANIZATION PROCESS

Management at all levels at SCE realized as early as the mid-1960s that they needed something different. Top management started to look for a better way to organize because they recognized that there were duplication problems, budget and schedule overruns, interdepartmental squabbles, and project overlaps and gaps.

The problems came to a head in 1972, when engineering management decided that they were not properly organized to get their job done, and they needed to improve their working relationships with the other major company division—Power Supply (operations). Engineering management formed a task force of key people (not management) who were to work with a consultant and outline his or her work. A consultant was hired and his first task was to interview key people and gather sufficient data on which to base a reorganization proposal. He pinpointed the real conflicts and eliminated the unjustifiable complaints. A number of meetings were then held with middle management and the consultant, which resulted in a report containing a proposed reorganization which was eventually approved by top management.

Objections immediately surfaced from middle management; the proposed reorganization did not really solve the problems of SCE. The consultant had been specifically asked how SCE should reorganize. He was not asked how they should handle projects, and he did not address this problem in his report. The consultant was looking only at the problem of fragmented disciplines, and there was considerable realignment of disciplines after his report was implemented. Instead of further centralizing disciplines, there was some decentralization to get disciplines closer to the activity. For instance, transmission design and substation design had their own problems, both technical and administrative, that were different from the power generation side of the house. That was the major type of discipline realignment.

The need for better management of projects was not recognized by either management or the consultant. However, when the consultant's report was received, SCE was just getting into a major nuclear project. A member of middle management, the chief of Nuclear Engineering, was perceptive enough to see that something major was missing—the project management concept. He read the report and pointed out to his management, department head vice presidents, that this element was really missing here, and that the consultant had not addressed this important point. As a result, the consultant returned, the projects and prospective project managers were identified, and the implementation of project management was put in motion. Top management approved the action with a wait-and-see attitude, indicating that they wanted to see how it worked out.

SCE found that the consultant was of little help in implementing the process, either because project management was not within his scope, or because he did not have the expertise to advise on the implementation—he had not provided management with a game plan for getting the ball rolling. They realized that they had the ball, and had to come up with their own game plan. Under the leadership of the chief nuclear engineer, who later became manager of projects or manager of project managers, a staff group was formed to develop a game plan. The initial implementation was not company-wide since the problems of being recognized by the other departments still existed. The game plan was adapted primarily for the Engineering Department and the reorganization affected only two departments—Power Generation and Engineering. Implementation of project management on a company-wide scale came much later after it had been thoroughly accepted in the Engineering Department and its advantages had been demonstrated.

The game plan provided plans for the implementation of the following actions:

1. To convert all projects in the Engineering Department to project management and assign project managers. There were nine active projects at this time.

2. To orient top management on the advantages of project management, and to obtain their commitment and firm support for the concept.

3. To give the involved people, i.e., engineering personnel and management, an understanding of what project management was all about so as to obtain their firm support. An outside training firm was to be brought in to aid in this activity.

4. To provide for the preparation of project charters, revised organization charts, new jurisdiction statements and job descriptions, and project manager salary levels.

The effort to implement project management was directed by the chief nuclear engineer with help from the previously mentioned staff group. The chief nuclear engineer served as a forcing function in that he personally kept up the momentum and pushed for rapid implementation of project management. He recognized that help was needed in obtaining the unqualified support of all people who would be involved in project management. Therefore, a training organization was given a contract to carry out the effort.

It was recognized that the function of the educational or training effort would be to adjust the attitudes of management and project personnel. Next it was recognized that the place to start is with top management since the rest of the job is much easier if an unqualified top management commitment has been obtained. Top management had to understand what project management means, and that they now must depend much less on line management for information and for assignment of responsibility. Top management must also relinquish some of their authority and decision-making prerogatives. As is often the case, top management was very receptive to the training consultants' arguments, and firm top management support was obtained.

The SCE staff group then worked with the training team to develop an orientation program for the rest of the organization. The training was to be conducted at two levels: (1) the line managers and supervisors along with the project managers, and (2) the workers who would be involved with projects. Because of the help of the outside training organization, this orientation period was relatively short.

PROJECT ORGANIZATION

A matrix organization was utilized for all of the projects. The SCE engineering organizational structure (simplified) prior to the implementation of project management is shown in Figure 13-2. Engineering and Construction were the two major subdivisions under the V.P. of Engineering. Construction was divided into its two major areas of effort, Transmission and Substations (T/S), and Generation (Gen.); and Engineering was broken down into the four basic engineering disciplines. As indicated in Figure 13-2, T/S and Gen. were subdivisions found in a number of the lower-level hierarchical units such as costing and the engineering disciplines. It can be seen that a great deal of coordination and negotiation was necessary on either a T/S or Gen. project, and the lead-discipline engineer was at too low an organizational level to do it effectively.

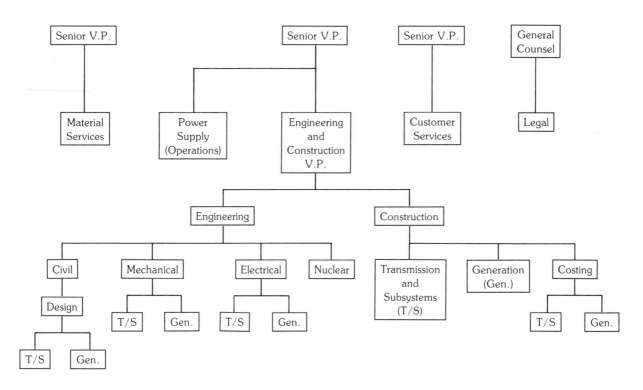

Figure 13-2. Southern California Edison—Prior to the Implementation of Project Management

The organization that eventually developed at SCE after the implementation of project management (after two years) is shown in Figure 13-3. It is a typical matrix organization, although confined to the engineering part of the SCE organization. However, the projects are primarily engineering in nature and seldom interface with organizational units outside of Engineering. Major projects had a single full-time project manager, while a number of small projects were handled by a single project manager utilizing minimal control as a multiproject manager.

ORGANIZATIONAL FINE TUNING

Because the basic implementation process was relatively short, and the organization jumped directly into project management without really adequate preparation, a certain amount of organizational fine tuning and juggling of organizational units was necessary. For instance, considerable experimentation was conducted to determine how best to organize within the project. The effect on project performance of the use of a tight matrix (the project team put together in a single location) or a loose matrix

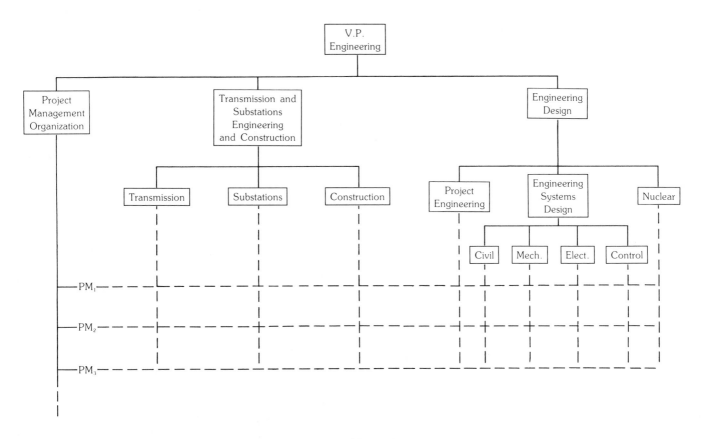

Figure 13-3. Southern California Edison—After Implementation of Project Management

(the project members remaining in their line "homes") was observed. Both types of matrix organizations had advantages, and each was excellent for certain types of projects, depending upon importance, urgency, and relationship with an engineer/constructor (if any). In general, the tighter the matrix, the better it worked, although in cases where personnel had to work on more than one project, the tight matrix was infeasible. The organization continued to make frequent changes in personnel and organizational form for approximately two years after the implementation process started. At this point in time, project management had achieved full recognition throughout the company, and project managers had more recognition and the full responsibility to make decisions involving dollars.

It was very interesting to observe that one year after beginning the implementation of project management most managers perceived project management to be at a higher level than it actually was. In one case, a project manager got a promotion (to chief of Nuclear Engineering), and many people perceived this move as a demotion because of the effective way that project management had been sold in SCE.

PROBLEMS ENCOUNTERED

The major types of problems encountered at SCE during the implementation of project management included the following:

1. Resolving conflict.

Very few problems were encountered in conflicts between project management and top management. Since the initial orientation had been very complete, top management was thoroughly committed. The critical problems occurred during the process of "selling" middle management, and working out the operational details. Many bitter battles occurred during the long conferences involving middle management and the chief nuclear engineer and his staff. Some middle-line managers proved to be completely intractable and had to be put into positions where they were not involved in the project matrix. Others became project managers where they had to completely reorient their line of thinking and their management approach. During the implementation period, there were a few power struggles primarily between project and line managers over who was really in control of some aspect of the project. Some of the line managers felt that they had been deserted by top management and that the rug had been pulled from under them. Top management's strong support of the project managers was necessary during this implementation phase, but did cause some difficulties and animosities.

Another reason for conflict was the tug-of-war over the utilization of resources, particularly people. The manpower shortage was a very critical problem; there were just not enough people to meet all the demands. The first action that had to be taken was the initiation of a manpower reporting system, which solved some of the problems since management now knew what everyone was working on. It was not that project management necessarily required more people, but that leadership was coming from two directions, and a tug-of-war resulted. The usual line activities went on continually, responding to the company's needs, and pulled on the line people and their management. On the other side, the project manager pulled on the same people for project work. Demands could not be ignored and an apparent manpower shortage resulted. In addition, there were shared people—people who worked on more than one project. These conflicts proved to be symptoms of the need for better monitoring and forecasting of manpower needs, better project planning, and better allocation of priorities.

2. Achieving acceptance of the two-boss situation.

This problem varied considerably from project to project, and seemed to be a direct function of whether the matrix was loose or tight. If the project team was housed together and spent most of its time together, it was no problem at all. The loose matrix, with the project team physically located in its disciplinary "home," did result in some reluctance to accept project directions.

3. Picking project managers.

The problem of how to pick project managers was not faced early in the implementation process. SCE management felt that the best people to lead a project were the same people who had been doing it all along. Therefore, most project managers were picked from the ranks of line managers. This procedure caused some problems at first, but for the most part those preferring to be line managers returned to the line and people that liked project work gravitated to the project office. Some of the best project managers who have remained in project work were coordinators before the implementation of project management.

4. Project management career path.

The problem of providing a career path for project managers did not arise immediately after implementation of project management because there were so many projects and they were all of fairly long duration. In addition, during the early implementation phase everyone was highly motivated and swept up into the excitement of a new job, and little thought was given to career paths. After the first year or so, as projects began to phase in and out and as the turnover of project managers increased, there began to be considerable apprehension over project career progression. A project manager job description had been written, but project management did not have a defined level in the management hierarchy or a defined salary scale. Most project managers went back and forth between middle management and project management, and there was always the worry of, if they became a project manager, what would happen when the project ends. Therefore, there was often a reluctance on the part of a manager to go into project management. A satisfactory career path for project managers still remains a problem.

5. Picking project management tools.

The major problem encountered during the implementation phase with project management tools involved the search for adequate reporting techniques. The original manager of projects wanted a consistent format for reporting (i.e., the same format for the reports from each project), providing him with sufficient visibility to take corrective action. He wanted to know how well his project managers were functioning, as well as communicating information. The staff group was assigned to develop a format which originally required a rather large report. However, once the project management concept had achieved company-wide acceptance, it became a one-page report, and today it has practically disappeared. The need for a common format disappeared once other lines of communication were opened and the project managers developed their own reporting styles.

Another problem that developed during the implementation phase was the utilization of planning and scheduling techniques. A consistent format again proved to be unnecessary, and the tools utilized differed widely, depending on the project. Small projects required only simple barcharts, and larger projects utilized critical path scheduling, although usually uncomputerized. It was not until approximately two years after the initial implementation of project management that computerized methods were in general use.

CONCLUSION   Project management has been accepted as a "way of life" at SCE. All projects are planned and controlled by project managers utilizing a matrix mode in the overall organization. Project managers function either for a single large project or as a multiproject manager for small, uncomplicated projects. The manager of projects serves as a coordinator of all projects, a manager of priorities, and an allocator of resources.

CASE HISTORY NUMBER 3: IMPLEMENTATION OF PROJECT MANAGEMENT AT GRAND ATLANTIC UTILITIES (GAU)

IN THE
BEGINNING   Early in April 1969, the Chief Executive Officer of Grand Atlantic Utilities Company called his Operating Vice President to discuss some alarming news he heard at a seminar about GAU's construction projects. It seems industry rumors painted GAU's largest project as disorganized and way behind schedule despite the glowing progress given by the "official" company-published reports.

"How could this be?" the Operating Vice President asked the Chief Engineer after his brief encounter with the CEO. If this were true, these conditions usually translated into budget overruns, but more important, any delay in the schedule increased the risk of overload conditions and possibly blackouts for GAU's customers.

"I don't know of any delays," replied the Chief Engineer. "Sure, there have been some changes, but Engineering is on schedule. The Architect Engineer is handling all of these things directly with Construction. It must be them."

The Superintendent of Construction was livid when he heard about the rumor. "Damn," he said, "based on our schedule we are three weeks ahead of Engineering. In fact, we were seven weeks ahead until the production people changed their minds and added another pump and two miles of pipe to the circulating water system."

"It wasn't us who added the pump and two miles of line," cried the Manager of Production. "It was the Permitting and Licensing Department that said we couldn't get our cooling water from Catfish Creek."

Cat Creek . . . the V.P. remembered that very well. There had been a public hearing followed by some pretty bad publicity about the terrible things that the company was going to do to Cat Creek. Then the General Counsel of the company came up with a stroke of genius. She and the Director of Licensing and the Chief of the State Environmental Regulation Agency got together and hammered out a compromise—easy permit approval for a two-mile tunnel to the lake, instead of a fight, adverse publicity, and a possible stalemate on the Cat Creek Dam.

The V.P. pondered the events leading up to the rumor. You know, this wasn't the first rumor about the construction project, nor would it be the last. The problem was that these types of misguided messages were happening more frequently. Not just on this one job, but all six of GAU's large capital projects. Fingers were pointed every which way. All the departments— engineering, construction, permitting, production—were working their tails off, but the harder they worked to meet their own objectives, the more problems they caused each other. The results were wasted time and lost dollars suffered by the company as a whole.

Just about every project problem, whether it was technical or some personal squabble between two department heads, landed right on the V.P's desk. There just didn't seem to be enough time left to manage the affairs of producing power and serving the customers. But you need power plants to serve customers, too.

DALLAS SEMINAR

A need to manage projects "better" prompted GAU's Operating V.P. to participate in the Dallas seminar on project management. It wasn't easy getting everybody together at first—everyone seemed to have problems getting away (the same kinds of problems with their capital projects). Naturally there were several consultants ready, willing, and able to host such a seminar. And so, a year later, an April meeting was held in Dallas to focus on the concepts of project management for building power plants.

The agenda included load forecast to startup, corporate policy and organization structure, project coordination, and techniques and tools needed to control the magnitude and variety of these power plant projects. There was a lot of talk at the meeting. Even together the utilities and consultants didn't have all the answers, but they had learned enough of the right questions from each other to see the need for project management.

What they discovered was most significant despite all the new technology and innovation with planning and scheduling techniques such as CPM and PERT. Their conclusion was stated as: "Project management is the person, not the tools." This statement was based on a list of questions which every department needed to answer for themselves. More important, each department recognized the need to plan the answers to these questions on a *parallel timetable* with the planning and budgeting of the physical plant. The project manager questions were:

1. Does the project need a full-time manager?

2. When should a project manager be selected?

3. What criteria should be used to select a project manager?

4. At what level in the corporate structure and to whom should the project manager report?

5. What should the project manager be accountable for, and how can performance be measured?

6. How should the corporation back up the project manager with staff and tools?

7. What should the corporation do with retired, successful project managers?

What about the project itself? What kind of criteria should be used? One of them is scope, the magnitude and geography of a project. The second one is corporate involvement. Do you turn a project over to an A/E and let him or her build it without getting involved? How much involvement is necessary for owner control? The third criterion is impact on corporate financial position. How does this capital project affect cash flow, long-term debt, and interest during construction? The fourth and final criterion is the impact on the corporate image. What are the various environmental considerations such as community affairs and the local and industrial labor market? How should they be handled?

There was a lot of concern on how to organize for the various degrees of corporate involvement and at what level the project manager should report in the company organization. Everyone agreed that the greater the scope of the project and the higher the financial and image risk, the greater was the accountability of the project manager, and the higher the reporting level should be in the company organization. If there were enough ongoing projects, perhaps a dedicated project organization, completely separate and apart from the traditional engineering and construction functions, might be warranted.

There were other concerns—staff size, skill level, and controls needed to monitor the progress of the architect and engineering design firms and the prime contractors. Perhaps stiffer contract specifications for project control, on-site witness testing, and penalty clauses were needed. But these didn't seem to be acceptable as substitutes for an effective project manager and an adequate staff. In the final analysis, project management was proclaimed as only input; power plants completed on time and on budget are supposed to be the results.

 PROJECT MANAGEMENT PROPOSAL

It wasn't long after the Dallas meeting that the Operating V.P. asked the consultant for a formal proposal recommending project management at GAU. The letter was written to the company President.

Dear Mr. Wellington:

In our initial contact with GAU early this year, you mentioned a concern in connection with the construction of your Atlantic I Plant. Your Operating Vice President asked us to establish a team and provide consulting assistance to review the company's planning and scheduling efforts. During the past three months we have made considerable progress in support of Atlantic I Task Force by initiating critical path planning and control of this construction project.

Based on this experience and on our prior consulting work in project management we feel that we have properly identified and assessed the problems the company faces in building new generating capacity. We are therefore recommending a project planning and control organization to be formed at GAU and from now on all major construction projects be managed by project directors. We believe this activity should report to the Operating Vice President since a substantial portion of this effort required in planning, construction, operating new plant facilities, engineering, construction, purchasing and operations, are already under his direction.

We are also recommending a more formal approach to meeting short-range needs in support of major projects currently in process, and the design of a comprehensive project planning system to cover all projects planned in the future. These efforts are described in Phase I and Phase II.

Phase I involves a continuation of fact-gathering and network planning to formalize and monitor progress on Atlantic I and implementation of the same control methods for all of the remaining projects.

Phase II should be initiated concurrently with Phase I and involves:

1. Defining the interface between the newly established Strategic Planning Department and the project planning and control function.

2. Developing a formal program of critical path planning which describes and documents the complete corporate planning process.

3. Developing policies, procedures, and guidelines to be followed by each group in the company responsible for a segment of the planning effort.

4. Preparing a project planning and control manual, incorporating much of the material in summary form obtained and developed in the above steps. This manual will serve both as a policy and procedure statement, as well as an educational and instructional guide.

5. Developing management reports and reporting systems required to monitor both the planning and construction process.

6. Defining the interrelationships and ultimate responsibilities of the different departments directly involved in supporting or monitoring construction and operational services.

7. Preparing job descriptions for personnel involved in the construction management process.

If you concur with these recommendations, we are prepared to organize and staff for this engagement within two weeks. Consultant resume, professional service fees, and tentative schedules are attached for your review.

Sincerely yours,

Samuel B. Arthur
Arthur & Arthur Company

Dear Mr. Arthur:

We are pleased to accept your proposal letter recommending project management for GAU. Please work out the engagement details with Mr. Hoover, Operating Vice President, who will be the corporate officer responsible for this effort.

Looking forward to getting some favorable and timely results.

Sincerely,

F. Brooks Wellington
President & Chief Executive Officer

ORGANIZING AND STARTING PROJECT MANAGEMENT

When project management was first introduced at Grand Atlantic Utilities, it was envisioned that a staff organization would be required to support the project managers in the planning, scheduling, and cost control of the projects. This staff, named project planning and control, was the first organization group to be established in project management. Started under consultant supervision, the initial idea was to create a computer-type project control system and perform all the cost and schedule work in parallel with the A/E and the prime contractors. It was intended for this group to perform planning and scheduling functions. Many position descriptions were written for planning people and computer specialists who could handle the day-to-day work.

To demonstrate the concept, an initial project planning team was mobilized and trained to develop a schedule for Atlantic Unit 1. Personnel were interviewed by the consultants and transferred to project planning and control from such places as the commercial department, engineering, computer programming and systems, and industrial engineering departments. The intent was to train these people in project control systems, organizational work, developing policies, writing guidelines and procedures, and implementing the project management support systems. At the same time, the initial project planning team would "test out" parallel planning and scheduling at Atlantic Unit 1 and gradually transfer this experience to the other projects. These two groups were called Phase I and Phase II, as identified by the consultant's letter. Phase I was called the projects group and Phase II, which contained several systems teams, was dubbed the "Blue Sky" systems. It was intended that when the systems and procedures were completed, the systems personnel would have been trained and would blend naturally into the projects group. By then all GAU major projects would be included in the project planning and control systems. This total effort was planned to take approximately two years to complete.

Company analysts and consultants participated in interviewing project-related department heads, soliciting their input to identify their ideas and areas of concern, and gaining their cooperation for effective project management. It also provided them with a means for smoothing out interfaces between other project-related departments. A matrix management concept was adopted and the systems group was directed to explain and promote this concept throughout the company. An executive bulletin was issued in January of 1974 establishing the project management concept and explaining the role of the project manager.

Executive Bulletin No. 36
Grand Atlantic Utilities Company

To: All Managers, Department Heads, Superintendents, Supervisors, and Outlying Districts

SUBJECT: Project Management Organization

The construction of large power plants is becoming increasingly complex and difficult to control. In order to more effectively manage these projects, GAU is establishing a project management organization. Mr. W. W. Josephs was appointed project manager for the Atlantic Units 1 and 2 effective July 1, 1974, reporting to me. Other project managers will be appointed as the project management organization develops.

The role of the project manager is to manage any and all activities associated with a project from the time of his assignment until the project is completed. He is delegated all the authority necessary for the accomplishment of this task. The scope of his responsibility and authority includes engineering, scheduling, budget and cost control, quality control, procurement of equipment and services, obtaining necessary licenses, construction, and other related functions necessary for the completion of a project. To accomplish this he will have assigned to him specific representatives from any other departments involved, such as environmental, engineering, construction, and production. These representatives will work with the project manager to assure that the project is completed on time, within budget, and in compliance with technical, contractual, and licensing requirements. Personnel assigned to the project, under the direction of a project manager will report to him for project direction, but will continue to report to their departments for functional and technical matters. The project manager may use the services of various departments in accordance with the functions assigned to those departments. He is the focal point for all groups involved with the project, both within and outside the company. No major decisions, technical, cost, schedule or performance, etc., concerning the project will be made without his approval.

Martin J. Hoover
Operating Vice President

Approved:

F. Brooks Wellington
President & Chief Executive Officer

OBSTACLES OF THE FIRST KIND

During this time, the projects group was attempting to identify the planning, scheduling, and cost ingredients for Atlantic Unit 1 and some of the other projects, and producing monthly status reports to management.

However, Atlantic I parallel effort proved unsuccessful and it was determined that the computer-assisted critical path scheduling would be deemphasized in favor of developing some general project planning and control methods for monitoring project status. It was in the second quarter of 1974 that the supervision of the projects group was turned over from the consultants to the company. Meanwhile, the systems group continued in project management policy development—preparing procedure outlines and planning a special organization interface with the various departments within the organization.

The Project Management Manual, which was expected to be published in late 1974, wasn't ready for another six months, and considerable effort was being expended in selling the matrix management concept in order to gain acceptance of the new procedures. No one seemed to understand just exactly what matrix was all about. The systems group efforts to complete detailed project control procedures, to organize special construction department interfaces, and to gain acceptance for standardizing the contractual specifications also failed.

When expectations and original promises were not realized, a credibility gap developed. Conditions did not improve when the fledgling staff control group made an eleventh-hour discovery about another schedule slippage on the Atlantic I project. But that wasn't the only problem—while the project manager's authority was defined, it was not fully recognized by other managers. Functional departments experienced difficulty in yielding the traditional authority. Construction site personnel who had been accustomed to operating without a project manager considered him and his new staff group to be greenhorn intruders around the site. This situation caused staff support emphasis to change from doing the planning and scheduling to monitoring and coordinating contractor's efforts.

EXPERIENCE IS *STILL* THE BEST TEACHER

The complexity and the scope of project activities established the basis for a more formal project management organization structure. Modification to existing procedures, new procedures, mission statements, job descriptions, scheduling systems, and reporting systems resulted in a rather complex organization. In fact, project management itself was split into two departments. One was a department of project managers and the other was a department of the project management services. Up until this time, the effort had been staffed with GAU people and consultants. However, things weren't really working that well with all of the company personnel, so authorization was given for recruiting experienced project planning and cost personnel from industry.

Credibility began to improve somewhat when the project management information system was created and the first report was issued. This was the first report of its kind which provided a single source for all the official schedule and budget information of GAU's major power plant projects. Much progress was being made when the project control group further became involved in developing specifications for the cost and schedule systems for Atlantic Unit 2 contract, which was later included as an Appendix to that contract. The project management budget system followed closely behind the Atlantic Unit Contract with the first formal capital expenditures budgeting system implemented at the company. Credibility continued to improve as experienced planning and scheduling personnel were recruited and began problem solving at the project level. The project management report became a regular monthly issue, and the other departments such as financial, management, and budget and the system planning group began to consistently check with project management for official project status and cost information. Then it happened. The project management report identified still another schedule slip and a corresponding overrun for Atlantic Unit I. The fact that this situation was not forecasted and reported earlier by project management dampened their recently acquired stature. Management said, "This happened because of poor estimating, over-optimism, and lack of knowledge as to the true job status." It became evident that more industry-experienced personnel were needed in the cost and estimating areas. While the consultants had acted as a catalyst for organization analysis and system development, it appears that they did not provide the staff with enough prescriptive tools for handling scheduling or cost problems at the project level. It was a significant event when the Operating Vice President said, "I don't give a damn how good your systems are, you better check that estimate." Almost immediately an estimating group was formed within the project management organization.

THE HUMAN EQUATION

As the problems with getting accurate information and true project status subsided, attention focused on another hotbed of controversy—the project manager and his "so called" team. It seemed that despite the meticulous and lengthy procedures, job descriptions, and executive bulletins written to tell how project management was supposed to work, there were certain key people who didn't know, or elected not to understand the company's project management concept.

By looking at the job description of the project manager, one might perceive that he was a superman. He was in charge of everything, made all the decisions, and told everybody what to do—or at least that's what the functional department managers thought.

Meanwhile, any display of hostility shown by the functional managers intimidated the project manager. Nobody really reported to him, so the project manager felt that he had no authority. He couldn't tell anybody to do anything, and he just thought of himself as a super-coordinator.

Discussions about who reported to whom were followed by written memos describing full-time team members and the part-time team members. Lengthy position papers explained the definitions of dotted-line, solid-line, staff, functional, and administrative reporting relationships. Things seemed to be very confused.

Project managers held team meetings to make decisions about the project, but the team members couldn't make decisions until they talked to their department heads. But that's not the way it was supposed to work. In the project manager's staff meeting even the project managers couldn't get together to decide how each project would work and what the common problems were. Things seemed to go from bad to worse. The procedures were so tight that they were unlivable, inconsequential, and nonsequitor.

"What do you mean we need project management training? We are already project managers!" It was Martin J. Hoover, the Operating Vice President, who suggested that perhaps some training and philosophy sessions would improve the working relationships of the project managers and the functional department heads.

A series of workshop seminars were developed and conducted by the staff group from project control services. The project management workshop was an eight-hour introductory training course on how Grand Atlantic Utilities conducts its project management business. The workshop was aimed at fostering better understanding of the project management organization by project managers, professionals, and others who are directly involved in day-to-day project activities.

A training manual was published which contained the basic material needed to conduct the workshop on the fundamentals of project management at GAU. The manual, divided into six sections, contained prework reading and grid learning tests. The prework material was developed for independent study and self-instruction. The grid learning tests were designed to encourage group discussion and team building in a workshop environment.

>   Section 1: Survey of Project Management
>   Section 2: Project Control Services
>   Section 3: Project Scheduling
>   Section 4: Project Estimating
>   Section 5: Project Budgeting & Cost Control
>   Section 6: Project Control Measures

While each section could have been handled alone, the material was covered in training manual sequence. The independent reading of the prework material and answering of the grid learning tests was followed by group participation and team answers during the workshops.

The project management workshop produced several other benefits. At one of the final critique sessions, the Director of Projects summarized the findings of the project management program at the company. He said, "At

Grand Atlantic Utilities there were seven critical success factors in implementing our project management program. If I had it to do over again, this is what I'd do:

1. I'd hire a consultant with a good track record and lots of project management experience. This is extremely important in implementing a program of this size and importance.

2. I would buy some experienced cost and schedule personnel. Yes, we have many young, bright systems analysts and engineers in the company, but without the right kind of experience it takes a lot longer and it's a lot harder to implement effective project control systems.

3. I'd start out with the estimating group as part of the project management organization. The best project control system in the world won't save a bad estimate.

4. I'd start with the architect/engineer contracts and gear them up for project management. The ones that GAU had didn't consider the project manager or how project management operates.

5. I'd hire a Madison Avenue image-maker and mount a campaign to market the project management philosophy and sell the advantages to all the people in the company, as well as those outside the company.

6. While it's important to sell project management to the functional managers and others, it's equally important and more time-efficient to dictate in some instances—knock a few heads together to get the job done.

7. The key to multiproject work is having an effective matrix organization. Matrix won't work just anywhere and won't work with just anybody. You have to select the people very carefully and you need to work very hard in order to operate in a

matrix organization. I wouldn't bother writing down all those details and having finicky procedures. It's very simple, when you have project management, to give the project manager *project direction* authority. The project manager tells the project team members what to do. It's the department head who gives them their *functional direction* authority. The department head tells them how. If we all remember that, project management will work."

APPENDIX A

CORPORATE
POLICY
STATEMENT—
PROJECT CHARTER

PROJECT MANAGEMENT

A. PRINCIPLE Project authority is established to provide an effective and uniform approach to manage projects, on an interdepartmental basis, utilizing company-wide and outside resources.

B. ACTION RULES

1. Project Establishment. Company projects shall be established by the responsible officer and/or department manager, and, as appropriate, subject to the approval of the Management Committee.

   a. A project manager shall be designated for a project or a group of projects by the authorized officer and/or manager. The project manager shall be given the responsibility and commensurate authority for the execution of the project, in accordance with established budget, schedule, and performance objectives, as defined in the project plan.

b. A formal project plan shall be prepared under the direction of the project manager to define the project objectives to be achieved and method of accomplishment. Such plan shall be revised, as necessary, for project implementation. Project plans will contain, but not be limited to: scope of work, objectives, schedules, budgets, project organization, and other information necessary to guide implementation and to serve as a basis for controlling performance.

2. Project Manager Responsibility. The project manager, or designated alternate(s), shall manage across organizational lines under the direction of the next higher level of project authority and shall operate within the context of authorized jurisdictions and corporate policies.

a. General support organizations under whose jurisdiction are such activities as those of accounting, legal, land acquisition, procurement, insurance, and public relations, are responsible for compliance with project requests within their respective jurisdictions and in keeping with priorities and resource limitations imposed by higher authority.

b. The project organization will specify the support requirements by utilizing established company procedures and forms.

c. Under the direction of the project manager and subject to higher approval, a project management team of appropriate size and organization shall be established for each authorized project to direct, or coordinate, activities such as the following:

1. Detailed development of project objectives, schedules, cost data, project control, and adaptation of existing information systems.
2. Authorization and agreement activities (e.g., regulatory permits, licenses, variances, service contracts, etc.).
3. Development of specific technical parameters, project specifications, quality control, and performance criteria.
4. Negotiation, procurement, contractor and vendor liaison, and inspection/evaluation of materials/services.

5. Project activities (e.g., engineering construction, subcontracting, and design).
6. Testing, start-up, conversion, and implementation activities.
7. Coordinate with Customer Service field management and others, as necessary, the implementation of actions required to gain local governmental approval and public acceptance for the project. Project managers will advise Customer Service field management in advance of specific action, such as filing with, or response to questions raised by, federal governmental agencies.

3. **Project Initiation.** Projects shall be initiated under the guidance of the formal project plan, with the prerequisite of an approved budget and work order for accumulating costs. Required approvals for the project plan, if any, shall be decided by the project manager in concert with his or her reviewing authority.

4. **Project Direction/Accountability.** Project direction is exercised through the project organization and requires support of all company organizations. Changes to the total authorized budget, schedule, technical specifications, or cash flow (allocation of budget) require approval of the responsible organization manager and the project organization. If the approval is not obtained, the matter will be resolved by higher authority.

5. **Project Personnel.** The company executes each project by a dual management system whereby project objectives are accomplished by (1) project management which defines, plans, budgets, directs, and monitors the performance of the participating functional organizations, and (2) management of personnel on an interdepartmental basis in support of the project, so as to provide operational and/or technical direction and control to complete assigned project tasks.

a. The project management concept provides for personnel to be assigned on either a full-time or part-time basis. Such personnel shall normally communicate or report functionally to the project manager and administratively to their parent organization.

b. Full-time personnel will be assigned to and released from the project only with the advance notification and concurrence of both project manager and the manager of the function organization involved.

c. Performance appraisals for personnel assigned to work on specific projects shall be initiated by the responsible manager of the functional organization involved with supporting performance input provided by the project manager(s).

d. Project personnel will be selected from appropriate organizations to utilize all company resources effectively.

6. Project Communication. Project managers shall communicate internally across company departmental lines, as necessary, to discharge effectively their jurisdiction responsibility. Such managers shall provide, or arrange for, appropriate interfacing with the public on project matters which pertain to the public interest. Project communication shall be subject to the provisions of the Corporate Policy Statement. "Publicity and Public Release of Information" and all such plans will be requested by, and coordinated through, the Customer Service field management as required by the Corporate Communications Advisory Committee Programs. The project manager shall review all items of such plans prior to release and will review and approve items that may represent commitments to the project which could affect cost, schedule, and/or environmental interfaces.

C. DEFINITIONS

1. Company projects. A set of activities with a definite project scope, objective, budget and schedule, which is defined as a project by the responsible officer and/or department manager.

2. Project organization. The organization headed by the project manager, which may include the project staff, support organization representatives, and additional support organization personnel.

3. Project reviewing authority. The manager, office, or designated representative, to whom the project manager reports. Such authority shall conduct reviews and implement action to:

a. Resolve problems identified by the project manager.

b. Monitor and guide the project manager in the conduct of the project.

D. REFERENCES

1. Project Plan, as amended.

2. Corporate Policy Statement 18.5.1, Publicity and Public Release of Information.

3. Corporate Communications Program Plan, as amended.

APPENDIX B

WORK BREAKDOWN STRUCTURE (WBS)

300 Document and Analyze Current REL & E Operation

 310 Analyze banking office

  311 Examine the operations at two banking offices

  312 Perform a file/document analysis

  313 Document task flow and operations—in narrative form

  314 Layout a task-oriented flowchart

  315 Document findings

 320 Analysis Service Center cost contributors

  321 EDP—analyze operation

  322 EDP—perform document/file analysis

  323 EDP—document task flow in flowchart

  324 EDP—document task flow and operations—in narrative form

  325 Corporate Banking—analyze operation; perform document/file analyzis; document in flowchart and narrative form

  326 Consumer Finance—analyze operation; perform document/file analysis; document in flowchart and narrative form

  327 Operations—analyze operation; perform document/file analysis; document in flowchart and narrative form

  328 Document findings

 330 Analyze Real Estate Finance Department

  331 Appraisal—analyze operation and perform document/file analysis

  332 Appraisal—document task flow and operation in flowchart and narrative form

  333 Sales—analyze operation and perform document/file analysis

  334 Sales—document task flow and operations in flowchart and narrative form

  335 Servicing—analyze operation and perform document/file analysis

  336 Servicing—document task flow and operations in flowchart and narrative form

  337 Interim Tract—perform a cursory overview analysis; brief documentation on operations

  338 Document findings

340 Analyze Division Administration/other Head Office cost contributors

    341 Division Administration—analyze operation; perform document/file analysis; document in flowchart and narrative form

    342 Other Head Office areas contributing to costs—analyze operation; perform document/file analysis; document in flowchart and narrative form

    343 Document findings

350 Perform cost analysis

    351 Review findings from tasks 310 thru 340 and 1976 functional costs

    352 Define the purpose of the costing, costing object, cost data, and allocation process

    353 Controller's Department—perform cost analysis

    354 Interface with Controller's Dept. on cost analysis

    355 Evaluation of Controller's costing

    356 Formalize final report—Controller's

    357 Write evaluation report

400 Analyses/Evaluation—Short-Term Payoffs/Test Assumptions

  410 Study loan origination—procedures

    411 Visit/interview vendors; e.g., SREA, TRW, Dart

    412 Secure current and proposed cost

    413 Validate task—310 data

    414 Evaluate use of title company in lieu of loan escrow

    415 Perform cost/benefit analysis

    416 Write evaluation report

  420 Study loan origination—alternatives

    421 Identify and contract with vendors for live test

    422 Set up live test and monitor vendors; e.g., SREA/TRW/PCS

    423 Perform cost/benefit analysis

    424 Write evaluation report of live test

  430 Evaluate loan servicing—impounding

    431 Secure current and proposed costs

    432 Perform cost/benefit analysis

    433 Write evaluation report

  440 Evaluate loan servicing—mail payments

    441 Secure current and proposed costs

    442 Design payment ticket and LTF statement format

443 Set up mail payments test and monitor

444 Perform cost/benefit analysis

445 Write evaluation report

500 Define Centralized Concept

  510 Develop overview scenario

    511 Identify who will be involved in developing concept

    512 Interview designated people from task 511

    513 Analyze responses from task 512

    514 Evaluate competition and document finding

    515 Review charge card centralized operation and document finding

    516 Document scenario

  520 Develop detail scenario and draft operating procedures/forms for test site

    521 Develop detail scenario

    522
    523 } Develop application procedures to be defined after
    524 } task 521
    525

  530 Establish test site

    531 Select site

    532 Set up/coordinate

    533 Establish quantity/quality goals

    534 Establish test organization

    535 Select staff

  540 Evaluate test site data—measure results

    541 Monitor quality of work

    542 Collect and analyze data from task 541

    543 Monitor quantity of work

    544 Collect and analyze data from task 543

    545 Adjust operating procedures/methods

    546 Write evaluation progress/final report

  550 Finalize evaluation of centralized concept

    551 Perform cost-effectiveness tradeoff

    552 Finalize Center concept

    553 Write evaluation final report

600 New Computer System—Statement of Requirements

700 610 Identify and document all existing computer systems

800 620 Gather input forms and output reports for each computer system

630 Gather file layouts on permanent files for each computer system and input/output files on system interfaces

640 Identify and document any external (outside SPNB) input sources to existing computer systems

650 Identify and document all existing internal computer system interfaces

660 Identify and document any external output sources to existing computer systems

670 Flowchart interrelationships of existing computer systems

680 Determine and document planned enhancements to existing computer systems and planned new computer systems

690 Analyze existing output reports
691
692
693   To be defined after task 620 data is received
694

710 Analyze existing input documents
711
712   To be defined after task 620 data is received
713

720 Gather information as to the number of report lines

730 Gather information as to the volume of transactions

740 Identify and document major processing functions of each of the existing systems

750 Identify and analyze requirements for compliance with regulations (outside SPNB) and policies (SPNB) that would affect the computer system

760 Determine/document plans and time frames for BTS plans relating to Real Estate Loans

770 Identify and document information needed by the branches, Center, and others on an inquiry basis—for centralized concept

780 Identify new elements/processing needed for computer system
781 Past studies/interviews
782 Trust
783 Interim tract
784 Document

790 Build, on a continuing basis, a log of needed data elements for a new system

810 Interview competition to determine their method/goals of processing Real Estate Loans

820 Document requirements for new system

821 ⎫
822 ⎪
823 ⎬ To be defined after task 780 is completed
824 ⎪
825 ⎭

830 Identify/evaluate software packages

831 Out-of-state review and preliminary evaluation
832 Out-of-state review and preliminary evaluation
834 Critical review of findings

840 Document required changes to the existing systems before the centralized concept can be implemented

850 Investigate use of mini computers

860 Recommend new computer systems, software and hardware

900 Prepare Project Documentation

910 Status reporting

920 Final APC report

921 Document current system
922 Document short-term payoff
923 Document centralized concept
924 Document new computer system
925 Prepare final report/recommendations

1000 Present Study to Management

APPENDIX C

PROJECT
MASTER
SCHEDULE

PROJECT TASK PLAN AND SCHEDULE

PROJECT NUMBER ___0002___

PROJECT TITLE ___REL & E OPERATION___

WORK UNIT/DESCRIPTION ___300 Document and Analyze Current REL & E Operation: Harold Einstein___

DATE 8/23/77

PREPARED BY ___Hal Einstein___

REV. BY ___Jim Ketchum___

PAGE ___3___ OF ___13___

TASK SCHEDULE: PERIOD ENDING

YEAR 1977   1978

TASK NO.	TASK DESCRIPTION	RESPONSI-BILITY	HOURS TO PLAN DATE	DATE PLAN	DATE ACT.
310	Analyze banking office				
311	Examine the operations at two banking offices	MILLER	24	9-2	
312	Perform a file/document analysis	MILLER	24	9-2	
313	Document task flow and operations--in narrative form	MILLER	24	9-16	
314	Layout a task oriented flowchart	MILLER	24	9-16	
315	Document findings	MILLER	16	9-23	
320	Analysis Service Center cost contributors				
321	EDP - analyze operation	WEINSTOCK	40	10-21	
322	EDP - perform document/file analysis	WEINSTOCK	16	10-21	
323	EDP - document task flow in flowchart	WEINSTOCK	24	10-28	
324	EDP - document task flow and operations--in narrative form	WEINSTOCK	32	11-4	
325	Corporate Banking - analyze operation; perform document/file analysis; document in flowchart and narrative form	EINSTEIN	32	9-16	
326	Consumer Finance - analyze operation; perform document/file analysis; document in flowchart and narrative form	EINSTEIN	16	9-16	
327	Operations - analyze operation; perform document/ file analysis; document in flowchart and narrative form	EINSTEIN	16	9-16	
328	Document findings	EINSTEIN	24	11-4	
330	Analyze Real Estate Finance Department				
331	Appraisal - analyze operation and perform document/file analysis	WEINSTOCK	40	9-9	
332	Appraisal - document task flow and operation in flowchart and narrative form	WEINSTOCK	40	9-9	

LEGEND

△ SCHEDULE EVENT ONE TIME

◬ RESCHEDULED EVENT NUMBER INDICATES RESCHEDULING SEQUENCE

▲ COMPLETED EVENT

△─△ SCHEDULED EVENT TIME SPAN

▱▱▱ PROGRESS ALONG TIME SPAN

△─→ CONTINUOUS ACTION

◇ ANTICIPATED SLIPPAGE

◆ ACTUAL SLIPPAGE (COMPLETED)

PROJECT TASK PLAN AND SCHEDULE

PROJECT NUMBER __0002__

PROJECT TITLE __REL. & E. OPERATION__

WORK UNIT/DESCRIPTION __300 Document and Analyze Current REL & E Operation: Harold Einstein__

DATE __8/23/77__

PREPARED BY __Hal Einstein__

REV. BY __Jim Ketchum__

PAGE __4__ OF __13__

YEAR 1977 / 1978

TASK SCHEDULE: PERIOD ENDING

TASK NO.	TASK DESCRIPTION	RESPONSI-BILITY	HOURS PLAN	DATE TO PLAN DATE	DATE PLAN	ACT.
333	Sales – analyze operation and perform document/ file analysis	WEINSTOCK	40		9-9	
334	Sales – Document task flow and operations in flowchart and narrative form	WEINSTOCK	40		9-16	
335	Servicing – analyze operation and perform document/file analysis	MILLER	40		9-23	
336	Servicing – document task flow and operations in flowchart and narrative form	MILLER	40		9-30	
337	Interim Tract – perform a cursery overview analysis; brief documentation on operations	WEINSTOCK	16		9-30	
338	Document findings	WEINSTOCK	30		9-30	
340	Analyze Division Administration/other Head Office cost contributors					
341	Division Administration – analyze operation; perform document/file analysis; document in flowchart and narrative form	WEINSTOCK	32		10-7	
342	Other Head Office areas contributing to costs – analyze operation; perform document/file analysis; document in flowchart and narrative form	WEINSTOCK	32		10-14	
343	Document findings	WEINSTOCK	16		10-14	
350	Perform cost analysis					
351	Review findings from tasks 310 thru 340 and 1976 functional costs	EINSTEIN	32		11-4	
352	Define the purpose of the costing, costing object, cost data, and allocation process	EINSTEIN	48		11-4	
353	Controller's Department – perform cost analysis	KANTZ	80		11-25	
354	Interface with Controller's Dept. on cost analysis	EINSTEIN	80		12-2	
355	Evaluation of Controller's costing	EINSTEIN	80		12-16	
356	Formalize final report – Controller's	KANTZ	60		12-16	

LEGEND

△ SCHEDULE EVENT ONE TIME

△ RESCHEDULED EVENT NUMBER INDICATES RESCHEDULING SEQUENCE

▲ COMPLETED EVENT

◁—▷ SCHEDULED EVENT TIME SPAN

◀——▷ PROGRESS ALONG TIME SPAN

◁ CONTINUOUS ACTION

◇ ANTICIPATED SLIPPAGE

◆ ACTUAL SLIPPAGE (COMPLETED)

APPENDIX D

PROJECT AUTHORIZATIONS AND AGREEMENTS SCHEDULE

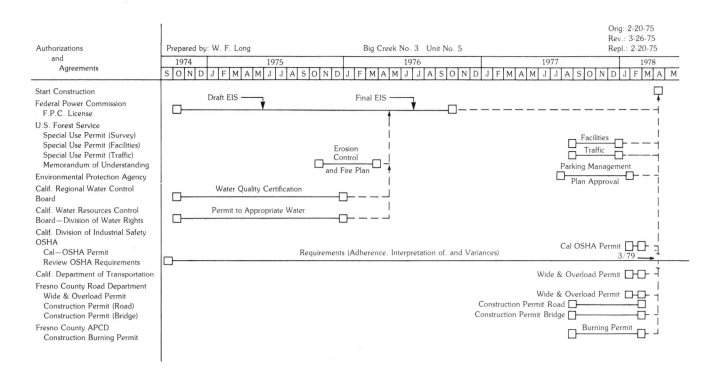

APPENDIX E

PROJECT
MATERIALS
AND EQUIPMENT
FORECAST

DPB-3198
PREPARED 01/30/80

MATERIAL/SERVICE FORECASTING REPORT
MATERIAL TRACKING SYSTEM

(1) (2) 1169   (3) POTTER/MALONE MTS PROJECT   (4) 1234A   (5) 1234-5678   (6) E   (7) ELECTRICAL

(8) MATERIAL ID / BM ITEM SPEC	(9) DESCRIPTION QUANTITY	(10) UOS	(11) P.O. NO. REQN NO/PCO SUPPLIER	(12) C H	(13) S SPEC ISSUE	(14) FINAL B/M ISSUE	(15) BID PKG PREP	(16) BID PKG APPVL	(17) QUOTES TO E&C	(18) AWARD PKG APPVL	(19) BID EVAL TO MS	(20) P.O. ISSUE DATE	(21) ON-SITE DEL DATE	(22) DWG RQD	(23) MI	(24) QC CL
SUBSTATIONS																
PINTER	1234 NEW 66KV SUB	CENTRAL		S												
				F												
				A												
PINTER	1234 CIVIL/STRUCTURAL	CENTRAL	B/M	S		100179					100879		020180			
				F		100179					100879					
				A		100179					100879					
PINTER	1234 ELECTRICAL ENGR	CENTRAL	PRELM	S		040180					040780		080180			
OD010181				F		040180					040780					
				A												
TRANSMISSION				S												
				F												
				A												
101	TOWER STEEL 12345		B9876543 / A TOWER CO	S	010579	030180	012079	012579	022579	032579	040179	050179	050180			
				F	010579	030180	012079	012579	022579	032579	040179	050179				
				A	010579		012079	012579	022579	032579	040179	050179				
102	HARDWARE		B/M	S		030180					030780	040180	080180			
				F		030180					030780					
				A												
GENERATION				S												
				F												
				A												
201	SWITCHGEAR 67890		A1234567 / A SWGR CO	S	020179		022579	030179	050179	070179	070779	080179	090180	Y		
				F	020179		022579	030179	050179	070179	070779	080179				
				A	020179		022579	030179	050179	070179	070779	080179				
202	CABLE WK SH 1/15		B/M	S		020180					020780		050180			
				F		020180					020780					
				A												
203	CONTROL SWITCH		M REQ	S		020180					011080	021580	050180			
				F		020180					011080					
				A												
204	GROUND CABLE EG01		B/M	S		082079					090179	090179	120179			
				F		082079					090179	090179				
				A		082079					090179	090179				

MATERIAL/ SERVICE FORECASTING REPORT (DPB 3198)

Keypoints

1. Date report was produced
2. Project Identifier
3. Project Name
4. Project Job Order and Phase Letter
5. Project Work Order Number
6. Discipline Code
7. Discipline Description
8. First Line Entry — Material Identifier
   Third Line Entry — Bill of Material Item No. (composed of Job Section Number and Job Section Item No.)

9. First Line Entry — Description of Material or Service Item
   Second Line Entry — Quantity Ordered
   Third Line Entry — Specification Order Number
10. First Line Entry — Purchase Order Number
    Second Line Entry — Requisition Number or Procurement Change Order Number (Requisition Number is printed until Purchase Order is issued. Procurement Change Order Number is printed when additional items are added to the Purchase Order.)
    Third Line Entry — Supplier/Contractor Name
11. Work Breakdown Structure
12. Schedule, Forecast and Actual Indicator
13. Specification Issue Dates
    First Line Entry — Scheduled Date
    Second Line Entry — Forecast Date
    Third Line Entry — Actual Date
14. Final Bill of Material Release Dates
    First Line Entry — Scheduled Date
    Second Line Entry — Forecast Date
    Third Line Entry — Actual Date
15. Bid Package Preparation Dates
    First Line Entry — Scheduled Date
    Second Line Entry — Forecast Date
    Third Line Entry — Actual Date
16. Bid Package Approval Dates
    First Line Entry — Scheduled Date
    Second Line Entry — Forecast Date
    Third Line Entry — Actual Date

17. Quotes to E&C for Evaluation Dates
 First Line Entry   -Scheduled Date
 Second Line Entry -Forecast Date
 Third Line Entry   -Actual Date

18. Award Package Approval Dates
 First Line Entry   -Scheduled Date
 Second Line Entry -Forecast Date
 Third Line Entry   -Actual Date

19. Bid Evaluation Received by Procurement Dates
 First Line Entry   -Scheduled Date
 Second Line Entry -Forecast Date
 Third Line Entry   -Actual Date

20. Purchase Order Issue Dates
 First Line Entry   -Scheduled Date
 Second Line Entry -Forecast Date
 Third Line Entry   -Actual Date

21. Onsite Delivery Dates
 First Line Entry   -Scheduled Date
 Second Line Entry -Forecast Date

22. Drawing Approvals Required Indicator
 N = no
 Y = yes
 P = yes, and proprietary or confidential information involved.

23. Inspection Required Indicator
 Letters "QC" will be entered first to indicate that quality control inspection will be required. Letters "SI," "FI," or "WI" will be entered as inspections are completed:
 SI = Source Inspection Performed
 FI = Field Inspection Performed
 WI = Waived Inspection

24. Quality Assurance Class (Nuclear Projects Only)

APPENDIX F

CROSS-IMPACT
MATRIX

PROJECT FUNCTIONAL CROSS IMPACT MATRIX

ORGANIZATION

TASK NO. 001	TASK DESCRIPTION	Audit	Bank Locations	Bnk.Term.System	Bnkg.Off.Adm.	Cons.Finance	Controller's	Corp.Bnkg.	Corp.Tax	Credit Servs.	Economics	Elec.Data Proc.	Ind.Eng.	Legal	Marketing	Operations	Opers.Plng.	Personnel	R.E.Finance	Special Assets	Trust	Fin.Committee	SPC-Ins.Agency
100	Planning Stage																						
110	Initiate study												X					X					
120	Structure project control system																X						
130	Prepare task milestone schedules and cross-																X						
	Impact matrix																						
140	Develop format for final APC documentation																						
150	Document planning stage																						
200	Preliminary Fact Gathering																						
210	Examine current SPNB operating policies,	X			X					X													
	practices and constraints													X							X		
220	Visit/interview other lenders (operations)																		X				
230	Visit/interview loan investors, brokers																		X				
240	Identify/interview software vendors											X			X								
250	Review long range real estate plans																						
260	Gather and review guidelines on costing,						X			X	X				X				X	X			
	accounting and overhead rates																						
270	Document fact gathering																					X	
300	Document and Analyze Current REL & E Operation									X	X						X						
310	Analyze banking office				X								X	X									
320	Analysis Service Center cost contributors					X		X				X				X							
330	Analyze Real Estate Finance Department																		X				
340	Analyze Division Administration/other Head				X													X	X	X	X		
350	Office cost contributors						X						X	X									
	Perform cost analysis																						
400	Analyses/Evaluation – Short Term Payoffs/Test												X	X									
	Assumptions																						
410	Study loan origination – procedures				X	X	X					X							X				
420	Study loan origination – alternatives				X		X												X				
430	Evaluate loan servicing – impounding				X		X					X		X					X				X
440	Evaluate loan servicing – mail payments				X		X					X							X				
500	Define Centralized Concept		X																	X	X		
510	Develop overview scenario				X														X	X	X		

APPENDIX G

PROJECT
ORGANIZATION
CHARTS

Phase: Construction/Start-Up

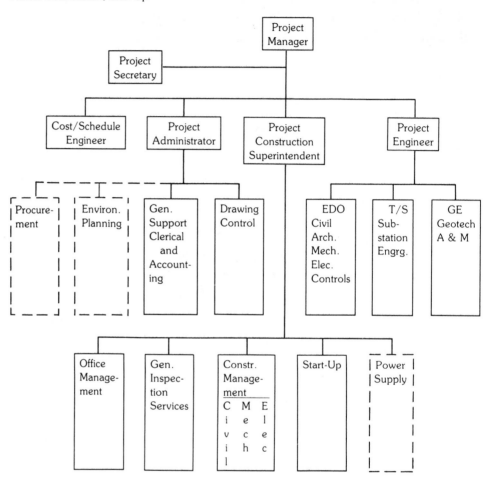

Phase: Completion

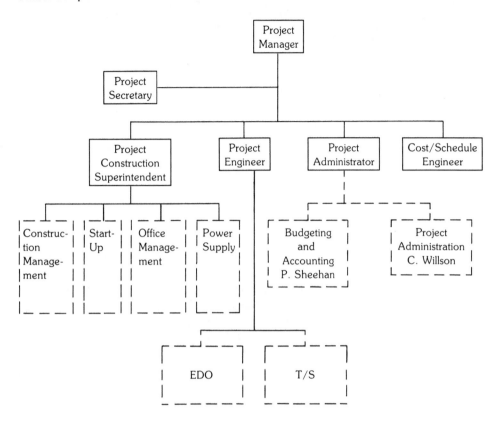

APPENDIX H

PROJECT
DOCUMENTS
MATRIX

Project Documents

Assigned Responsibilities	Engr. Design/ Criteria. Parameters and Studies	Basic Flow/ P&T Diagrams	Design and Detailed Design Drawings	Vendor Drawings	Specifications	Bills of Material	Proposal Evaluation and Purchase Recommendations	Line Designation List	Valve List	Drawing Progress Report	Calculations	One-Line Diagrams	Control Logic Diagrams	Elementary Diagrams	Major Equipment Material Control Schedule	Plant Manuals
1. Preparation: Lead Design Engineer	X	X	X		X		X	X	X		X	X	X	X	X	X
Construction Superintendent					X										X	
Designer(s)/Draftsmen			X			X		X	X	X				X		
Cost/Schedule Engineer															X	
2. Drafting: Designer(s)/Draftsmen		X	X		X							X	X	X		X
3. Checking: Lead Discipline Engineer	X	X	X		X	X	X	X	X		X	X	X	X	X	X
Designer(s)/Draftsmen		X	X		X	X		X	X	X		X	X			X
Project Administrator					X										X	
4. Review and Comments: Steam Generation Engr(s).	X	X		X	X						X	X	X	X		X
Lead Design Engineer	X			X	X	X	X	X	X	X	X	X	X	X		X
Cost/Schedule Engineers					X	X	X								X	
Construction Superintendent				X	X	X	X			X					X	X
Project Engineer	X	X	X	X	X	X	X	X	X	X	X	X	X	X	X	X
Project Administrator																
5. Approval: Construction Superintendent					X	X	X									
Project Lead Discipline Engr.	X	X	X	X	X	X	X	X	X	X	X	X	X			X
Project Engineer	X	X	X	X	X	X	X	X	X	X	X	X	X	X	X	X
Project Manager	X	X		X	X	X	X			X		X	X			X
Engineering Design Organization	X			X	X										X	

INDEX